SELF-HELP
AND SUPPORT
GROUPS

SAGE SOURCEBOOKS FOR THE HUMAN SERVICES SERIES

Series Editors: ARMAND LAUFFER and CHARLES GARVIN

SELF-HELP AND SUPPORT GROUPS

A Handbook for Practitioners

Linda Farris Kurtz

Sage Sourcebooks for

the Human Services
Volume 34

SAGE Publications
International Educational and Professional Publisher
Thousand Oaks   London   New Delhi

For information, address to:

 SAGE Publications, Inc.
2455 Teller Road
Thousand Oaks, California 91320
E-mail: order@sagepub.com

SAGE Publications Ltd.
6 Bonhill Street
London EC2A 4PU
United Kingdom

SAGE Publications India Pvt. Ltd.
M-32 Market
Greater Kailash I
New Delhi 110 048 India

Printed in the United States of America

Library of Congress Cataloging-in-Publication Data

Kurtz, Linda Farris.
   Self-help and support groups: a handbook for practitioners/author,
Linda Farris Kurtz.
      p. cm.—(Sage sourcebooks for the human services; v. 34)
   Includes bibliographical references and index.
   ISBN 0-8039-7098-6 (cloth: alk. paper).—ISBN 0-8039-7099-4 (pbk.: alk. paper)
   1. Self-help groups. 2. Group counseling. I. Title. II. Series.
  BF637.C6K87 1997
361.4—dc20   96-35630

97 98 99 00 01 02 03 10 9 8 7 6 5 4 3 2 1

Acquiring Editor:	Jim Nageotte
Editorial Assistant:	Nancy Hale
Production Editor:	Michèle Lingre
Production Assistant:	Karen Wiley
Typesetter/Designer:	Marion Warren
Cover Designer:	Candice Harman
Print Buyer:	Anna Chin

CONTENTS

PREFACE

Self-help, mutual aid, and reciprocal support have benefitted members of the human community for centuries. Most strikingly in the United States, the 20th century has witnessed the beginning of many such efforts to resolve human problems. The most recent of these has been the self-help movement that swelled in the 1970s and is characterized by federations of small groups oriented to assisting fellow sufferers of diseases, compulsions, and interpersonal problems. Closely related to these self-help associations are support groups, which are often confused with them. The self-help and support group movement responds to an immense unmet need for the application of experiential knowledge to problem solving, for community interaction, and for social advocacy. Millions of people in the United States and around the world are potential beneficiaries of such groups.

The self-help and support group phenomenon reminds us of the importance of groups in meeting human needs. Self-help and support groups occupy an important place among a wide array of types of groups, such as psychotherapy groups, educational/didactic groups, focal-group therapies, social and recreational groups, and task groups of all kinds. Students and practitioners in the human services need to know about the dynamics of such groups and how to use them.

One purpose of this book is to inform human service practitioners, educators, and students about the theories, concepts, and research related to self-help and support groups. Another purpose is to impart practical advice and directions for working with these groups—guidance solidly based on theory and research. Both conceptual understanding and practical competence begin with clear definitions of the two kinds of groups, a differentiation that helps dispel misunderstandings and inaccurate assumptions about how each functions, whom they attract, and how they help participants achieve goals.

I have chosen to focus on both self-help and support groups in this text for two reasons. First, most people think of self-help and support groups as one and the same; treating the two in one volume clarifies comparisons and contrasts between them. Second, the similarities between the two mean that research and theory on the one are often applicable to the other. Although there is more research on self-help groups, I have attempted to give equal treatment to both types of groups.

This book is organized around three levels of analysis. Part I examines self-help and support using the *group* as the unit of analysis. Part II examines the *member* who chooses (or chooses not) to affiliate with the group. Part III considers the *practitioner* in his or her interactions with self-help and support groups. The last section describes representative associations that illustrate various types of self-help and support groups, including a final chapter on telephone and computer-based, on-line groups.

Individual, group, and professional levels of analysis conform loosely to an ecological paradigm (Maton, 1993) that avoids overemphasis on psychological variables and reinforces recognition of the group as a valuable community resource over and above its use as a type of treatment. This approach aims to do justice both to the complexity of individual differences among participants and to the variety and complexity of group processes found in self-help and support groups.

The literature of the past 25 years has tended to present the self-help movement either as encompassing a very broad array of groups for social action, self-actualization, and problem resolution, or as being an alternate treatment that reinforces and augments professional services. Another, more recent view contends that self-help associations are potential communities. As communities, they are not alternatives to professional care, although they may reinforce and sustain the effects of social welfare, health care, and mental health services. As communities, they offer members far more than weekly doses of "self-help" contained in a small face-to-face group meeting. As communities, neither self-help nor support groups are amenable to evaluation by randomized, control-group design, nor can they take the place of the nation's health care system, community mental health centers, and departments of social services.

This book thus takes shape at mid-decade within a context that redefines self help, that questions the assumptions of traditional experimental research, and that views self help and support as potentially independent community resources. I hope students and practitioners who read this book will realize the empowering force of community self-help associations and understand the role that they as professional practitioners can play to initiate and sustain self-help impulses among client populations.

ACKNOWLEDGMENTS

I would like first to express my gratitude to Eastern Michigan University for granting me a year-long sabbatical so that I could concentrate on writing this book. Secondly, I wish to thank Charles Garvin, coeditor of the Sage Sourcebooks for the Human Services Series, for his editorial help and support. I am grateful to many individuals who have reviewed my writing, given me information, or otherwise assisted me in this endeavor. These include Harvey Bertcher, Donald Blain, Don Lee, and Mark Chesler, who read parts of the manuscript. Ed Madara has repeatedly taken time to provide information from the American Self-Help Clearinghouse. The same can be said for Frank Riessman of the National Self-Help Clearinghouse. One of my students, John Furey, assisted with graphics. Rose Kurland (of Evanston, IL), Grace Powers Monaco and Julia Sullivan (of Washington, DC), Carol Rees (of Ann Arbor, MI), and Dian Wilkins (of Southfield, MI) have given me information about the groups with which they are associated. I am grateful to Tom Powell, Director of the Center for Self-Help Research at the University of Michigan, who helped me gain access to needed library resources.

I owe a special thanks to the students in SWK 681, Spring 1996, who read the manuscript, completed some of my suggested assignments, and tested many of the classroom exercises. Many of the class members, especially Christine Houghton, gave useful recommendations for revision and clarification of the written text.

Most importantly, I thank Ernest Kurtz for his contributions, which included research in libraries and electronic databases, drafting Chapter 11's discussion of on-line resources, and critiquing the entire manuscript. Any errors that remain are entirely my own responsibility.

—*LINDA FARRIS KURTZ*

PART 1

THE GROUP

Chapter 1

INTRODUCTION

In the practice of mutual aid, which we can retrace to the earliest beginnings of evolution, we thus find the positive and undoubted origin of our ethical conceptions; and we can affirm that in the ethical progress of man, mutual support—not mutual struggle—has had the leading part.
—Kropotkin, 1955, p. 300

The most important fact about both self-help and support groups is that they are made up of fellow sufferers. Beyond that, the two are not the same kind of group, though they have many characteristics in common (Lavoie, Borkman, & Gidron, 1995; Schopler & Galinsky, 1993; 1995). This chapter offers definitions of self-help and support groups and will suggest ways of differentiating between the two as well as between them and psychotherapy groups. It will review what is known about the prevalence of self-help and support groups and briefly summarize research on them.

WHAT ARE SELF-HELP AND SUPPORT GROUPS?

Definitions

Any definition of either a self-help group or a support group describes an "ideal type"—a pure form that rarely represents reality adequately; actual groups have some, but not all, of the characteristics found in the ideal type. With that caveat in mind, the differences between these two types of groups can be examined. Among the major differences between self-help and support groups are the role of professionals in group activities, the size of the organization's membership, the extent and type of the group's change orientation, the degree of local group autonomy, and the complexity of the organization's program and philosophy (Powell, 1987; Schopler & Galinsky, 1995; Schubert & Borkman, 1991).

Self-help and support groups may be seen as existing on either end of a continuum, with self-help being the larger and more complex form of group, having a clear mission of helping members to change some aspect of themselves (see Figure 1.1). At the other end of the continuum, support groups are smaller and less complicated forms of gatherings that seek more to support and comfort than to change members. Fleshing out the continuum, we move from groups, both Twelve Step and non-Twelve Step, that attempt to reform and transform their members, to advocacy groups primarily focused on changing aspects of society, to mixed groups that support primarily by educating and building up coping skills, to groups that simply bring together fellow sufferers. As the continuum image suggests, such a definitional taxonomy does not mean that support groups do not produce personal change, but rather that reform and change are not their primary purpose. Likewise, change-oriented groups also educate and support, but these are not their primary goals.

With that complexity of group reality in mind, the following are working definitions of self-help and support groups:

Definition of Self-Help Groups

A self-help group is a supportive, educational, usually change-oriented mutual-aid group that addresses a single life problem or condition shared by all members. Its purpose may be personal or societal change or both, achieved through the use of ideologies for dealing with a situation. Its leadership is indigenous to the group's members; participation and contributions are voluntary—it charges no fees. Professionals rarely have an active role in the group's activities, unless they participate as members. Boundaries include all who qualify for membership by having the problem, the situation, or an identity in common with other members. Meetings are structured and task-oriented and use specific methods of help for the basic problem or condition. Local groups are usually relatively autonomous from their national headquarters.

Definition of Support Groups

Support groups meet for the purpose of giving emotional support and information to persons with a common problem. They are often facilitated by professionals and linked to a social agency or a larger, formal organization. Membership criteria often exclude individuals not served by the sponsoring organization. Behavioral and societal change are subordinate

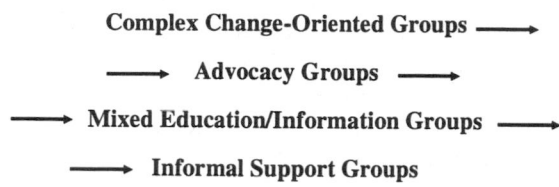

Figure 1.1. Continuum

to the goals of emotional support and education. Meetings are relatively unstructured, and the group's program is unlikely to espouse an ideology. Support groups usually do not charge fees or collect dues.

Differences Between Self-Help, Support, and Psychotherapy Groups

Many practitioners have difficulty distinguishing among self-help, support, or psychotherapy groups. A major difference between self-help and support is that the former aims at effecting change. Since both self-help and psychotherapy groups help members to achieve personal change, they differ in their inclusion of a professional therapist rather than relying on the group. A professional therapist conducts a psychotherapy group, whereas self-help groups seldom have professional facilitators in meetings (one reason that they are referred to as self-help). Professionals may relate to self-help groups as behind-the-scenes helpers, as linkages to potential members, as consultants, and occasionally as invited guests; but not as facilitators, leaders, or therapists, as with therapy groups. Using the continuum image, Schopler and Galinsky (1995) place self-help groups on one end and psychotherapy groups on the other, with support groups in between. They view support groups as potentially overlapping with models on either end of the continuum.

Lieberman (1990) offers a useful analytic framework for comparing the internal processes in self-help and psychotherapy groups. Its five dimensions are

- a view of the group as a "social microcosm"
- the group's technological complexity/simplicity
- the psychological distance between helper and helpee
- the specificity-generality of helping methods
- the degree of differentiation among members

Lieberman explains that by *social microcosm,* he means that "underneath activities in therapy groups lies the assumption that cure or change is based on the exploration and reworking of relationships in the group" (p. 265). The group provides a microcosm of society in which members examine dysfunctional ways of relating to the world. The self-help group, on the other hand, de-emphasizes transactions among members and does not focus on these transactions as a therapeutic device.

Psychotherapy relies on complex technologies introduced by the group therapist. By *complex technologies,* Lieberman means therapeutic methods based on human behavior theory and professional skills applied by the therapist in work with the group. Self-help groups rely on nonprofessional helpers who represent specific group ideologies "that define the problem and direct specific interventions" (p. 266).

Specialized training and use of professional settings emphasize *psychological distance* between professionals and group members. Professionals refrain from bringing up their own problems, limit contacts between themselves and group members, and emphasize their role as expert. In self-help groups, each member is both helper and helpee, thus limiting psychological distance.

Professional helping methods are *more specific* than those offered by peer counselors in, for example, a support group; but they are less specific than help offered in self-help groups. The techniques in self-help groups are "codified" and designed to alleviate a specific problem with a specific method (p. 267). For example, the "will training" applied in Recovery, Inc. is a very specific method, described in a manual and applied for very specific difficulties (Low, 1950).

Psychotherapy group members are usually relatively *undifferentiated* (different from one another) and deal with a variety of problems. If they share a common problem, they also are expected to grow in their view of themselves as unique individuals. In self-help groups, the common core problem is the raison d'être of the group and is emphasized consistently (p. 268).

To these five points, I would add three additional factors: *open versus closed boundaries, the charging of fees,* and *dependence on extraorganizational support.* Self-help groups typically admit anyone who qualifies for membership; therapy groups do not. Professional psychotherapists charge fees for their services in the group; self-help groups rarely charge a fee, although they may ask for small donations. Self-help groups rarely depend on outside organizational support except for their own national federations; professional therapy groups often meet in social agencies and mental health facilities.

Therapy groups, of course, may vary from this ideal-type definition. Some therapists do not think of the group as a social microcosm and initiate time-limited, didactic groups for individuals with a common problem (McKay & Paleg, 1992). Professionals in non-mental-health settings initiate and work with groups that set behavior-change and therapeutic goals but are not defined as psychotherapy groups. With these considerations in mind, the following definition is offered as a means of clarifying the nature of professionally led, change-oriented groups, referred to here as "psychotherapy" groups.

Definition of Psychotherapy Groups

Psychotherapy groups seek to produce individual growth and change through the relationships established among members with the help of a professional therapist. Using professional methods, therapists encourage and interpret "here and now" events among members to produce insight and change. Members pay for the professional's services. Therapists limit the number of members and have control over who is invited to the group. Similarity of problem is not a qualification for membership in therapy groups, and heterogeneity among members is often valued.

Organizational Typologies

Self-help groups also vary in the degree and type of change desired by members. Some groups, such as Twelve-Step programs, may be primarily behavioral-change-oriented. Others are primarily educational and supportive (see Figure 1.2) without using behavioral-change ideologies. Many of the latter pursue advocacy objectives as well. The matrix shown in Figure 1.2 portrays two major dimensions on which groups differ—professional leadership/facilitation and personal change orientation—and divides the various types of groups into four cells. It classifies groups into three categories: self-help, support, and psychotherapy. Within self-help, it shows the two sub-categories of personal-change groups and supportive/educational, advocacy groups.

The groups described in Part 4 of this book exemplify the three self-help and support categories (shown in Figure 1.2). Twelve-Step programs, Recovery, Inc., and Parents Anonymous illustrate personal change organizations. The National Alliance for the Mentally Ill (NAMI), Candlelighters, and The Compassionate Friends illustrate the supportive/educational variety of self-help groups. Support groups for caregivers sponsored by the Alzheimer's Association illustrate more closely the ideal type support-group model.

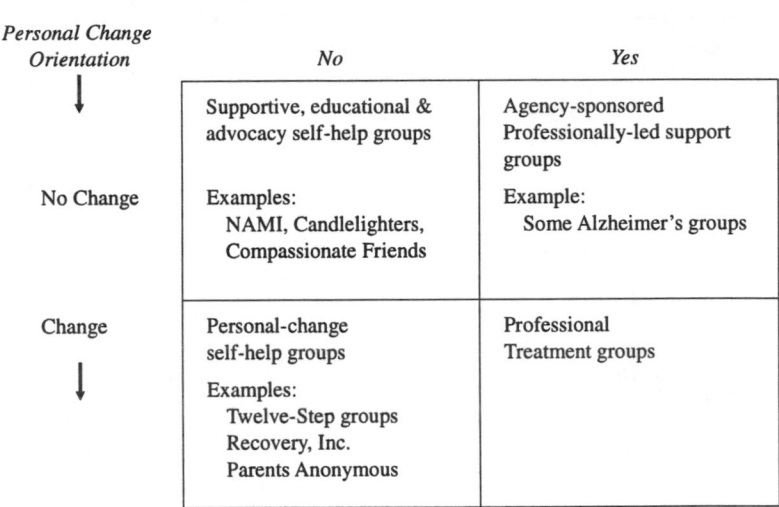

| | Professionals | |
Personal Change Orientation	No	Yes
No Change ↓	Supportive, educational & advocacy self-help groups Examples: NAMI, Candlelighters, Compassionate Friends	Agency-sponsored Professionally-led support groups Example: Some Alzheimer's groups
Change ↓	Personal-change self-help groups Examples: Twelve-Step groups Recovery, Inc. Parents Anonymous	Professional Treatment groups

Figure 1.2. Matrix Differentiating Self-Help, Support and Treatment Groups by Change Orientation and Relationship to Professionals

Another typology (Schubert and Borkman, 1991) classifies local-level self-help groups (support groups are not included) according to the degree of their dependence on a larger organization. This classification is based on two dimensions: resource dependence and authority to make decisions. It identifies five patterns of dependency on external sources and decision-making authority. Table 1.1 reflects the five types of dependency illustrated in the groups described in the last section of this book.

Five Patterns of Dependency

1. Unaffiliated groups—independent local groups that have no relationship with an outside source of leadership, funding, or policy.
2. Federated groups—groups that relate to a larger association but have complete autonomy from it. They benefit from resources provided by the national organization.
3. Affiliated groups—groups that are subordinate to higher levels of their own organization, which has power to dictate policy and authorize the groups to act as an affiliate.

Table 1.1

Part 4 Illustrations According to Classification Based on Organizational
Autonomy (Schubert & Borkman, 1991)

Unaffiliated	None
Federated	Twelve-Step Groups
	Candlelighters
	NAMI
Affiliated	Recovery, Inc.
	Compassionate Friends
Managed	Alzheimer's Association
Hybrid	Parents Anonymous

4. Managed groups—groups that are monitored and controlled by professionals. These groups use a combination of self-help and professional techniques but are under the control of a non-self-help organization.
5. Hybrid groups—groups that combine features of affiliated and managed groups. These groups are organized by a higher level of the same organization, as are affiliated groups, but use professionals, who introduce professional expertise, along with the peer helpers' experiential knowledge, to resolve member difficulties.

Sources of Confusion

In 1987, Powell delineated what self-help is not. Self-help groups are not cooperatives, such as food cooperatives; they are not foundations engaged in research and social policy; they are not self-help books, although they may use such books; and they are not agency support groups. Yet their similarity to other voluntary associations, as well as the factors discussed below, contribute to continuing confusion.

Hybrid Groups. Despite numerous definitions and classifications in the literature, many people continue to use the terms "support," "self-help," and "therapy" in ways that confuse them with each other. One reason for this is the relatively large number of hybrid groups spawned within social agencies. Professionals begin many groups with the intention of giving them independence at a later date; therefore, in their creators' expectations and imaginations, these groups have already become self-help groups.

Self-Help as Human Service Agency. Another source of confusion is the widespread impression that self-help groups are a type of human service agency. For example, literature on self-help and support groups refers to the "treatment" given by Parents Anonymous groups and Alzheimer's support groups (Hunka, O'Toole, & O'Toole, 1985; Wasow, 1986). The term *treatment* used in this way is likely to refer to the services of professionals in Borkman and Schubert's "hybrid" category, such as Parents Anonymous, or their "managed" category, such as many Alzheimer's groups. But these fine distinctions are not obvious to practitioners.

Experimental Outcome Study. Efforts of researchers to study outcomes of self-help group participation in order to evaluate effectiveness offer another example of the confusion caused by the human service agency paradigm. Social scientists tend to judge outcome as though the self-help group were an expertless and leaderless psychotherapy group. Applying experimental methodology requiring random assignment to experimental and control conditions, researchers seek to determine if the self-help group is successful. Because controlled research methods are hard to impose on independent self-help groups, researchers sometimes simulate self-help conditions or examine phenomena they believe are comparable to self-help (Kaufman, Schulberg, & Schooler, 1995). Findings from these efforts tell us very little about the actual effectiveness of community-based self-help associations.

It is important to understand that self-help organizations and support groups have goals that differ from those of psychotherapy and treatment. Their goals may be to prevent relapse or to help in rehabilitation, but self-help groups are not treatment in the sense that they perform a professional service. In fact, the self-help ethos is that it is the helper who receives the greatest help (Riessman, 1965; Riessman & Carroll, 1995).

A New Self-Help Paradigm

Some authors are calling for a new self-help paradigm to replace that of self-help as an alternative treatment service (Borkman, 1995; Humphreys & Rappaport, 1994). Rappaport (1993), discussing his research with GROW International for persons with serious mental illness, contrasted the alternative treatment perspective with one that views the self-help organization as a normative community. He reflected that, in his study of GROW, he had operated as though the group were a human service and in so doing had failed to capture the total experience of GROW's members.

He noted that members experienced a change in their social identities that could not be attributed to meeting participation alone, but could be understood as deriving from "the organization's narrative about itself (community narrative) and how that narrative influences the personal life stories of members" (p. 121). As the organization's story becomes a part of one's identity, one's own story, a person comes to understand his or her identity in terms of that story. People who choose to join a mutual-help group are not deciding to obtain a treatment; they are joining a voluntary association, just as they would join a social club or a neighborhood organization.

In their book, *Redefining Self-Help*, Riessman & Carroll (1995) suggest that all examples of self-help, whether they be individual, group, community, or nation, have one thing in common: promotion of latent inner strengths. Self-help emphasizes self-determination, self-reliance, self-production, and self-empowerment. It mobilizes the internal resources of the person, the group, or the community. This is an important distinction because we tend to think of the word *self* as being synonymous with *individual*. In this redefinition, the word *self* becomes, instead, a synonym for *internal*.

The Self-Help Ethos

One way to understand the essence of self-help is through an understanding of the self-help ethos. Riessman and Carroll (1995) define *ethos* as "a constellation of norms and sentiments, a series of themes that underlie behavior" (p. 5). Referring to their characterization of the self-help ethos as an "ideal type" construction (p. 5), its themes are "anti-big," anti-bureaucratic and anti-impersonality (p. 6). In contrast to formal organizations, self-help is highly personal, nonhierarchical, and without division of labor. Self-help favors experience over expertise.

A second theme of the self-help ethos is the reaffirmation of basic core traditions of community, neighborhood, spiritual values, and self-reliance. Other themes, according to Riessman and Carroll, are empowerment, new age psychology, and democratization of everyday life. Democratization includes demystification of mental and physical illness, "anti-elitism," and "anti-expertism" (p. 8).

The self-help ethos in North America may not correspond to the ethos of the self-help movement in other parts of the world. Gidron and Chesler (1995) point out that nations have differing arrangements for caring for people. In countries with a welfare state orientation, the government assists self-help groups as part of the state's responsibility. In contrast, in the United States, self-help groups conform to an anti-social-welfare ideology that prohibits dependence on government service. The ethos of self-help groups in the United States thus favors peer leadership that is independent of formal authority.

PREVALENCE OF SELF-HELP
AND SUPPORT GROUPS

Gussow and Tracy (1976) estimated in the 1970s that self-help groups were growing at an annual rate of 3%. A later analysis of self-help group growth in one state found the annual rate of growth to be 8.4% (Leventhal, Maton, & Madara, 1988). In 1989, Jacobs and Goodman, thinking of mutual help within a human service paradigm, predicted that self-help will become the major form of mental health care in the 1990s and will involve over 10 million members by the year 2000. In 1993, two research groups independently estimated that there were 7.6 million self-help group members in the United States (Goodman & Jacobs, 1994; Lieberman & Snowden, 1993). Canadian researchers determined that about 2% of the Canadian population or 420,000 individuals had participated in a mutual-help group in the previous 12 months (Gottlieb & Peters, 1991). A survey of the U.S. population in the early 1980s compared with a similar survey in the 1990s documenting incidence of mental illness and mental health service use found a dramatic increase in self-help group attendance—0.7% in the 1980s versus 3.2% in the 1990s (Kessler et al., 1996).

The largest self-help group, Alcoholics Anonymous, reported 1,307,803 individual members and 58,084 groups in the United States and Canada as of January 1, 1996 (AA, 1996). An estimate of world-wide membership in 1995 was 1,790,528 individual members and 89,239 groups (AA, 1995). Room (1993), in a national random survey of the U.S. population, found that 3.1% of the U.S. population had attended a meeting of AA for their own problem, 9% had attended an AA meeting for any reason, and 13% had attended a Twelve-Step meeting of some type.

A 1991 California survey (which excluded substance abuse groups such as AA) found that of 4,000 self-help/support groups in that state, 40% addressed physical illness and 9% addressed emotional problems (Lieberman & Snowden, 1993). There were approximately 500,000 participants of such groups in California at that point. The average group had 94 members, and the average meeting consisted of 21 participants. Characteristics of typical participants in self-help associations will be discussed in later chapters.

RESEARCH ON SELF-HELP
AND SUPPORT GROUPS

The research on self-help and support groups has progressed over the past 20 years from anecdotal descriptions to outcome studies and ethnographic analyses. An edited work by Morton Lieberman and the late Leonard Borman provided the first large compendium of research reports on self-help associations. It contained reports of quasi-experimental outcome studies, observations of group processes and ideologies, and descriptions of many community self-help organizations (Lieberman & Borman, 1979). In the 1980s most self-help research focused on how professionals related to self-help associations, described and classified helping processes in such groups, and evaluated the effect of such groups on members (L. F. Kurtz, 1990a). Surveys examining professionals' attitudes toward self-help found them receptive to the idea, although it is important to remember that definitions of the term "self-help" may have varied among those surveyed. This research found professionals lacked information about how various self-help associations worked and how professionals might coordinate with them. Surveys of self-help group members' impressions of professionals' reaction to their groups were consistent with findings in surveys of professionals; i.e., professionals were receptive but uninformed (Goodman & Jacobs, 1994; L. F. Kurtz, 1990a).

Evaluations of outcome, which almost invariably viewed self-help and support groups as alternative human service agencies, most often employed cross-sectional designs that elicited retrospective self reports from convenience samples. More extensive evaluations used such methodologies as before-after measures, comparison groups, and time-series designs. A common finding was that more intense and longer term participation contributed to better outcomes. Useful outcomes of self-help participation included reduced psychiatric symptomatology, reduced use of professional services, increased coping skills, increased life satisfaction, and shorter hospital stays. Members of health-related groups reported better adjustment, better coping, higher self-esteem, and improved acceptance of the illness than self-assessments of less active and nonmembers (L. F. Kurtz, 1990a).

Current Research

The current decade's research has continued to focus on helping processes and outcome, but has increasingly recognized that self-help is not treatment and that outcome evaluations and clinical trials may be a misuse of research resources (Borkman & Schubert, 1995; Kennedy &

Humphreys, 1995; E. Kurtz, 1992; Rappaport, 1993). Researchers have expanded investigations to include organizational variables (L. F. Kurtz, 1992; Maton, 1993; Moos, Finney, & Maude-Griffin, 1993), worldviews and ideologies (Kennedy & Humphreys, 1995; Humphreys & Kaskutas, in press), minority participation (Humphreys, Mavis, & Stöfflemayr, 1995; Medvene, Lin, Wu, Mendoza, Harris, & Miller, 1995), and international and multicultural phenomena (Lavoie, Borkman, & Gidron, 1995; Mäkelä, 1996). Research has focused more intensely on the factors that contribute to affiliation and participation in self-help and support groups, recognizing that groups cannot remain in existence without new members and that members cannot benefit without attending (Luke, Roberts, & Rappaport, 1993; Kurtz et al., 1995; Powell et al., 1995). Detailed discussion of these findings will be found throughout the balance of this book.

Theoretical Understanding of Self-Help and Support Groups

Much of the research on self-help and support groups is atheoretical, adhering to no particular point of view or approach. Theoretical understanding nevertheless remains possible and useful (Stewart, 1990). Small group theory, stress theory, and behavioral and cognitive theories contribute to the conceptual understanding of mutual help. Theories of group attraction and social comparison provide some understanding of how members are attracted to and affiliate with self-help groups (Arkin & Burger, 1980; Clore & Byrne, 1974; Festinger, 1954; Thibaut & Kelley, 1959).

Stewart (1990), in an overview of theories used in the literature on self-help groups, found that theories of affiliation, attribution, change, coping, deviance, loneliness/social-isolation, and self-esteem had been included in the research, but inconsistently. She found that equity, reference group, social comparison, and social movement theories predominated. As additional conceptualizations for consideration by self-help group researchers, she offered psychoneuroimmunology and social-learning theories. *Psychoneuroimmunology* concerns the relationship of emotions and resistance to disease. Through social support, the disease-fighting ability of the immune system is strengthened. Disruption to one's social network, on the other hand, weakens the immune system. Stewart argued that although social buffering and social learning theories have been mentioned in the literature on self-help, they have not been tested through empirical research.

Social learning employs three major ingredients that one can identify in self-help and support groups: instruction, reinforcement, and modeling (Kurtz & Powell, 1987). Many groups have guest speakers who educate members in their area of expertise. Interactions among members provide natural reinforcers for approved behavior. Groups publish and promote literature, and veteran members serve as role models for newcomers. One well-developed group, Recovery, Inc., teaches a method by which behavioral and cognitive habits are addressed (Lee, 1991; 1995). Cognitive theory holds that thinking determines feelings and behavior—that by changing one's interpretations and understanding, new responses can emerge. The worldviews of groups become a means of reeducating or reframing how members think of and define their difficulties (Collier, 1991).

Sociological theories have also been used to explain what happens in a self-help organization. For example, Kempe and Helfer's theory on the etiology of child abuse has added to understanding of how Parents Anonymous assists parents who abuse their children (Hunka, et al., 1985). The concept of "social world" and symbolic interactionism has been used in understanding Alcoholics Anonymous (Smith, 1991; 1993). Social movement theory has offered explanations of the growth and impact of self-help on society (Katz, 1993; Mäkelä, 1996; Room, 1993) As researchers move away from simple descriptions and views of self-help as a treatment paradigm, theoretical understanding of self-help and support groups grows. With that comes new appreciation of the mutual-aid phenomenon as it evolves and takes shape.

SUMMARY

This chapter clarifies differences among various kinds of groups that address personal and social problems and provides "ideal type" definitions of self-help, support, and psychotherapy groups. It explains the self-help ethos and highlights the significance and growth of the self-help and support group movement. Anecdotal studies and descriptions of self-help groups have given way to theoretical applications and more rigorous outcome research, although many have questioned the appropriateness of the human services paradigm used to evaluate self-help groups. The next chapter will focus more intensely on the beneficial elements of self-help and support groups and how these elements affect group members.

DISCUSSION QUESTIONS

1. Discuss the definitions of self-help and support groups by applying them to groups with which you are familiar. Decide how well the definitions provided apply to these groups.
2. Compose a hypothetical group and describe how the group would function as each of the three types of group described in this chapter: self-help, support, and psychotherapy. For example, if the group were composed of people who believe they have been abducted by UFOs, how would the group differ within the three categories (self-help, support, therapy)?
3. Discuss the theories mentioned at the end of the chapter and advance other social science theories that might be applied to self-help or support groups. How might the theory be used in the study of self-help and support? What research questions might be asked?

CLASSROOM EXERCISE

Divide the class into three groups, each of which representing one of the three types of group discussed in the chapter. Choose a common problem across all three groups. Have members of each subgroup develop a role play depicting a segment of a meeting as it might occur within each of the three definitions.

ASSIGNMENT

Perform a literature search on a self-help group or on support groups, in which you examine how the authors defined these groups. Identify the major research themes found during a particular time frame, e.g., 1993-1994. Write a five- or six-page paper on what you found.

Chapter 2

HELPING CHARACTERISTICS AND CHANGE MECHANISMS IN SELF-HELP AND SUPPORT GROUPS

Our need for *mutuality* arises from our very flawedness and imperfection; it originates in the fact that by ourselves we are never enough. We need others to help us; we need others in order to help them. Thus the question "Who am I?" carries within itself another, even more important question: "Where do I belong?" We find self—ourselves—only through the actual practice of locating ourselves within the community of our fellow human beings.

—Kurtz & Ketcham, 1992, p. 86

Most self-help and support groups exist for the purpose of helping and sometimes changing their members. They help members in ways that are both similar to and different from psychotherapy groups (Lieberman, 1990; Yalom, 1995). After first reviewing some of the therapeutic factors in psychotherapy groups, this chapter will emphasize how and whether these and other helpful factors are manifested in self-help and support groups. The chapter will conclude with a discussion of possible dangers in self-help and support groups and how to create and sustain helping factors.

THERAPEUTIC FACTORS IN PSYCHOTHERAPY GROUPS

Yalom (1995) identified 11 therapeutic factors in psychotherapy groups. Because many of these are also found in self-help groups, Yalom's list will be used as a starting point for discussion. The first factor is the *instillation of hope*. The belief that therapy will help is fundamental to the individual's willingness to engage in the therapeutic process. The second is *universality*. It is painful to believe that one's dilemma is unique and that one is alone with a seemingly unsolvable problem. Realizing that others in the group are "in the same boat" comes as a welcome relief. A third factor is *information or direct advice*. Much that is learned in groups, according to Yalom (1995), is implicit. However, many groups also impart information didactically. A fourth factor, *altruism,* is generated through opportunities to help others.

Yalom termed his fifth factor the *corrective recapitulation of the primary family group*. One interacts with members of the group as one has with one's family. In so doing, one learns that family history may shape present relationships in ways that do not fit current circumstances. New and better ways of relating can be learned within the therapy group.

Basic social skills may be acquired in the group, learned explicitly or implicitly. A seventh factor is *imitative behavior.* Listening to and watching group members, one learns vicariously from their experiences and from interactions with them. *Interpersonal learning* evolves from relationships formed within the group through which members pursue goals such as being more loving or more assertive. *Group cohesiveness,* Yalom believes, is the "analogue of 'relationship' in individual therapy" (p. 48). It is the degree to which members feel trust and closeness to one another. The tenth factor, *catharsis,* is the ventilation of feelings. The last factor, Yalom terms *existential factors,* meaning recognition of such realities as that life may be unfair, that everyone is ultimately alone, that everyone must face death, and that one must take responsibility for one's life.

THERAPEUTIC FACTORS IN
SELF-HELP AND SUPPORT GROUPS

Practitioners and researchers have seldom recorded exactly how the group processes of self-help and support groups occur. As Goodman and Jacobs (1994) comment, the field "lacks a psychology of its intimate method" (p. 500). The next section reviews the literature on helping processes found in many studies of self-help groups. We begin by considering Yalom's helping factors within the framework of what goes on in self-help and support groups.

Yalom's Factors in Self-Help
and Support Groups

Members of Alcoholics Anonymous (AA), Emotions Anonymous, Al-Anon, and Parent-to-Parent groups, responding to a survey, regarded three of Yalom's factors: *group cohesiveness, instillation of hope,* and *universality,* as those most helpful to them (Heil, 1992). Members of a group for people with depression reported *cohesiveness* as the most helpful factor in the group (Llewelyn & Haslett, 1986). Llewelyn and Haslett also found that *universality* was experienced as the most helpful by members of a group for widows. A study of members in a computer-mediated support group found that *instillation of hope, group cohesion,* and *universality* were the most helpful factors; *catharsis* and *altruism* were less frequently identified as helpful (Weinburg, Uken, Schmale, & Adamek, 1995). Group climate studies reveal that *cohesiveness* is higher in self-help and support groups than in other types of groups, including psychotherapy groups (Moos, Finney, & Maude-Griffin, 1993).

Research on the storytelling activity in self-help groups supports the importance of *instilling hope.* Hope comes when newcomers listen to veteran members tell their stories of recovery (E. Kurtz, 1979; Rappaport, 1993). Newcomers identify with the "what we used to be like" portion of the story. They realize that the veteran was once in the same desperate state that the newcomer currently experiences. They attain hope when they hear the "what it's like now," or recovery portion of the veteran member's story. The following testimony by a member of Parents Anonymous illustrates how the group engendered hopefulness:

My first meeting replaced hopelessness with hope. My second meeting replaced helplessness with new ideas. It's now been three years and I am the parent leader of my group. Just taking home even one small bit of information once a week has given me an entire treasure chest full of hope to turn to when times are stressful. (Parents Anonymous, 1995b, p. 3)

Numerous authors have noted the importance of *universality,* the finding of similarity in self-help/support groups (Goodman & Jacobs, 1994; L. F. Kurtz, 1994; Lieberman, 1979; Llewelyn & Haslett, 1986; Medvene, 1990). "Similarity of suffering from a specific common problem creates environments with a high frequency of expressed empathy" (Goodman & Jacobs, 1994, p. 501). Feelings of belonging, similarity, and willingness to self-disclose were expressed by more than half of the members of an Alliance for the Mentally Ill group studied by Medvene (1990) and were among the helping factors identified by a similar proportion of members in L. F. Kurtz's (1994) study of family groups.

Most groups impart *information,* either through outside speakers or through the sharing of their experiential knowledge by members (Borkman, 1990). Levy (1979) found the provision of "normative and instrumental information and advice" prevalent in all the groups he and his associates studied (p. 250).

Altruism evolves through efforts to carry the message of recovery to others, which is generally seen as an advanced stage of participation (see chapter 4) (Jurik, 1987; Rudy, 1986). Imparting help is beneficial to the giver as well as to the receiver. In fact, some contend that such helping of others is not purely altruistic because it is undertaken as a means of continuing one's own recovery (Rudy, 1986; Smith, 1991).

Imitative behavior takes place in many groups. For example, the Society of Compassionate Friends (for parents who have lost a child) asks members to imitate others who introduce themselves in meetings by giving the name of the child who died and the circumstances of the child's death. This helps the parent learn to relate these facts more calmly outside the group (Sherman, 1979).

The remaining five of Yalom's factors are less likely to occur in a self-help or support group. For example, without direct effort by a psychotherapist, who teaches group members that the meaning of their interactions *recapitulates the original family group,* it is unlikely that this factor will become salient in self-help or support group meetings.

Basic social skills may be acquired in a support group, but again, it is unlikely that they will be explicitly taught or be the focus during self-help group gatherings.

Interpersonal learning occurs when the relationship of group members with each other becomes the focus of group discussion. This kind of interaction is unlikely in either a self-help or a true support group (Yalom, 1995). Self-help groups maintain a safe and nonconfrontive environment in which there are few if any instances of back-and-forth exchange among members about their relationships with each other.

Catharsis might occur in a support group, but is not one of the factors typically identified by members as helpful. In fact, intense discussion of feelings can be overwhelming and harmful to participants (Chesler, 1990; Galinsky & Schopler, 1994). Yalom's (1995) discussion of catharsis indicates that this factor is helpful only if it occurs after the group's members have formed a cohesive bond. He further suggests that catharsis must be combined with some form of cognitive learning. Although catharsis may occur in self-help groups, if it is to be experienced positively, feelings must be connected to the group's cognitive understanding of the difficulty and its resolution. Most often, feelings are expressed superficially and in a manner restrained by the structure found in most self-help groups.

Some self-help and support groups meet *existential concerns,* although not by intended focus or even with any explicit intent. An analysis of AA suggests that by its avoidance of self-centeredness and its urging one to accept one's limitations, AA and imitator groups bring to bear the insights of existential philosophy and crisis theology, but in the vocabulary of the pragmatic Twelve Steps (E. Kurtz, 1982).

Helping Factors Common to Both
Self-Help and Support Groups

Research on group processes and change mechanisms discloses five processes that appear in both support and self-help groups. They are: *giving support, imparting information, conveying a sense of belonging, communicating experiential knowledge,* and *teaching coping methods.*

Giving Support

Support is the primary purpose of a support group and is the benefit most often mentioned by members when asked what they received from their group (Katz & Maida, 1990; L. F. Kurtz, 1988; Maton, 1988). But what is support? Studies present it as a combination of words and silent attention, personal disclosure and empathy. Support groups enlarge the social network of members (L. F. Kurtz, 1994; Toseland, Rossiter, Peak, & Smith, 1990). Gottlieb (1982) defines support in self-help groups as encompassing the learning of coping strategies, having a sense of community, coping with public attitudes, getting factual information, attaining a spirit of hope, attaining self-confidence, and meeting others with similar problems (Gottlieb, 1982). Support, it seems, encompasses most of the other factors discussed here.

One analysis of communicating in meetings found that supportive help-giving comments, direct guidance, and suggestions correlated with members' positive evaluation of meetings (Roberts, 1985; 1987). In contrast, negative comments and probing, personal questions resulted in negative meeting evaluations. The key ingredient of support thus appears to be crucial to group success, whereas criticism and intrusiveness will damage it.

Imparting Information

Research on helping factors in support groups shows that information is another of the most important factors (Abramowitz & Coursey, 1989; L. F. Kurtz, 1988). Support groups often rely on professional information brought to the group by outside experts. For example, the National Alliance for the Mentally Ill (NAMI) and other support groups for relatives who have mental illness publish newsletters, compile bibliographies, stage conferences, and invite speakers to educate their membership. Levy (1979) noted that information comes to members in two ways: as part of the formal meeting, and in informal socializing after the meeting. In a survey of members in 65 disease-related groups, the researcher found that with participation, members became more competent in finding additional professional help and in using prescribed medications (Trojan, 1989). Although self-help is often viewed as an alternative to professional service, Trojan's findings indicated that members are more likely to increase their use of professional services after participating in self-help and support groups. This is likely due to the information received about available helping resources.

Conveying a Sense of Belonging

Joining any group is an exercise in affiliation; group participation offers opportunities for gaining a sense of belonging. Studies of GROW, a group for persons with serious mental illness, reveal that GROW is more than just a self-help group; it offers an entire social network and an interdependent collective that values community over autonomy (Salem, Seidman, & Rappaport, 1988). Similarly, many of those interviewed for a study of family self-help thought that people in their ordinary support system could not understand their situation (L. F. Kurtz, 1994). Joining the group offered contact with people who knew what they were enduring. As one group member put it in an interview, "Without the group I wouldn't have any social life at all" (p. 305).

Recall the discussion of self-help as community rather than self-help as alternative treatment in chapter 1. Rappaport (1993) proposed that the mutual-help organization is a normative structure similar to a family, a religious organization, or other voluntary association. He writes that "members are not clients . . . rather they are people having lives" (p. 123). Helping people connect is a first step in their belonging to a group of other people. Achieving a sense of belonging in the self-help community becomes a measure of successful identity change.

Communicating Experiential Knowledge

The specialized information and perspective that people gain when they live through and resolve a problem differs from both the expertise of professionals and the common knowledge of the lay person; Borkman (1990) termed this *experiential knowledge*. For example, members of a group for people with affective disorders shared information regarding their diagnoses and the medications they used (Karp, 1992). They created a conceptual framework for each other that enlightened and gave meaning to their personal trouble. Learning that many productive and brilliant people are suffering or have suffered from manic depressive illness, members developed an ideology in which they construed themselves as gifted but unusually sensitive people—an attitude that reframed their illness as contributing a positive aspect to their self images.

Experiential knowledge is conveyed through personal stories of learning to cope and using the group's support. The typical story begins with "what we used to be like." The storytellers then tell about joining the group, after which they have experienced improved coping, relief from shame, and a growing ability to help others. In some groups this process is ritualized. For example, in Twelve-Step groups, members tell their story as the main part of the program (in some locales this is referred to as "giving a lead"). In Recovery, Inc., each meeting consists of members offering panel examples consisting of four parts: the circumstances at the time of the example, how the individual began "to work her- or himself up," how the spotting of symptoms occurred and the Recovery methods used, and what would have happened before the Recovery training. In other groups, experiential knowledge is conveyed in less formal ways through the exchange of conversation. For example, in one Alliance for the Mentally Ill (AMI) group, the program alternated between informational meetings and support meetings in which members took turns relating how things were going. When problems and crises arose in the exchange, others, who had faced similar situations and overcome them, described their experiences, what worked for them, and how they coped with the same problems or crises.

Teaching Coping Methods

Drawing on both expertise and experience, group members develop new methods for coping with their situation. For example, when asked how they had learned to handle problems, interviewees in an Al-Anon group described learning to detach (L. F. Kurtz, 1994, p. 303). They gave the term a particular meaning, a behavior that involved letting go of the situation and not trying to control either the person or the course of that person's illness.

Developing the ability to communicate in ways that are conducive to harmonious relationships is another skill sharpened in self-help and support groups. Families with both alcoholic and mentally ill members come to realize the need to reduce the feeling intensity in their communication with the other person. For example, an AMI member said, "I've learned that I have to soften my voice, watch my body movements, and avoid arguments" (Kurtz, 1994, p. 304). Similarly, an Al-Anon member described herself:

My sponsor told me that when I talked to him just keep to the facts. Before that, I would have been crying and screaming and yelling and everything. So I was talking to him really factual and part of me was looking at this and saying, is this really me? (Kurtz, 1994, p. 304).

Members of Recovery, Inc. learn to "spot" instances of temper, moments when unnecessary fears or anger threaten to move them to behavior they will later regret. Spotting requires mindfulness of when those episodes are about to happen and an ability to replace a habitual way of thinking and self-talk with new ways learned in the Recovery program (Low, 1950). For example, a tendency to imagine what another person is thinking or feeling is replaced by the thought that one does not, in fact, have "the vanity of knowing" what actually occurs in the mind of another. Overreactions to episodes of discomfort are replaced with the "will to bear discomfort." (See chapter 9 for a description of the Recovery, Inc. method.) Members are enjoined to avoid involvement in upsetting interactions in order to "put one's mental health first." Learning to cope in new ways is transmitted through exchange with persons who have learned to use these methods through experience and practice.

The five processes just discussed can be found and nurtured in both support and self-help groups. Five additional processes associated with personal change also may be present in either kind of group, but are more likely to be found in self-help associations that have larger memberships, longer histories, and more complex programs.

Change Mechanisms in Self-Help Groups

Self-help groups, with their focus on change, produce five change-oriented skills that help members to achieve life-altering goals: *identity transformation, empowerment, insight, reframing,* and *formation of a new way of life.* Although all of these are rarely present in any one group or at any one time, to understand self-help groups and their capacity to change, one must be alert to these diverse manifestations.

Transforming Identities

Twenty years ago, Katz and Bender (1976) proposed that the major contribution of a self-help group to people with deviant labels was the reconstruction of a positive identity. The newcomer first identifies with group members through the sense that they have gone through a similar experience (i.e., the newcomer is still what the speaker once was). In time, the recognition that she or he can achieve what the veteran member has attained moves the recruit to acquire the characteristics of the older member. Veteran members construct and model new ways of coping and being.

Identity transformation is a kind of *conversion*; characteristics of the process of conversion include biographical reconstruction (i.e., mentally rewriting one's life story) and finding a causal interpretation of the condition or behavior (Snow & Machalek, 1983). For self-help group members, this often requires accepting a diagnostic label as part of one's identity. In so doing, members attain a clearer conceptualization of what had once been a bewildering set of symptoms that had caused harm to self and others. The process of attaching a label to one's problem often serves to define who can be a member of the group and who cannot.

Labeling is controversial. Does adopting a label mean acceptance of a stigmatized or "spoiled" identity (Goffman, 1963)? Challenging the negative connotations of diagnosis, Karp's (1992) ethnographic study of a group for people with manic depressive illness found that "group discussion centering on cause, responsibility, and the correctness of the mental illness label . . . provided plausible explanations for members' difficulties while helping to protect their diminished selves" (p. 166-167). It was important that members had a label for symptoms that for years had been without a name. "The creation of an illness reality was, then, a first and critical step in the effort to make sense of things" (p. 149).

One cannot take steps to help oneself if one does not know what is wrong. Also, the group protects one from further identity damage. Group members attempted to repair their identities by discussing famous individuals who had an affective disorder. In addition, their talk provided a vocabulary through which members could both conceptualize and communicate about their illness. The social scientist's "label" is the members' *way of talking about*. "Members learned to navigate between rhetorics . . . in a way that accounted for their situation while empowering them to do something about it" (p. 167).

The alcoholic (illness) identity is only a beginning in AA (as well as in other Twelve-Step Groups). In Twelve-Step groups, the ultimate transformation is expressed as having had a *spiritual awakening*. AA's Twelfth Step reads, "Having had a spiritual awakening as the result of these steps, we tried to carry this message to alcoholics and to practice these principles in all our affairs" (AA, 1976, p. 60). A spiritual awakening involves more than simple abstinence from alcohol ("putting the cork in the bottle"): It is a transformation that involves letting go of willfulness and surrendering control to a power greater than one's self. As a result, one becomes "able to do, feel, and believe that which he could not do before on his unaided strengths and resources alone" (AA, 1952, p. 110). The following quote from an AA member illustrates this calm and gradual conversion experience:

> I had been praying every night when I went to bed and in the morning, reading the *Twenty-Four Hour Book.* One night, it just seemed to be there when I was praying. I said, *God, I'm an alcoholic, and I can't drink or I'll die. But I'm turning my life over to You, and I'll do whatever You want me to do just to stay sober a day at a time.* After that, the obsession to drink just seemed not to be there anymore. (Smith, 1991, p. 98)

Spiritual transformation is only one kind of change. Other changes may have to do with being more assertive and able to assume more responsibility for coping with disability. For some, it is a transition to personal empowerment.

Becoming Empowered

Empowerment occurs when one becomes able to take action for oneself and in behalf of others. The first sign of it is a dawning belief in oneself; one experiences growth of self confidence, which is usually accomplished within a group of others facing the same ordeal (Kieffer, 1984). Members of family self-help groups reported gaining the ability to reach out to others, to tackle a problem a step at a time, and to convert the frustrated wish to help one's child to taking steps to change social policy (L. F. Kurtz, 1994). An AMI member said, "It is real important to me to start doing something. I had to be in a group that didn't see everything in completely negative terms." Another said, "You realize that you can't do for your child. By working with AMI, I can help her by changing the public's opinion, by getting legislation, by supporting research on medication to make her life more livable" (p.305).

Empowerment flows from the community aspect of a self-help group (Gidron & Chesler, 1995). The group is a place where one joins with others to mobilize resources in the pursuit of needs and interests. The members' common sense becomes validated and relevant. The feeling of empowerment is enhanced by having indigenous leadership and peer governance. Some groups focus on social change. Others, particularly groups in the Twelve-Step tradition, eschew social change as a goal in the group. This avoidance of an external focus and the reference to powerlessness in the first of the Twelve Steps lead some observers to interpret these groups as favoring helplessness or even infantile dependency. More sophisticated thinkers recognize the potency of knowing what is possible and focusing one's energies in that direction. As Gregory Bateson (1972) pointed out a quarter-century ago, and others have elaborated since, recognizing powerlessness over those things that cannot be changed is the first step to empowerment (Bateson 1972; Kurtz & Ketcham, 1992).

Joanne Hall's (1994) study of lesbian experiences in AA provides an example of how that fellowship can become an experience of empowerment. She quotes one of her research subjects:

> I have always conceptualized higher power as inside me. And I never bought that I was powerless, like they try to teach you in AA. So for me, AA hasn't taken any energy away from political work. I think it adds to it. Once you get clean and sober you have so much more ability to see the world clearly.
>
> Being a sober lesbian is a very political thing. It is important that lesbians wake up from the fog of alcohol in our community. And there is a lot of activism you can do inside AA if you get on committees, take responsibility. Even having a lesbian chair an AA meeting, that's a little political triumph right there. (p. 9)

Even though this individual misunderstood what AA says about powerlessness, she realized that she had become empowered through her sobriety and through the fellowship of other alcoholics. Understanding the meaning of powerlessness and the role it plays in one's lack of self-efficacy is an insight that comes when a person recognizes that individual effort will not produce control over the use of alcohol, but surrendering that use, in the context of the group, empowers the member to remain sober one day at a time.

Achieving Insight

Goodman and Jacobs (1994) hypothesize that insight comes more easily in self-help groups than in formal therapies where denial and avoidance are more typical. In self-help groups there is less skepticism; the presence of the problem is taken for granted, since it is a condition of membership. The group's typical response is "bland, patient, and instructional" (p. 501). Detailed self-disclosure is minimal, and one's problem is discussed abstractly and as being the same as that of other members, rather than in terms of one's individual failings. Even difficult disclosures bring forth empathic understanding and expressions of identification (a "me-too" response). This nonthreatening atmosphere allows members to arrive at insights in their own time and on their own terms.

Insights take time to develop. The following quote comes from an older woman with several years of sobriety, who almost drank again. It serves as an example of insight gained through a combination of group membership and a sudden threatening experience:

Life had been the pits for me that year. I was feeling lonely, since my family was all scattered. A woman at work invited me to a party, and the booze was flowing. I figured I might try to have just one glass of punch. But something came over me just as I was about to pour it. I thought . . . I'm an alcoholic . . . and this could *kill* me! I left the party and drove to an Alkathon (AA event). And all the way over I kept saying, "Thank you, God!" (Smith, 1991, p. 111)

This woman had been attending AA meetings for 3 years and presumably had accepted the label *alcoholic,* but this incident gave her sudden insight into the "cunning, baffling, and powerful" nature of alcoholism (AA, 1976, p. 58-59).

Reframing One's Understanding of the Problem

In addition to facilitating the letting go of futile efforts to effect improbable change, self-help groups can give new insights through cognitive redefinitions and new language to articulate what is wrong and how to fix what is wrong. The most explicit example of cognitive therapy in self-help is found in *will training,* the method used by Recovery, Inc. (Low, 1950). Once Recovery members learn the method of will training, they begin to reframe upsetting events as instances of fearful or angry temper, rather than as dangers or wrongdoings. Acquiring a new understanding of temper, the member learns to think with a new vocabulary. For example, Recovery, Inc. members learn that they cannot control what is in their "outer environment," but they can control what is inside them, the inner environment. This frees energy to use in more effective ways.

In an example of temper, Low (1950) tells of a woman who from a young age learned to openly correct anyone she heard make a mistake. If her neighbor pointed to crabgrass in the yard and referred to it as ragweed, the woman would correct her. She became unpopular with other people because of this annoying habit. As a Recovery member, she learned to reframe this habit of correcting people as an example of "temper." She learned to spot such examples and to keep her mind on her goal of achieving inner and outer peace, a goal impeded by her practice of correcting the mistakes of others. Once the woman learned to spot this habit, she curbed her practice of correcting and began enjoying more harmonious relationships.

In a study of family self-help groups, many subjects mentioned the benefits of redefining the problem (L. F. Kurtz, 1994). Members learned to define the alarming and embarrassing behaviors of mental illness or alcoholism as symptoms of a disease rather than as intentional, immoral, or foolish actions. The disease definition relieved members of blame and helped them to act compassionately toward the sick person. An AMI member illustrated the importance of the disease definition: "The major feeling is guilt, so the group takes the guilt away. You're supposed to take care of your children, and you feel you've done something to cause it, but you learn it's just part of the illness" (p. 305).

New Community for Living

Rappaport (1993) presents GROW as a *normative narrative community.* The group has its own narrative; in choosing to join the group, a member adopts the community narrative as a template for his or her own story and begins to shape his or her identity within the frame of the community narrative. Rejecting the tendency of social scientists to see self-help groups as alternative treatments, Rappaport pointed out that "when membership leads to significant change in a person's identity and behavior, it could be understood as a change in community of membership and lifestyle rather than as a 'treatment outcome' " (p. 124). When people join a self-help group of this kind, they are making a change that has large consequences for their entire way of life, just as if they were changing careers or converting to a new religion. For some, the new community will not appeal, and membership will be aborted; for others, the community will inspire continued investment and the recruit will come to see himself or herself within the context of community membership and begin to develop a personal narrative that reflects the new way of life and new way of thinking.

Rudy's (1986) qualitative study of AA described members deeply immersed in that program, some having begun their participation by attending 90 meetings in 90 days. Because AA has many meetings and is intensely social, it is literally possible for a participant to attend a meeting every day or even more often. Some members encircle themselves with other members as friends. Some may become employed by another AA member who routinely hires other members, so that even at work he or she is surrounded by recovering people. If the spouse and children desire, they may become involved in Al-Anon and Alateen. The AA member may also take on responsibilities, attend workshops, conferences, and weekend retreats. Rudy designated this as an example of "encapsulation," an extreme form of community experience.

Mutual-help groups have also been viewed as social worlds (Smith, 1991). The social world perspective defines the group as a universe or cultural arena with no formal boundaries, in which there is a perception of a common bond among members. Those who join the social world attach definitions and symbolic meanings to things usually unknown to outsiders (Smith, 1991). Smith's analysis suggests that AA involvement leads many to a "redefinition of self" within the AA social world (p.101).

Unhelpful Characteristics in Groups

Galinsky and Schopler (1994) observed that people value the idea of support groups so highly that they often assume no harm can come from them. Although there is little evidence of pervasive harmful effects within self-help or support groups, it is unwise to think that harm cannot occur in these groups. Readers of this book need to be alert to the practitioner's obligation to help people find a suitable group, to assure safety in groups they facilitate, to structure groups in ways that offer stable procedures and expectations, and to cultivate norms that assure positive discussion.

Possible dangers in self-help and support groups fall into six general categories (Galinsky & Schopler, 1994; Chesler, 1990):

1. There is concern that people in non-professionally-led groups may give misguided and misinformed information to members. This risk can be diminished by establishing norms that prohibit members from giving advice. In AA, for example, members emphasize that all they have to offer is their collective experience, strength, and hope (Taylor, 1977).

2. Expression of intense feelings in groups can overwhelm members who are struggling with pain and fear. Exchange of purely negative emotions surrounding the situation, although helpful in small doses, will depress members and convey that the situation is hopeless. Group members need to be alert to the need to emphasize positive, concrete help, and demonstrations of coping.

3. Irregular attendance has been cited as a problem by both professional facilitators and peer leaders (Meissen & Volk, 1995). To some extent, this must be accepted and dealt with by continuing to recruit newer members and by maintaining a welcoming, comfortable group climate. The open-endedness of groups is a positive feature for people who may not need to attend every meeting, but need to know the group is there when needed, although this reality does make for some instability of member attendance.

4. Groups for people with fatal medical conditions are distressing to members in early stages of the illness because they overexpose newer members to people in terminal stages of the disease. One solution to this concern is to establish separate groups for people in varying stages; for example, people with cancer can be separated by the type of treatment they are receiving as well as the stage they are in (Glajchen & Magen, 1995).

5. There is concern that peer leaders, who are not professionally trained, may seek to provide therapy, for which they are not prepared. Support groups are not therapy groups, and as such, peer leaders should not offer therapeutic interventions, such as exploration of feelings, interpretations of unconscious material, encouragement to examine interpersonal relationships within the group, and the like. It is partly for this reason that

professionals have been cautioned not to "train" peer helpers in therapeutic methods.

6. Some have cautioned that self-help groups may pressure newcomers to accept stigmatized identities and cult-like beliefs (Wechsler, 1960). Although most groups encourage newcomers to identify with members and to accept the group's way of thinking, most do so in ways that reframe the condition as a manageable and temporary concern. It is possible, however, that forceful individuals in some groups or norms in certain groups can operate in ways that may be discouraging or stigmatizing. For example, a person who has occasional drinking problems but is not alcoholic may be convinced that he or she is alcoholic and thus may unnecessarily accept a stigmatized identity.

For a wide-ranging but somewhat unbalanced critique of recovery groups and recovery literature, the reader should examine Kaminer's (1992) *I'm Dysfunctional, You're Dysfunctional: The Recovery Movement and Other Self-Help Fashions.* She targets high-profile but frivolous aspects of the self-help/support group phenomenon; that is, codependency, recovery books, talk shows, positive thinking, new age fads, and Twelve-Step groups, although those she describes seem to have little acquaintance with the Twelve Steps. Her approach is valuable in that it points out the excesses and distortions that can occur within self-help groups, particularly the Twelve-Step variety, when they evolve away from the philosophy on which they were originally established.

IMPLICATIONS FOR PRACTITIONERS

Because professional roles differ with regard to self-help and support, the discussion of implications for practice will focus first on support groups and then on self-help groups.

For Support Group Facilitators

The first rule of thumb is to be clear about the nature of support, which is the essence of a support group. We know from Roberts (1985; 1987) that members prefer meetings in which they hear positive, supportive comments and where negative, critical comments and intrusive questions are absent. Achieving this atmosphere often depends on role modeling by a facilitator; a supportive atmosphere also depends on the personality style of the group's formal and informal leadership, who should minimize focus on intense feelings. Support group facilitators can enhance supportiveness by setting ground rules, such as not criticizing other members, not asking personal questions, and respecting confidentiality. Facilitators should remember that support groups are more social than therapeutic in nature; they are a place to belong, not a treatment to undergo.

Group cohesiveness can be promoted by facilitators through increasing opportunities for members to become acquainted with one another. Facilitators can suggest that members come a little early to meetings in order to meet newcomers and engage in conversation. For the same reason, refreshments and conversation after the formal meeting can be made a part of the meeting routine.

Hope is instilled when newcomers see positive changes in more experienced members. For this to happen, those members should have an opportunity to tell their success stories. Experienced members, who may be uncomfortable about giving the impression that they are bragging, can be helped to understand the importance of their success as a means of instilling hope. Oldtimers can attribute success to the group rather than to themselves. The facilitator can explain this and suggest structured ways of including positive storytelling in meetings. In groups where the reason for the meeting involves the eventual death of members, facilitators should be particularly careful about including those who are in late stages with those who are not yet facing that prospect.

Universality is achieved through self-disclosure and the recognition of similarity among members; structuring group meetings in ways that allow for recognition of similarity can enhance this factor. This can be accomplished through going around the group and offering members an opportunity to tell of their situation. In listening, others can realize how their situations compare with their own.

Information is probably the most frequent contribution of facilitators. Information can be transmitted through presenting it didactically, recommending experts to speak to the group, and providing literature for members. Facilitators may want to be on guard that they do not allow the group to pressure them into being the only source of information (members' experiential knowledge should also be reflected in group discussions); on the other hand, knowledge requiring expertise should not be imparted by lay persons.

Facilitators can encourage members to share their own success stories by reassuring them of the value of experiential knowledge. The professional's own attitude can be an important model of this behavior: do we listen to learn, or to judge? Likewise, facilitators can emphasize to members that coping methods are important to discuss in the group. For example, a new member may ask how to handle a difficult situation. After waiting a moment for other members to speak, the facilitator can ask, "Has anyone else dealt with that kind of situation?" The facilitator may on occasion have to remind the group that his or her task is to bring them together so they can share their experiences, not so that the facilitator can give instructions.

Altruism occurs in the process of mutual aid. It is important that professional facilitators and group leaders promote opportunities for members to help each other and not view this helping as the sole responsibility of the facilitator or group leader. This will be further discussed in Chapter 6.

Social learning takes place through instruction, reinforcement, and modeling. Facilitators and group leaders provide instruction through simple explanations and factual information. Reinforcement can be given by recognition of improvements and efforts. It is important that the group's discourse be steered toward a focus on successes rather than on complaints and failures. Effort should be recognized, even if the effort is not initially successful. Modeling is important in giving hope, but also important for the purpose of demonstrating how change was brought about. Facilitators can support modeling by identifying for more advanced members when their experiences can serve as examples for newer members.

Linking With Self-Help Groups

Self-help groups do not have professional facilitators; practice implications for working with such groups thus differ from those of support group facilitation. Professionals are most often involved in referring or linking clients to groups. In order to do this, it is most important to be aware of the group's helping capacities and to recognize when someone with whom you work may benefit from them.

Research suggests that people who join self-help groups are also more inclined to use professional therapy (Kessler et al., 1996). Therapists and case managers who are informed about the groups their clients attend can help them understand how the groups help them change. For example, practitioners who understand the process of identity transformation, in which one rewrites one's life story, can reassure the client who wants immediate change by explaining the gradual nature of identity change and the subtle ways in which that happens. Insights that develop without the interpretations of a therapist occur gradually and require that the group member listen patiently with an openness to identification with those who are more experienced members. Beliefs and worldviews held by self-help communities reframe the meaning of the member's problem and in this way relieve him or her of emotional pain by normalizing the condition and showing that one is not alone in having it. Finally, professionals can recognize that a self-help group is not a "treatment," but rather offers the member an association that becomes an entirely new way of life within the group's community.

SUMMARY

In this chapter, we have seen how self-help and support groups contain many of the same helping processes found in psychotherapy groups. We have also seen that there are differences between helping in therapy, self-help, and support groups. We have discussed in detail how helping factors manifest themselves in self-help groups. Suggestions for creating and sustaining these factors have been offered.

The next chapter discusses group ideologies, group climate, organizational structure, and professionalization of self-help associations. Readers will be offered some analytic frameworks that have been used to analyze ideologies and climates.

DISCUSSION QUESTIONS

1. What is your position on the view of self-help as an alternative form of human service as opposed to the view of self-help as a new community for living? Discuss the pros and cons to each of the two points of view.
2. Imagine yourself as a professional who is advising members of a support group. The group's leader comes to you asking how to set an agenda for discussion in meetings. Consider the various helping elements possible, and list suggestions for the group's leader that would facilitate the emergence of those elements.

CLASSROOM EXERCISE

Watch one or more of the videos listed at the end of chapter 4, and have each class member rate the helping factors discussed in this chapter on the rating sheet at the end of this chapter.

ASSIGNMENT

The following observation form gives space for observations of the helping mechanisms discussed in chapter 2. With a group's permission, attend one of its meetings. After the meeting is over, go over the checklist and identify examples of helping processes that you observed. Describe them in the space provided, and discuss this experience in a short paper.

OBSERVATIONS OF THERAPEUTIC FACTORS IN SELF-HELP GROUPS

When you are observing a group in action, watch for indications of the following factors and make notes after the meeting about how you observed the factor you noticed.

Giving Support _____

_____

Imparting Information _____

_____

Teaching Coping Methods _____

_____

Conveying a Sense of Belonging _____

_____

Communicating Experiential Knowledge _____

_____

Transforming Identities _____

_____

Becoming Empowered _____

_____

Achieving Insight _____

_____

Reframing the Problem_____

_____

New Community for Living _____

_____

Chapter 3

IDEOLOGY, CLIMATE, STRUCTURE, AND PROFESSIONALIZATION IN SELF-HELP AND SUPPORT GROUPS

In a very important way, the self-help approach represents an extension of the worldwide movement toward democracy.
—Riessman & Carroll, 1995, p. 8.

Established self-help organizations typically teach understandings that define both cause and cure for the condition to which they address themselves. Yet groups can develop very different climates. Some groups are tightly organized, while others are loose and casual. Some welcome professional experts in their midst, while others ask professionals to keep silent or to stay away altogether. This chapter addresses these issues: (a) ideologies and worldviews, their effects, and their significance as means of transforming members; (b) organizational climate, the social atmosphere in self-help and support groups; (c) organizational structure, how self-help groups differ from more formal, bureaucratic organizations; and (d) professionalization, the role of professional staff as employees of the association.

IDEOLOGIES AND WORLDVIEWS

Paul Antze (1979) wrote that a "group's teachings are its very essence. . . . Participants absorb group ideas, not just as a creed, but as a living reality that is reconfirmed in each day's experience" (p. 273-274). Antze asserted that these teachings, tailored to the specific group and its members, are more influential in the lives of members than any other of the group's processes. Other researchers have agreed, and there is now a beginning body of knowledge about self-help ideologies and worldviews (Borkman, 1996; Humphreys & Kaskutas, 1995; Kennedy & Humphreys, 1995; Norman, 1983-1984).

Ideologies as Cognitive Antidotes

Antze (1979) defined ideology as "the group's explicit beliefs . . . rituals, rules of behavior, slogans, and even favorite expressions" (p. 273). Reporting findings from studies of Alcoholics Anonymous (AA), Recovery, Inc., and Synanon, Antze argued that a group's ideology is the feature that members take most seriously. He believed that stories members share contribute to beliefs. Experience with others who have the same beliefs becomes a subtle form of indoctrination. Regular contacts within "communities of belief" maintain and reinforce change (p. 274).

Of the analytic frameworks offered for the study of self-help ideologies, Antze's remains the simplest (Antze, 1979; Borkman, 1996; Kennedy & Humphreys, 1995; Norman, 1983-1984). He proposed that ideologies are cognitive antidotes to the basic condition that the participant wishes to change and that these antidotes work to block relapse (Antze, 1979). For example, alcoholics have an exaggerated sense of their own ability to exert independence and control. AA teaches that one must replace one's belief in an omnipotent self with belief that there is a power greater than the self. Recovery, Inc., members believe they are helpless victims of their pain, fear, and anger. Recovery's antidote is Abraham Low's method of will training, which removes the belief in helplessness (see chapter 9). Hard drug addicts in Synanon (now defunct), were closely attuned to their feelings and to controlling those feelings with drugs. Synanon redirected their attention to standards of behavior and forced members to vent their feelings rather than anaesthetize them.

In another study of ideology, Norman (1983-1984) contrasted the beliefs about cause and cure in two weight-loss groups: Overeaters Anonymous (OA) and another group he referred to as "Lose Extra Weight Sanely" (LEWS) (not the association's real name). His analysis focused on the groups' definitions of causality and their methods of changing the tendency to overeat. The two associations differ in how they define the cause of overweight. OA views overweight as a type of illness or compulsion for which the person bears little responsibility. LEWS, in contrast, views the condition as a failure of willpower. The two associations differ in other ways as well. LEWS has no explicit program beyond sponsoring contests in which participants compete with one another over the rapidity of weight loss. OA bases itself on AA's Twelve-Step model. With the latter model, self-blame is reduced or eliminated; while in the LEWS model, participants are exhorted to control their eating tendencies and to view them as examples of individual weakness.

Ideology as a Template

In her study of a group for stutterers, Borkman (1996) termed the group's teachings its "frame" or "template." The template emerges from the exchange of stories and ideas. These gradually create a core of meanings, perspectives, and beliefs about the condition that have been tested and evaluated in the lives of members. Borkman lists four components in a template: (a) how the condition is defined; (b) how the condition modifies identity; (c) how one resolves problems stemming from the condition; and (d) how the group should be structured in order to resolve problems.

Application of Borkman's framework to AA illustrates its use. AA *defines the problem* as self-centeredness that has resulted in a physical, mental, and spiritual disease (AA, 1976; Miller & Kurtz, 1994). The alcoholic's *identity* is thus that of a person with "defects of character," a self-defined "alcoholic," who suffers from an incurable disease that can be held in check "one day at a time" through participation in AA. The problem of alcoholism is *resolved* by practicing the Twelve Steps, especially by carrying the AA message to alcoholics who still suffer, which is to be done for an indefinite period of time, possibly for the rest of one's life (AA, 1976). AA's rules of *structure* are found in its Twelve Traditions and its well-known meeting format in which members tell their stories of "what we used to be like, what happened, and what we are like now" (p. 58).

Worldviews

Like others just discussed, Kennedy & Humphreys (1995) regard ideologies as means of shaping how members define and deal with their difficulties. Referring to self-help groups as "communities of belief" (p. 182), the authors outline four life domains that reflect the group's worldview:

1. Experience of self as a result of the condition and how the group changes that experience.
2. How the group inculcates beliefs about a universal order and Higher Power.
3. Relationships with others because of the condition and how these change as a result of the group's beliefs.
4. Understanding of the problem or affliction which changes as one assumes the worldview of the group.

Using this framework, Humphreys and Kaskutas (1994) compared three self-help associations: AA, Adult Children of Alcoholics/Al-Anon, and Women For Sobriety (WFS). Table 3.1 contrasts the worldviews of the three associations as analyzed by Humphreys and Kaskutas. As the comparison moves from AA on the left to WFS on the right, one can see that the experience of self becomes less concerned with the member's character defects and more concerned with raising self-esteem. In reference to "universal order," both of the Twelve-Step programs recognize some form of power greater than the self, whereas WFS regards successful sobriety to be a direct result of personal effort. Relationships with others in AA are oriented around the Twelfth Step, giving service to others. In WFS, one is urged to first love oneself. In AA, the problem is rooted in the alcoholic's own being. In the other two associations, the source of the problem is located outside the self.

Group ideologies, templates, and worldviews represent a compelling means of explaining and resolving a problem. They provide explanations of life situations that have baffled and distressed new members and offer them hope through following specified steps. Thus, well-articulated worldviews and teachings can be powerfully attractive to potential members. They reinforce a group's ability to influence its members in attaining the goals for which the group was formed.

Another source of attraction, as well as an indication of group functioning, is the group's social climate. While ideologies represent the thinking aspect of the group, climate represents the feel of the group to its participants. Is the group calm and accepting or exciting and innovative? The next section explains the concept of climate and offers a means of assessing it.

SOCIAL CLIMATE IN
SELF-HELP AND SUPPORT GROUPS

The concept of group climate comes from social-ecology theory (Moos, 1974). Moos, Finney, and Maude-Griffin (1993) explain that "the social climate perspective assumes that each environment has a unique quality that gives it unity and coherence" (p. 253). Human beings interact and shape one another. Groups and other human aggregates have personalities just as individuals do, and these personalities have an important impact on their members (Moos, 1986; Moos, Finney, & Maude-Griffin, 1993).

Moos (1986) and his associates have developed standardized instruments to assess social climate (Group Environment Scales or GES). These instruments aggregate individual member ratings of the group's internal

Table 3.1

Comparison of Worldviews of

AA, ACoA/Al-Anon and Women For Sobriety

AA	ACoA/Al-Anon	Women For Sobriety (WFS)
Experience of Self		
AA emphasizes deflation of the grandiose self and attributes alcoholism as being rooted in self-centeredness. Its approach attempts to instill humility and minimize egotism.	Members come with low self-esteem yet they also overestimate their personal control and must learn to give it up. Hence, members must increase their sense of self-worth but curb their sense of the self's power.	Women alcoholics experience chronic low self-esteem and should not be taught to accept humility. They need to assert belief in the self and affirm their worth.
Universal Order		
AA urges members to "turn over" to God those problems the alcoholic has been unable to solve alone. In relation to God, AA emphasizes that the alcoholic is "not-God" and members pray only for knowledge of His will for them.	Members are encouraged to surrender control to God. Rather than being too grandiose to accept God, the organization teaches that members feel unworthy of God's love and thus need to increase their sense of worth.	God is not mentioned nor is reliance on a Higher Power encouraged. Sobriety is viewed as a personal achievement, not a gift from God. Spiritual growth is seen as an outgrowth of emotional growth.
Relationships With Others		
AA shifts the member from a competitive symmetrical relationship with others to one that is complementary and oriented to helping others as a means toward sobriety.	Members are helped to achieve positive relationships with others. Love is valued as an exchange of rewards rather than as opportunity for self-sacrifice.	Members are encouraged to love themselves and once accomplished, loving others will follow.
The Problem		
In AA alcoholism is causally located in the alcoholic's character. To quit drinking, members must admit the need for help from others and from a higher power.	The problem is being from an alcoholic family; the source of the problem is not found within the self, but rather comes from damage done in childhood.	Alcoholism is a problem to be conquered, and this can be done by developing the mind. Triumph over alcoholism is achieved through learning cognitive reframing.

Adapted from K.Humphreys & L. A. Kaskutas, *Worldviews of Alcoholics Anonymous, Women for Sobriety, and Adult Children of Alcoholics/Al-Anon Mutual Help Groups.* Paper presented at a meeting of the Kettil Bruun Society International conference on Addiction and Mutual Help Movements in a Comparative Perspective, Toronto, Canada, September 12-16, 1994. Used with permission of the authors.

environment to assess 10 dimensions of group climate. The averaged ratings provide a profile of the group's climate. Ratings can identify for members what dimensions may be causing difficulties in the group and can measure changes brought about by efforts to alter its processes.

Subscales of the GES

There are 10 subscales on the GES: *Cohesion* taps commitment to the group and the friendship members show for one another. *Leader support* refers to the help and concern the leader expresses to members. *Expressiveness* refers to the emphasis on freedom of action and expression of feelings. *Independence* has to do with how much the group encourages independent action and expression among members. *Task orientation* concerns the emphasis on practical problem solving and learning specific skills. *Selfdiscovery* reflects orientation to self-revelation and discussion of personal information. *Anger and aggression* have to do with how much the group accepts open expression of negative feelings and disagreements among members. *Order and organization* concern structure and explicitness of rules and sanctions. *Leader control* refers to the extent to which the leader or chairperson makes decisions and directs the group. *Innovation* assesses how much the group facilitates diversity and change in its activities.

Profiles of self-help and support groups show them to be high on cohesion and leader support (L.F. Kurtz, 1992; Maton, 1988; 1989; Montgomery, Miller, & Tonigan, 1993; Moos et al., 1993; Tonigan & Ashcroft, 1995; Toro, Rappaport, & Seidman, 1987). Unlike psychotherapy groups, they are highly task-orientated and orderly. Anger and aggression ratings are typically low, and they rarely exhibit innovation.

Uses of the GES

GES profiles can be used to compare groups from different associations or from affiliates of the same association. For example, a study of one Al-Anon, National Alliance for the Mentally Ill (NAMI), and support group for families who have a relative with mental illness or alcoholism, found that the three group climates were very much alike, despite different goals, structures, and meeting formats (L. F. Kurtz, 1992). All were exceptionally cohesive, task-oriented, and orderly. All had high leader support. Anger, aggression, and innovation were low in all three groups (see Figure 3.1).

Conversely, a comparison of four AA groups found them to differ significantly on both the cohesion and the anger-aggression subscales (Montgomery et al., 1993). The two smaller groups were assessed by participants as highly cohesive and quite low in anger and aggression, while the two larger groups received mean ratings that demonstrated significantly lower cohesion and higher anger and aggression (although not low or high relative to the norms in other types of groups). This finding demonstrates that subgroups of the same organizational network, in this case AA, may have very different climates. Thus, the ability of any

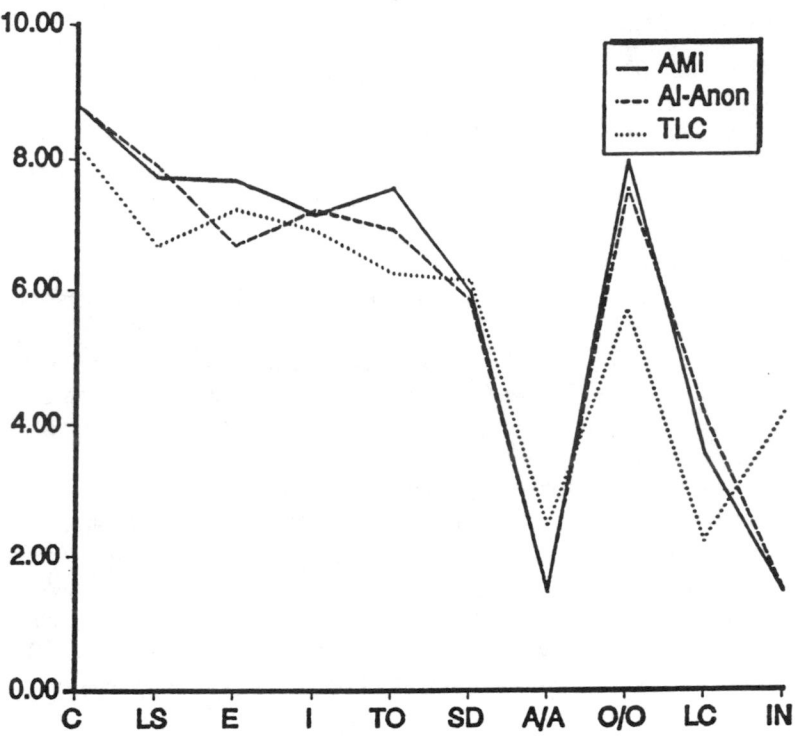

Figure 3.1. Social Climate Comparisons of Alliance for the Mentally Ill, Al-Anon, and Local Support Group (TLC)

particular group to help a specific individual may correlate with that group's climate.

Individual subscales of the GES can suggest how selected dimensions influence outcomes of group process. Three studies that gathered GES ratings of climate in self-help groups illustrate: First, Maton's (1989) comparison of eight self-help groups, four with high cohesion and four with low cohesion, found that people in the high-cohesion groups received more support, endured less depression, and possessed higher self-esteem than those in the low-cohesion groups. A second study correlated ratings of 22 NAMI groups with members' perceptions of the groups' effectiveness (Perkins, Lafuze, & Van Dusen, 1995). Social climate factors strongly and consistently correlated with member ratings. Groups in which members received the most support, in which leadership was strong, and in which meetings were seen as orderly and organized were rated as more effective than those without those features. And third, one of the studies of GROW, a group for people with mental illness, examined the effect of temporary professional leadership on GROW groups in which indigenous leaders had not yet developed (Toro, Reischl, Zimmerman, & Rappaport, 1988). Researchers found that groups with professional leaders experienced less free expression, less independent action, and less self-disclosure than groups where professionals had not assumed leader roles.

GES ratings of group climate can also help investigations of the group's problems. For example, one of the most common problems in self-help and support groups is that of declining membership (Meissen & Volk, 1995). Obtaining climate scale ratings from current and past members may suggest what needs to be altered to reverse that trend.

ORGANIZATIONAL STRUCTURE

Organizational structure is most relevant to members, leaders, and practitioners when they are involved in establishing, leading, and relating to larger self-help organizations that have aged and grown into national networks. These organizations have grown in size to a point at which structure in the form of regular procedures, careful division of labor, and lines of authority are necessary to prevent disorganization and inefficiency. Larger networks can be strengthened by the development of structure. Their stability provides a sense of community, and their procedures regulate the conduct of meetings (Powell, 1990). Structure sustains an organization and makes it more efficient. As subgroups of successful federations spread across the country and the world, the need for a headquarters and a leadership hierarchy increases.

Organizational Hierarchy

The self-help ethos (see chapter 1) inhibits self-help organizations from developing a formal hierarchy and encourages instead a more democratic form of administration. At their most formal, these national federations more resemble voluntary associations in which leadership flows upward from local subunits to state, regional, and national boards and committees. As Schubert and Borkman's (1991) typology of organizational dependency (chapter 1) shows, many national self-help organizations operate as federations; i.e., they have a national supportive network, but individual chapters are autonomous. Others have national bodies by which they are governed, but reserve leadership positions for fellow members rather than paid professionals. In still others, Schubert and Borkman's "managed" type, national bodies have become bureaucratized and are managed by professionals. Some become part of existing, professional human service organizations.

An example of how an organization has protected itself from formal hierarchy is Alcoholics Anonymous. AA's organizational hierarchy is purposely inverted so that representatives of local groups are at the top of the decision-making hierarchy, as shown in Figure 3.2 (AA, 1986). In addition, the General Service Board (composed of alcoholic and nonalcoholic trustees) cannot take action without the approval of the General Service Conference (composed of delegates who represent groups in their respective, defined geographic areas) (AA, 1990).

Delegates to AA's General Service Conference meet yearly to hear reports from board committees and the General Service Office. The conference recommends future directions through "advisory actions" generally agreed upon by the delegates: "It is the responsibility of the (General Service) Conference to work toward a consensus . . . on matters vital to AA as a whole" (AA, 1990, p. 41). Thus, decisions at the top of AA are made by consensus among representatives of geographic areas in the United States and Canada.

Alcoholics Anonymous presents itself as "a spiritual program." On the group level, this is nowhere clearer than in the fellowship's Second Tradition: "For our group purpose there is but one ultimate authority—a loving God as He may express Himself in our group conscience. Our leaders are but trusted servants; they do not govern" (AA, 1990, p. 45). The concept of "group conscience" means that controversial matters are decided, not by majority vote, but by an effort to attain unanimity. Votes are rarely taken at "group conscience meetings." Thus the ideal of spirituality, formulated in the concept of a "group conscience," plays a large role in allowing the AA Fellowship to avoid bureaucracy and centralized authority.

AA's non-hierarchical structure has been imitated by other Twelve-Step fellowships, but aside from these groups, it is atypical. Self-help networks are more likely to evolve in ways that are more hierarchical and more bureaucratized.

Evolution to Bureaucracy

Katz (1965) and later Traunstein (1984) described an evolutionary process through which a hypothetical self-help organization might go. This evolution progresses from origins and early survival, through development of formal procedures, to the hiring of professional administrators, and the establishment of formal policy (see Figure 3.3). Traunstein explained how the process of "legitimation" (acceptance) by the community can sow the

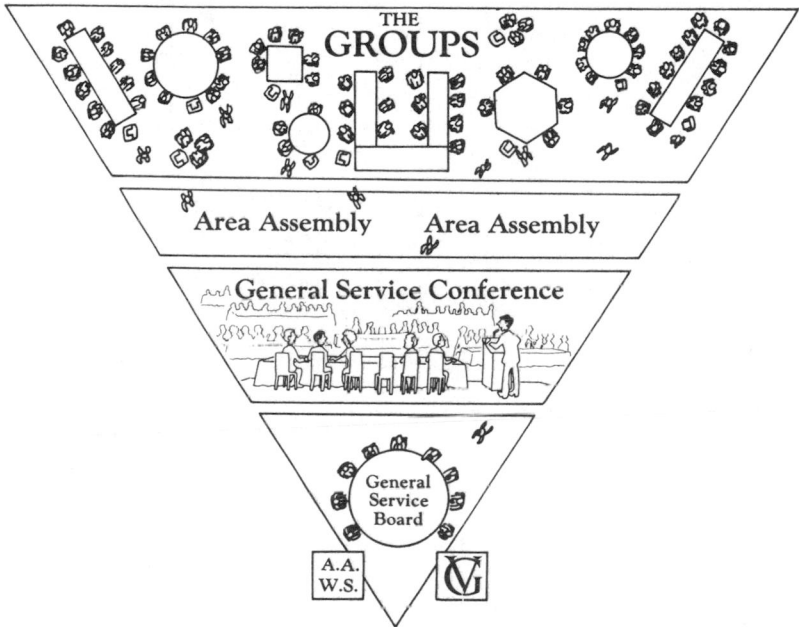

Figure 3.2. The Inverted Hierarchy of Alcoholics Anonymous (U.S. and Canada)
NOTE: From AA World Services. (1986). *The Twelve Concepts for World Service.* New York: Author. This material is reprinted with permission of Alcoholics Anonymous World Services, Inc. Permission to reprint this material does not mean that AA has reviewed or approved the contents of this handbook, nor that AA agrees with the views expressed herein. AA is a program of recovery from alcoholism only—use of this material in connection with programs and activities which are patterned after AA, but which address other problems, or in any other non-AA context, does not imply otherwise.

seeds of the professionalization process. Once the organization becomes sanctioned by human services personnel, demands for service by potential members stretch the program beyond its means; the organization hires staff, recruits influential citizens to boards of directors, and hires administrators. It may take public funds, which leads funders to make other demands that put the organization further along the road to professional bureaucratization.

A self-help organization, experiencing growth, may hover on the edge of this process, becoming a hybrid with some self-help and some human service organization characteristics. Traunstein (1984) identified the points of no return as: (a) acceptance of public monies, and (b) hiring of an administrator "whose organizational intelligence and control of resources makes her or him the single most powerful person in the agency" (p. 626). Despite these risks, it is not impossible for an organization to successfully

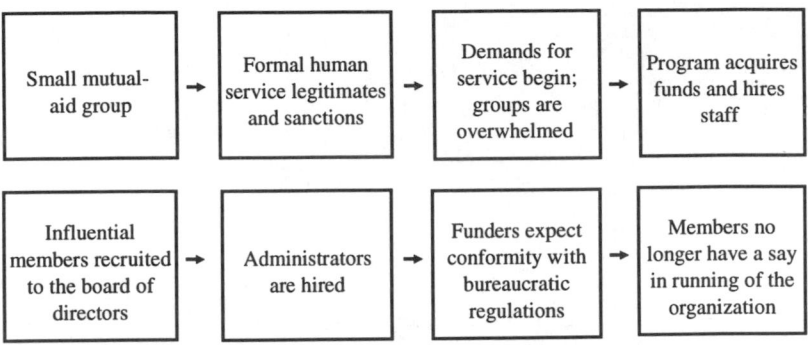

Figure 3.3. Progression From Mutual Aid Group to Formal Bureaucracy
Adapted from D. M. Traunstein (1984). From mutual-aid self-help to professional service. *Social Casework, 65,* 622-627. Used with permission from Family Service America, Publisher.

remain true to the self-help model with a hired administrator and with some public funding, as some of the associations examined in the last section of this book will illustrate. Furthermore, there are distinct advantages to the growth and differentiation of national self-help organizations that smaller, local, and informal groups forego.

In comparing national self-help organizations (NSHOs) with local self-help groups (LSHGs), Powell (1990) judged the national model superior in almost every way. The membership has more energy, greater sense of belonging, more diversity, more stable programs, more leadership opportunities, and "seasoned models" of leadership structure (p. 63). The trade-off is to remain small, tolerate a degree of chaos, and assist fewer people. A middle ground is for organizations to aim at greater efficiency while trying to preserve their self-help character and to avoid becoming just another professionalized human service agency.

Professionals relate to self-help and support groups typically as founders, consultants, facilitators, and linking agents, all of which will be the topic of chapters 6 and 7. The professional who takes a position working *within* a self-help association, however, has a very different role with such groups.

PROFESSIONALIZATION

When a group's success brings about more demand for services than volunteers can give, one solution is to hire paid staff. Later, the group may hire a director to supervise the staff. Often those with the larger responsibility possess professional credentials. Parents Anonymous may be a case in point.

When Parents Anonymous began in 1971, self-help was little known and was confined primarily to groups for people with addictions. Leonard Lieber, PA's cofounder and a social worker, took a big risk when he trusted a parent with a child abuse problem to assume responsibility for the leadership of a parent group (Parents Anonymous, 1975). Within this context, the cofounders decided to include a professional sponsor in all of its groups. As it has evolved, PA has become increasingly professionalized. For example, its first chairperson-sponsor manual asked the professional to set aside the traditional professional role and assist the parent chairperson to grow in assuming responsibility and leadership. It recognized that the parent leader offered other parents an important role model. A revision of the first edition also included a paragraph on overcontrol by the sponsor and instructed parent leaders to take problems of this nature to a regional coordinator, who could assist in resolving the problem. Later editions of the manual omitted discussion of Lieber's role or the recommendation to set aside the traditional professional role (Parents Anonymous, 1982). It gave less direction to parent leaders who experienced the professional as overcontrolling, focusing instead on the possible problems of parent leaders.

Professionals as Leaders

Some associations have policies requiring that board members and directors be from among the membership; others invite both outsiders and members to take part in leadership. For example, some require that leadership and staff be members or eligible members of the association. A social worker known to this writer is the executive director of a state-level unit of one well-known self-help association. She is professionally educated and accredited, but also, by virtue of problems in her family of origin, shares the same condition as the group's members, although this may not have been a condition of her employment.

A nationwide survey of self-help groups for persons with mental illness investigated the degree to which professionals were involved in activities of the association (Emerick, 1990). The investigator placed organizations into three categories: (a) "partnership groups" that allow professionals to participate in the leadership; (b) "supportive groups" that accept professionals in auxiliary roles; (c) "separatist groups" that reject professionals within their membership in any capacity, even as members. Emerick found that 62% of the groups fell into the supportive category; i.e, they allowed professionals a role in the group, but not as leaders. Twenty-one percent were "partnership groups" (with professionals as leaders) and 16% were "separatist groups." (The reader should keep in mind that many definitions of self-help would exclude the partnership groups.)

The Iron Law of Oligarchy

It may not be easy for group leaders to resist professional dominance. As Robert Michels described it in 1915, an "iron law of oligarchy" operates to transfer leadership in voluntary associations to a few elite members (the definition of "oligarchy") (Michels, 1915/1978, pp. 377-392). In Michels's view, leaders in any democratic association become a "political class" who detach from the rank-and-file membership and centralize leadership among a few. This evolution to oligarchy, he proposed, occurs inevitably in mass movements because people cannot influence leaders, especially when the leaders are seen to have special qualifications that set them apart from others.

This is not to suggest that professionals are a political class, but that when a group becomes professionalized, for example by hiring staff to offer services, its leadership tends to drift away from the original spirit of mutual aid and to lose the self-help ethos. Some situations encourage leader detachment. For example, a group that lacks a structured, democratic process may discourage ordinary members from influencing leaders. Moreover, when the organization hires outside experts, these experts gain control of the information used to make decisions, which is less available to ordinary members. Similarly, when decision-making and authority structures become centralized in one location or with a few individuals, members are further distanced from the organization's program and decisions related to it.

Whenever professional human service workers involve themselves in the workings and leadership of self-help associations, they encounter a style of service and operation that varies from the efficient, dispassionate, and formalized organization in which they are accustomed to working. It is important, therefore, to recognize the value of the esprit de corps and companionship that characterizes self-help groups and to hesitate before changing them, even though changes may increase order and efficiency.

IMPLICATIONS FOR PRACTITIONERS

There are a number of ways that understanding group ideologies, social climate, organizational structure, and professional leadership might influence practitioners. Awareness of these dimensions will contribute to planned, rather than haphazard, professional interaction with self-help group members. Such knowledge can also be applied to relationships between peer leaders and followers.

Understanding of self-help group ideologies, templates, and worldviews can help practitioners to be more sensitive to how groups may influence their members. If your client attends a self-help group, familiarity with the group's teachings can prevent dissonance between your approach and the group's. Furthermore, organizers can be aware of the need for groups to have teachings and understandings that develop experientially among the membership rather than relying on those borrowed from outside experts.

Although it is unlikely that practitioners will use the social climate scales in regard to self-help groups, these scales can easily be used within professionally-facilitated support groups either to assess all 10 of the dimensions or to measure only those dimensions that are pertinent. The GES is simple to obtain, administer, and score (see below for ordering instructions). The scales allow assessing the ideal and the expected group climate as well as the actual climate.

Climate ratings give group leaders direction for change. Ratings of each dimension can suggest strategies to increase or decrease it (see Chart 3.1).

Recognizing that self-help groups differ from professionally sponsored and led groups, leaders of independent self-help groups should be wary of centralizing authority that reduces the democratic atmosphere of the group. Decisions made through consensus are preferable to majority rule because they increase group cohesion. Successful associations, however, must develop some formal structure in order to handle growth. With knowledge of how to develop procedures, practitioners can assist successful groups to incorporate some structure without becoming overly formalized. Moreover, developing procedures and instructions can simplify the tasks of leadership and allow relatively inexperienced members to acquire leadership roles.

It is important to avoid compromising the mutual aid philosophy and self-help ethos of a group. For example, accepting government grants, taking funds from formal organizations, and hiring staff to perform tasks that previously were the domain of indigenous members indicate a group's transition to a professional social service agency. Practitioners can help the group's leadership to understand the consequences of these decisions and to consider whether they are making the right choices.

Formal service providers need to realize that, while self-help groups depend on new members to stay alive, they are not formal service delivery systems and may not be able to cope with large numbers of potential new members demanding services. Once you have discovered a community group that is effective for clients you serve, be circumspect in the number

CHART 3.1

Changing Social Climate Dimensions

Dimension	Method
Higher Cohesion	Increase homogeneity of membership
	Emphasize commonalities among members
	Plan social events
Leader Support	Increase supportive comments
	Move chair closer to members
Increased Order/Organization	More formal presentations
	Use meeting agenda
	Develop standardized procedures
Increased Expressiveness	Use free floating communication patterns
Increased Independence	Encourage members to take action
Increased Task Orientation	Introduce structured exercises to meetings
Increased Leader Control	Train leadership
	Use meeting agenda
Reduced Anger/Aggression	Verbalize ground rules and norms against anger
Increased Innovation	Use less structure
	Ask for new ideas

of referrals you make at a given time. Meet with representatives of the group to determine how it can respond best to client needs.

You may find that independent self-help is not a realistic solution for self-help and support groups with which you interact. In that case, agency-based or small, local, support groups fit well within a larger organization's formal bureaucracy and may be more suited to the needs of your clientele. If the group with which you interact desires this kind of sponsorship, concerns about organizational structure and professional leadership are less relevant. Groups have the right to trade independence for the security of professional staff and organizational support.

SUMMARY

Worldviews and ideologies convey understandings of members' concerns and plausible methods of dealing with their situations. This chapter presented three frameworks for examining the ideologies of self-help groups: they give understanding of the problem, methods of solving it, ways of organizing the group, and ways of interpreting the connection between the problem and the solution. They also sometimes give members new ways of viewing themselves and of regarding the universal order in life.

Social climate scales furnish a useful way to identify and measure the feel of the group to its members and visitors. Groups that are orderly, task oriented and stable can be distinguished from those that are innovative, expressive and lively, for example. Group environment assessments can help to uncover reasons for difficulties. They offer one means of evaluating groups and of evaluating their effectiveness.

Organizational structure develops naturally as an association grows and ages. Most national self-help associations are loosely structured federations in which the local groups operate relatively autonomously. When groups flourish and as they age, there is an inevitable demand for increased structure that can lead to an unintended professionalization.

Large self-help associations typically include professionals in some kind of role with the group, but a minority allow professionals to act as group leaders or to have formal leadership in the national association (unless the professional is also a legitimate member of the association by virtue of sharing the condition). Professional leadership occurs regularly with support groups, however, and this is one of the major differences between self-help and support groups. The "iron law of oligarchy" can take hold and transform a membership organization to one that has distanced itself from the members and is thus unresponsive to their concerns. Practitioners must carefully consider their relationships with self-help groups to avoid unintentionally transforming them into social agencies.

This chapter and the one before it have focused on the group. In Part 2, attention will turn to the member and how he or she fits into a group environment. The next two chapters will address what attracts a person to the group and what makes an individual remain active in the group.

DISCUSSION QUESTION

Think of a group to which you have belonged or that you have visited or studied. Take one of the frameworks for analyzing an ideology and apply it to that group's worldview or set of beliefs and teachings. Discuss your analysis with others in a small group.

CLASSROOM EXERCISES

1. Divide the class into groups of 8 to 10 members. Charge each group with developing a support-group-climate role play (see directions below).

- Choose a condition from which all suffer.
- Choose one person to play the facilitator role.
- Create a scenario that conforms to the following group climate:

HIGH:	Cohesion
	Leader Support
	Expressiveness
MODERATE:	Task Orientation
	Self-Discovery
	Independence
	Order and Organization
	Leader Control
LOW:	Anger and Aggression
	Innovation

- After about 5 or 10 minutes, figure out a way for the facilitator to increase or decrease one or more of the dimensions. Create another 5 or 10 minutes of group action demonstrating the change.

2. Divide the class into groups of 8 or 10 and develop a self-help group climate role play.
   - Simulate about five or ten minutes of a self-help group meeting. In this meeting depict a group that is having trouble attracting and holding on to new members (those who come for the first time). Choose one or more dimensions of group climate that may be alienating the newcomers. Some of your group should play the role of newcomers; the rest play oldtimers.
   - Once you have the problematic climate scripted, discuss what you think may be the problem and introduce activity that will change the climate to one that may be more attractive to newcomers. Create a scenario of about 5 or 10 minutes in which the changes are enacted.

ASSIGNMENT

1. Identify a group, attend a meeting with permission of its members, and after the meeting, use the group environment scale dimensions to do an informal assessment of the group's social climate. Discuss this assessment in a short paper.
2. Identify a self-help organization with which you are familiar. Do an analysis of the organization's ideology using either Borkman's template or Humphrey's and Kaskutas's worldviews. Discuss your analysis in a short paper.

RESOURCE

Moos Social Climate Scales can be obtained from The Consulting Psychologists Press, Inc., P.O. Box 10096, Palo, CA 94303-0979, Phone: (800) 624-1765, ext. 400. The test materials include a manual, a scoring key, a test booklet, answer sheets, and profiles.

PART 2

THE MEMBER

Chapter 4

BEGINNING PARTICIPATION

"As we sat in the parking lot outside the huge old house where the group met, we watched other people arriving for the meeting. After we saw that they didn't look uppity, sanctimonious or like guttersnipes either, we decided to go on in. If I had been alone, I wouldn't have gone."
—Anonymous, First AA Meeting

An essential element in the success of any open-ended community group is the ability to attract and retain new members. As practitioners, we want our clients to bond with the group in a way that will assure useful involvement. However, the majority of those who initially visit a self-help group do not continue participation. Dropouts during the first few months exceed the ranks of those who continue (Emrick, Tonigan, Montgomery, & Little, 1993; Luke, Roberts, & Rappaport, 1993; Meissen, Gleason, & Embree, 1991). Thus, group attractiveness is of immense importance to everyone. Without it, we are unable to link our clients with groups they need. Without some attractive elements, recruits will depart never to return, and the group will die.

As the opening quote suggests, negative stereotypes (and other forms of apprehension) often impede initial attendance. People under stress may resist group participation—self-help or otherwise. Once the individual attends a group, however, its benefits can be recognized when regular members attest to the group's useful effects. How might we as practitioners encourage people to attend that first meeting? This chapter addresses that question and introduces the complexities surrounding the process of linking people with groups.

Just thinking about going to the first meeting can activate feelings of intense dread, no matter who the person or what the problem. A social work student writes about her first AA meeting:

I didn't want to go alone, which was extremely out of character for me. I went everywhere alone—movies, weddings, funerals, bars, vacations— but I sure didn't want to go to AA alone. I was afraid for several reasons: they'd ask me to tell all about my drinking and I wasn't used to being very truthful about it; they'd think I was really down-and-out and miserable, which I wasn't; they'd try to control my behavior or my life, or I'd be asked to make a commitment of some sort.

Researching what attracts people to groups, social scientists have found that affiliation is more likely if newcomers perceive members to be similar to themselves and if they find that the group is able to meet their needs (Festinger, 1954; Wheelan, 1994). If participants are appealing in other ways, such as by being warmly welcoming, dependably present in meetings, open about past suffering, and explicit about how the group helped them, the newcomer will more likely bond with the group.

These general observations about groups hold true also for self-help and support groups. Member similarity is one of their most attractive features. Clear communication about how they can help also increases attractiveness. If the group can demonstrate helpfulness by giving needed information about the condition and support, so much the better. Broad participation, enabling all those present to say how the group has worked for them, allows recruits to decide how well they may fit in. Older members convey hope to newcomers by telling stories of successfully using the group's methods.

It is both intuitively apparent and empirically supported that those who are most likely to benefit from a self-help or support group are those who invest the most time and effort in participation (Emrick et al., 1993; Luke et al., 1993). We therefore need to understand how to encourage such participation when we deem there is need for it. The rest of this chapter discusses how characteristics of people are likely to influence affiliation, particularly in terms of race, gender, group fit, and stage of change readiness and offers a model depicting stages in the affiliation process. The chapter concludes with recommendations for connecting people with groups.

CHARACTERISTICS OF AFFILIATORS

Can we tell who will do well in a group and who will not? Is it possible to distinguish between those who will not respond to a group and those who will and then to develop an appropriate intervention strategy? The answer is yes—if we know which factors to consider. Five personal characteristics merit further examination: demographics, problem seriousness, size of support system, personal philosophy, and need for affiliation.

Demographic Characteristics

Demographic characteristics are important but must be understood within the concept of group fit, which will be discussed in the next section. The typical member of a self-help group is a middle-class, well-educated, middle-aged, European-American male (Lieberman & Snowden, 1993). Members in the groups profiled in the last section of this book fit this description, except that for most, their membership was predominantly female (Al-Anon, 1993; Chesler & Chesney, 1995; Galanter, 1988; Overeaters Anonymous, 1992; Videka-Sherman, 1982).

There are exceptions. Alcoholics Anonymous (AA) and Gamblers Anonymous (GA) members are disproportionately male (AA, 1992; GA, 1988). Parents Anonymous (PA) members are relatively young (median age is 29) and low-income (47% received incomes under $10,000 in 1988) (Post-Kammer, 1988). National Alliance for the Mentally Ill (NAMI) and Alzheimer's Association participants were somewhat older than members in the other groups (Gonyea, 1989; Jenson, n.d.). Members of particular groups thus may or may not fit the demographic description of the typical self-help group participant.

Studies of AA have attempted to correlate member characteristics with group involvement, drop-out rates, and outcome. In a comprehensive meta-analysis of findings from 107 evaluations of AA effectiveness and member involvement, Emrick et al., (1993) concluded that demographic characteristics of members do *not* predict involvement in or benefit from AA participation. These characteristics included age, gender, education, marital status, employment status, and socio-economic status. Only ethnic background (being of Irish descent) correlated positively with successful AA involvement. Thus, we must look further for accurate predictors of group attraction and affiliation. We will return to the question of demographics, specifically gender and race, but first we will examine other individual characteristics that may influence whether a person participates in self-help or support groups.

Problem Seriousness

Seriousness of the drinking problem consistently correlates positively with AA involvement (Emrick et al., 1993). Persons who report losing control of their drinking, consuming a higher quantity of alcohol when drinking, and drinking compulsively are more likely to continue with and benefit from AA participation. In one study of the use of Narcotics Anonymous (NA) by drug abusers, investigators found that more serious drug problems increased the likelihood of participation in NA (Christo & Franey, 1995).

Joiners of bereavement groups were significantly more distressed in their bereavement than nonjoiners and were also more likely to consult with professionals (Levy & Derby, 1992). Attendees of cancer victim support groups were more likely to consult with mental health professionals than were nonattendees, thus suggesting that they were more anxious about their illness (Bauman, Gervey, & Siegel, 1992). Psychological distress among members of cancer support groups correlated significantly with severity of surgery, radiation, and chemotherapy, concern about body image, and concern over recurrence (Silverman-Dresner, 1989-1990). Thus, what is intuitively felt to be correct, *is* in fact correct. People experiencing greater distress are more likely to attend a self-help group and to ask for help from professionals as well.

Personal Philosophy

Individuals whose personal philosophies are congruent with the philosophy and worldview of the group affiliate more readily with it. For example, affiliators with AA are more likely to be religious, more likely to view God as being in control of life's events, and more likely to have intense, personal religious experiences (Emrick, et al., 1993, p. 53). Although these findings suggest the influence AA has had on these individuals, they also tell us that openness to spiritual experience must also be present.

Size of Support System

People with adequate support systems may be less in need of a support group and therefore less likely to attend one. Levy and Derby's (1992) study of bereavement support groups found that adequate size of existing support system was one reason given by nonparticipants for their disinterest in joining a group. Similarly, cancer support group participants reporting lack of emotional support from their immediate circle were more inclined to use support groups (Bauman et al., 1992). At the same time, however, many who attended cancer support meetings rated their families as adequately supportive, suggesting that such groups add something unique to the existing helping system. More study is needed around this issue because the kind of support given by an existing system rarely meets the need for sharing experiential knowledge.

Need for Affiliation and Discomfort in Groups

Many people claim, "I'm not a joiner." Levy and Derby (1992) described persons referred to bereavement support groups who declined to participate citing fear of harm, lack of commonality with members, and difficulty opening up in a group as reasons for their disinterest. Trice (1957) and Trice and Roman (1970) found that those who affiliated successfully with AA were more likely to have high affiliation needs and to be more open to sharing problems with others. Similarly, Kurtz et al. (1995) found that dually diagnosed persons who were generally more comfortable in groups were more involved with AA than those who were not. Among cancer patients, those who had belonged to other voluntary organizations were also more likely to have participated in support groups (Bauman et al., 1992).

Despite this, it is reasonable to expect those with low affiliation needs to involve themselves in a self-help group. Smith (1991), in a study of AA, proposed that nonaffiliators can become convinced that they *need* the group. She observed that nonaffiliators, more than others, need a one-on-one relationship, such as with a sponsor, in which they are persuaded to participate. Once participation is established, the rewards of fellowship follow. She quotes one member.

> I wanted so much to be like my sponsor that I decided to follow in his footsteps and do whatever he did. So I made myself go around at meetings shaking hands with everyone there! (Smith, 1993, p. 699)

RACE, GENDER, SEXUAL ORIENTATION, AND GROUP FIT

Is it true that African-Americans do not use self-help groups as much as do European-Americans do? And are groups founded by men not good for women? Can gays and lesbians find acceptance in community self-help groups?

People of Color in Self-Help Groups

Practitioners often express concern about whether minorities fit in with groups that are composed mostly of persons of the majority culture. Demographic findings related to the groups in the latter part of this book illustrate the general underrepresentation of minority-group members in self-help and support groups (as narrowly defined and leaving out church, neighborhood associations, and social clubs). In addition, African-Americans were clearly underrepresented in the California groups surveyed by Snowden and Lieberman (1994).

This underrepresentation could, in part, be related to a concept called "racial fit," also termed "person-group fit" (Humphreys & Woods, 1993; Luke, Roberts, & Rappaport, 1993; Maton, 1993). The idea is that people feel more comfortable in groups where they have the same racial or other ethnic characteristics as most of the other members. Investigating outcomes of referral to AA or NA after substance abuse treatment, Michigan researchers followed up with people recently discharged (a majority were African-American) to determine, among other things, whether they attended AA or NA (Humphreys & Woods, 1993). These former patients were from urban Detroit as well as rural Michigan. Investigators found that participation was influenced by how well the recruit was matched with the racial makeup of the groups attended. In predominantly European-American, rural Michigan, European-American recruits were likely to continue attendance while African-Americans were not. In predominantly African-American, urban areas, African-American recruits were more likely to continue attendance, while European-Americans were not.

Further analysis after 6 months and again at 12 months showed that minorities and women dropped out of AA/NA slightly more often than European-American men at 6 months, but at 12 months both race and gender differences of the subjects who continued disappeared (Humphreys, Mavis, & Stöfflemayr, 1995). In addition, minority group persons who remained in AA or NA evidenced more improvement in measures of successful sobriety than persons who did not follow through with participation. This indicated that minority participants both attended and benefited from meetings.

Women in Self-Help Groups

Women are the majority in almost all the groups discussed in the latter part of this book: Recovery, Inc., Al-Anon Family Groups, National Alliance for the Mentally Ill, Candlelighters Childhood Cancer Foundation, Compassionate Friends, Alzheimer's Association, and Parents Anonymous. Groups like AA for alcoholism and GA for gambling, which are more typically male problems, are exceptions. Peer support programs for people with serious mental illnesses also report a more equal balance of males and females (Chamberlin, Rogers, & Ellison, 1996; Salem, 1987).

Some people question the appropriateness of AA for women because of the predominance of men in AA, although recent reports indicate the percentage of women participants has grown to over one-third of the total membership (AA, 1992; Beckman, 1993). In reviewing research on alcoholic women, Beckman (1993) concluded that despite her own beginning bias to the contrary, AA appears to be as or more effective for women than for men and that "there is no clear empirical evidence to suggest that certain types of women would fare better in other types of alcoholism treatment [sic]" (p. 246). Nevertheless, some women are not comfortable in AA. Jean Kirkpatrick founded Women For Sobriety (WFS) because she did not feel at home in AA (Kaskutas, 1994). She also thought AA's emphasis on powerlessness damaged women's self-esteem and that it was not a positive concept when applied to women.

Despite Kirkpatrick's opinion of AA, most of the women who attend WFS (89%) reported to researchers that they either currently attended or had attended AA (Kaskutas, 1994). They responded that they attended WFS for support and nurturance, freedom in choosing discussion topics, focus on self-esteem, and the positive emphasis they found there. The same women attended AA because they thought it was more likely to guarantee sobriety. In addition, they liked the availability of many meetings, they felt they fit in, and AA offered them a social life. They liked the spiritual focus, the structure, AA's literature, and the mixed gender meetings. A small percentage of WFS members (11%), who did not go to AA, thought they did not fit in or that AA was too negative and too male-oriented. Due to objections of this nature, many local AA districts list special AA groups that are solely for women.

In GROW International, an organization sponsoring groups for people with serious mental illness, the percentage of men and women members is roughly equal. Extensive study of over 100 groups of the Illinois GROW membership revealed that all-female groups were less attractive to both male and female members (Luke et al., 1993). Recruits of both genders who first attended mixed-gender groups were more likely to extend their participation than those who had first attended an all-female group.

Sexual Orientation

Identification with a gay or lesbian sexual orientation can have a profound effect on one's comfort with self-help or support group participation. Bittle (1982) estimated that the numbers of gay and lesbian members of AA were disproportionately lower than the proportion of homosexual alcoholics in the population. This finding suggests the need to reassure gay and lesbian clients that they will be welcome in such groups and to provide group environments in which they can feel at home. Experiences of some gay and lesbian alcoholics indicate that comfort and safety are increased when they attend special gay and lesbian AA groups (Kus, 1988; Kus & Latcovich, 1995).

Special gay and lesbian AA groups exist in all larger urban areas. One of their advantages is their ability to provide a setting in which members can work on ridding themselves of internalized homophobia while simultaneously achieving abstinence and a spiritual base for recovery (Kus, 1992). McNally (1989) described identity transformation of lesbian alcoholics who participated in AA. She recounts how these women were able to accept and integrate both lesbian and alcoholic subidentities in their recovery.

Examination of support groups for gay and lesbian individuals indicates that such groups produce higher self-acceptance and greater ease of association with straight populations (Vincke & Bolton, 1994). Lesbian support groups lead to larger social networks and more accessible social support (Hollander, 1989). One examination of support groups for gay adolescents on a college campus found that they provided their members with their only real means of emotional support (Westefeld & Winkelpleck, 1983). Support groups for HIV/AIDS patients and their caregivers have become a major means of assistance to this large subpopulation of gay men (Barouh, 1992).

The Concept of Group Fit

The concept of *group fit* clarifies the relationship between demographic characteristics and affiliation. Multiple studies of AA membership show that sheer demographics do not predict successful involvement. How well one fits with the members of the group, however, does predict successful affiliation. Fit may include demographic variables, but it can include other factors as well (Luke et al., 1993). It can be seen as one's fitting in with the "ideal" member for whom the group was designed, such as being an alcoholic in a group designed for alcoholics. It can also be defined as the context of the group that the recruit first attends. For example, the particular meeting or group may have primarily gay or lesbian members, even though this is not characteristic of all groups of the association. Another way of considering fit is the degree of similarity or dissimilarity of the new member and existing members on any specific dimension, such as educational attainment. Thus, how well an individual fits within the group can be determined by multiple factors that may or may not include demographic characteristics such as gender and race or lifestyle factors such as sexual orientation.

Research on 644 Illinois attenders of GROW provides an example of how group fit affected member characteristics. Researchers found that older, more educated, never-married persons experienced the best fit with the groups in the study. Presumably, because these groups comprised persons with serious mental illness, higher functioning recruits were more likely than lower functioning recruits to drop out. Different hospitalization history also influenced whether an individual remained involved. Persons with several hospitalizations were the norm in GROW groups; those without this history fit less well and were less likely to remain in attendance. As mentioned previously, groups with members of both genders more successfully retained new members.

All of these studies (the follow up with people referred to AA and NA, the study of WFS members, and the GROW studies) emphasize that one cannot easily make generalizations about who should or should not be expected to benefit from a particular self-help or support group. For gender as well as race, age, sexual orientation, marital status, socioeconomic class, problem seriousness, and other characteristics, predictions about appropriateness of the group must take into account the specific group in question, the goals of the member, and the fit between the member and the particular group. Although the research reported here focuses mostly on self-help groups, the same findings likely also apply to support groups.

In the foregoing discussion, we have examined individual characteristics that remain relatively stable, such as gender, race, problem seriousness, sexual orientation, and comfort in groups. The next section examines another important factor in the affiliation process—readiness to change. This factor is particularly salient for those who join a group in order to change themselves in some way. Group involvement requires sacrificing time. Practicing its teachings involves changing one's habits and ways of thinking. Willingness to become involved in the group is necessary. Because readiness implies personal transformation, it is more relevant, of course, to change-oriented groups, although participation in any group requires a change in one's scheduled activities.

STAGES OF CHANGE READINESS

Many who enter a self-help group for the first time are doing so because of curiosity or coercion. Many have not reached a point of readiness to change and as such will likely not follow through on participation in a group that encourages change. Here we examine the concept of change readiness and apply this understanding to the group participation process. Prochaska, Norcross, and DiClemente (1994) have proposed five stages of change readiness: (a) precontemplation, the individual cannot see a need for change; (b) contemplation, one recognizes and acknowledges a need for change, but is not ready to take action; (c) preparation, characterized by plans for taking action but also by ambivalence; (d) action, when the necessary steps toward change begin in earnest and visible changes take place; and (e) maintenance, preventing relapse to a former undesirable condition.

As people move through stages of change readiness, their progression is more like a spiral of back and forth motions gradually moving from a point of unreadiness to a point of taking action than like a straight and uninterrupted passage from stage one to stage five (Prochaska, 1994; Prochaska, DiClemente, & Norcross, 1992). In the first stage of change readiness, the person can be confronted with a need for change, but cannot be expected to immediately begin the process. In the second stage of change readiness, people can be taught about how to attain change, but still cannot be expected to take action. In the third stage, the person can begin to take small steps; for example, he or she might attend a few group meetings without making a commitment to regular attendance. When one is at the action stage, one can be expected to take immediate and dedicated action. At this point, participation will be wholehearted and one will try anything that veteran members suggest. In the final stage, ideally, the member can be expected to attend regularly over a period of time, devoting him or herself to maintaining the change.

When observing someone's participation in a self-help group, it is important to understand how people change and how they move through stages of change readiness. In the initial stage, one may be forced to attend, but cannot be forced to listen, to practice methods prescribed by the group at home, or to read the literature. A newcomer in the precontemplation stage can be expected to drop out after one or two meetings. That same person, having been informed about the group, however, may come back days, months, or even years later when he or she reaches the preparation and action stages.

In the contemplation stage, the individual may attend a few meetings, drop out, come back, then drop out again. In the preparation stage, participation will be more regular and will eventually lead to commitment when the individual reaches the action stage. Remember, the stages do not occur in a steady, linear pattern, but rather are more like taking a few steps forward, a few back or sideways, and then a few forward again.

The concept of change readiness can help to explain why many potential recruits drop out after one or two meetings. Readiness to change, interacting with any number of other personal factors, as well as unpredictable variations in group climate that may or may not be attractive, sheds light on possible reasons for membership attrition in early stages of participation. Stages of change readiness will be discussed further in the next chapter as they apply to longer-term participation. Next, however, it is important to recognize that there is also an affiliation process that roughly parallels the stages of change readiness but includes the additional considerations of what happens within the group as well as within the individual recruit.

STAGES OF AFFILIATION

Just as there are stages of change, there are stages of affiliation. Instead of being a static phenomenon, the process of joining a group may change from day to day and year to year. Thus, rather than looking at individual characteristics, a few researchers have examined the stages people go through when they join and involve themselves with a self-help group (Jurik, 1987; Klass, 1984-1985; Raiff, 1978; Rudy, 1986; Taylor, 1977; Trice, 1957). These studies have described phenomenologically how people choose to become involved.

Stages in the affiliation process resemble the stages of change readiness in many ways, but they are not identical. The two columns in Table 4.1 compare and contrast the two concepts. Research on stages of affiliation has focused primarily on three self-help associations: Recovery, Inc., The Compassionate Friends, and Alcoholics Anonymous. Investigators have identified from three to five stages of affiliation, which are reflected in Table 4.1.

The First Stage of Affiliation: Deciding

The period before attendance is critical to the process of affiliating. Many simply call this the "hitting bottom" stage. It is the first decision point: the decision to go to a meeting. One author divided this premeeting stage into two subparts: (a) life problem preemption (i.e., major losses brought on by the problem); and (b) readiness for recovery—a state of "hitting bottom" (Taylor, 1977, p. 9). *Hitting bottom* occurs when the individual reaches the point at which he or she is unable to continue and thus becomes ready to try new means of ending pain.

The Second Stage of Affiliation: First Meeting

The second stage involves first meetings, being a newcomer, and that all-important question, "Do I belong here?" At this point, affiliation depends on the newcomer's *ability to identify* with the group's members and whether he or she acquires a wish to be like the other people in this meeting. Moreover, the recruit must be able to accept the group's

Table 4.1

Stages of Change Readiness and Stages of Affiliation

Stage of Change Readiness	Stage of Affiliation
Precontemplation: Person sees no need for change.	No parallel.
Contemplation: Person acknowledges need to change, but doesn't take action.	Deciding: Person finds the condition intolerable and sees the need to take action by joining the group.
Preparation: Person begins to make small efforts to change and thinks about how to do it.	First Meeting: Person takes the first step by attending a meeting.
Action: Person is actively engaged in the change process.	Commitment: Person begins regular attendance.
	Taking action: Person accepts the problem and takes on an identity as a member of the group; Person can tell his or her story of recovery.
Maintenance: Person has changed and continues to work at sustaining the change.	Helping Others: Person continues group contact in a role of helping others, acting as a leader, thereby maintaining the change.

philosophy and beliefs. At this point, people who do not fit in and whose personal lives are quite different from those in the group are likely to drop out.

At this stage, newcomers need orientation and a good deal of attention. They need to know in advance what will take place in the first few meetings. It helps if recruits experience close contact with a member immediately following the first meeting and if they are quickly convinced that their problem is causing more pain than satisfaction (Trice, 1957). It helps if the recruit is comfortable with being of a different social class than those in the meeting, only one of several group-fit factors.

The Third Stage of Affiliation: Commitment

Once one has attended the first meeting or two, one enters a stage of being persuaded that one's concern fits the group's solution (Jurik, 1987). The recruit must then make the second important decision, that of *trusting the group*. Trust inspires commitment to participating (Raiff, 1978). Trusting the group to help usually comes about when recruits realize that recovery is possible, when they feel accepted by others, and when they have a little success with using the group's methods to cope with their situation.

Other conditions that may induce commitment include taking part in before and after meeting "chit chat" and obtaining support for attendance from other members of one's household (Trice, 1957). Taking small responsibilities, such as bringing refreshments or making coffee, can help to bind newcomers to groups. Affiliates make behavioral, ideological, and social commitments during this phase. For example, newcomers to AA may attend "90 meetings in 90 days," a radical but frequently prescribed behavioral strategy in early recovery.

The Fourth Stage of Affiliation:
Taking Action

After being persuaded that one's problem fits the definition given it by the group, one must next be persuaded that the group's activities will *lead to improvement*. In Recovery, Inc., this means that newcomers must practice the method of will training and apply it to situations that prompt episodes of "temper" (Jurik, 1987). Further, they must find this method to be helpful. As noted previously in the discussion of readiness, this practicing phase requires members to be willing to take action in everyday life, not just sit in a meeting once or twice a week. In Recovery meetings, members are expected to tell others about their efforts to practice the method. They report a situation, how they initially became "worked up" over it, how they applied the method, and what would have happened in such a situation before their Recovery training.

There can be two substages at this point in the process: *accepting one's problem* and *telling one's story*. Accepting the problem involves identification with others and possibly accepting a diagnostic label. Telling one's story involves describing the unpleasantness before and explaining how much better things have been since participation. The "story" stage continues in the final stage of helping others, as one's story becomes a powerful source of identification for newcomers.

The Final Stage of Affiliation:
Helping Others

Most of the research on affiliation identified the same theme in the last stage of affiliation—*helping others*. This may involve becoming a leader; sponsoring newcomers; speaking before community groups; bringing meetings to institutions, prisons, and hospitals—doing whatever may be the need wherever it exists. Klass (1984-1985), investigating The Compassionate Friends, quoted one parent: "I came to realize too that in trying to help others, I was helping myself, that a very important part of that healing was putting love back into my life" (p. 369).

THE SOCIAL
WORLD PERSPECTIVE

In many ways, affiliating resembles another concept with respect to bonding with groups—"social world integration" (Unruh, 1983). A *social world* differs from other organizational forms in that its boundaries are defined only by cognitive identification; it has little authority structure, and it can be quite large. Boundaries are extremely permeable, and there are no territorial limits. People enter and leave social worlds at will. Four social types reflect various levels of involvement in a social world: strangers, tourists, regulars, and insiders according to Unruh, 1983.

Strangers, though full-fledged members, stand at the boundary of the social world they have just entered. All participants begin as strangers; and as such, they are naive and uncommitted. *Tourists* are those who have gone beyond the level of stranger. They have penetrated the social world more deeply in search of an experience about which they are curious, but this involvement remains superficial. *Regulars* are well-integrated, and their participation is habitual. *Insiders* stand at the "very heart, or core, of social world activities" (p. 144).

Smith (1991) uses the social world perspective in her analysis of AA. The *stranger* in AA is the newcomer attending his or her first few meetings. *Tourists* have become more involved, but still question their identification as alcoholic. They attend meetings with curiosity and interest, but remain unconvinced. *Regulars'* involvement is habitual, but does not extend beyond a meeting or two each week. An AA *insider's* entire identity is that of being a recovering member. The participation of insiders helps to create the varied activities that give newcomers and regulars the option of more intense involvement. Intimate relationships can develop with other participants. Recruitment of new members and continuing integration of existing participants is a commitment of people adopting the insider stance (Unruh, 1983).

Group attachment can fall within a continuum with marginal interest at one end and intense commitment at the other. Belonging or not belonging is not an either/or proposition; efforts to build a membership base in any group must rest on understanding the formation of group attachment over time and through stages in the affiliation process. Personal characteristics, readiness to change, and group attractiveness all play a role in establishing the beginning stages of participation.

IMPLICATIONS FOR PRACTITIONERS

Predicting who will successfully bond with a self-help or support group can seem so complex as to be impossible. Research reveals the errors of assuming that men will bond and women will not, or that European-Americans will and African-Americans will not (Humphreys, Mavis, & Stöfflemayr, 1995; Humphreys & Woods, 1993). Nor can one assume that women will find the larger percentage of men in some groups unattractive or that an all women's group will be attractive to them. Each person must be given information and allowed to make such decisions on his or her own. Merely giving information, however, is rarely enough.

Linking people to a group in which they will most likely "fit in" requires hard work, but its importance is attested to by the research on individual characteristics as well as by that on the stages of change readiness and affiliation. Connecting to a group those persons whose racial identification differs from that of most other group members is especially difficult. Fear of nonacceptance by persons of other races is very high in our culture, and these initial fears cannot be minimized. Yet once the individual feels at home in a specific group, such misgivings tend to subside. Effort to locate a compatible group for each person will be rewarded when the connection is made. On such occasions, it is not unusual to hear a new member state, "The minute I walked in the door, I knew I belonged."

Certain personal characteristics can make group bonding more difficult for some people. For example, those who are less gregarious and more uncomfortable in groups will be more hesitant to become involved. However, if the need for the group is great, such individuals may be helped to discover that participation is necessary to achieve their goals. Recognition of need for a group may come from having tried other measures that failed. Need may arise because there is no other form of assistance or because the group offers the best solution for the specific situation.

When professionals ask their clients to use a self-help or support group as a supplement or follow-up to professional service, they must consider the person's readiness for change. Different aspects of the group will appeal at different points in their progression through stages of change readiness. Keep change readiness in mind, and use the old social work slogan, "start where the client is." For example, in a precontemplation stage, the individual can be exposed to the idea, can simply read about the group, or can attend one meeting. Institutions use this approach with AA by having "institutional meetings." These are informative sessions in which AA members from the community meet at the institution and "put on a meeting" so that those gathered may observe and be introduced to the AA program in this way.

Practitioners should not give up on linking someone with a group when at first he or she does not continue attendance. Nor should they assume that the person will not be helped by the group or that the group has nothing to offer. Realize that the individual may not be ready to take this action and that the individual may not have experienced a fit with the particular group but may with a different group. If there is no other group, explore the person's reasons for dropping out; discuss what occurred in meetings attended to correct misunderstandings about what took place. Help less extroverted people adjust to the group by linking them with temporary sponsors or companions with whom to attend the group. Many professionals accompany clients to their first few meetings. People must be prepared for the first meeting. Introduce them to a member, provide some reading on the group, explain the group's program, or show them a video made by the group (see resource listings at the end of the chapter).

Group facilitators should consider the fear people have of talking before strangers and should not force newcomers to say something unless they wish to do so. Independent self-help groups rarely ask the newcomer to say anything other than his or her name. Facilitators should note the need for safety, the fear of not fitting in, and the intense need for acceptance most people feel in a group of strangers. They can help the group keep a focus on positive steps and successful coping to let the recruit know that success is possible and that the group will benefit him or her. Finally, they can make sure new members link up with an experienced member, who can answer questions and offer to receive phone calls before the next meeting.

SUMMARY

In this chapter, we have examined aspects of group attraction, bonding with groups, characteristics of group members, and the importance to recruits of fitting in with the existing group's membership. We have recognized that people go through stages of change readiness before making commitments to participate in a group. Another way of understanding this process is one of stages of affiliation, from "hitting bottom," to initial exploratory attendance, to commitment to the group. Once ready to attend the first meeting, the newcomer is likely to be sensitized to whether he or she fits in and how warmly he or she will be received by other members. First impressions may determine whether the potential new member returns and attends regularly.

The next chapter will consider group processes and dynamics that affect whether the member commits to and is helped by the group. Additional discussion of readiness and stage of affiliation will highlight the dynamics of advanced readiness and regular involvement.

DISCUSSION QUESTION

Consider your own theories about who does and does not fit in particular groups or groups in general. Write them down. In a small group discuss your theories with other members. What has been your basis for referring people to groups in the past? Have your theories changed as a result of this chapter? If so how?

CLASSROOM EXERCISES

1. Consider the following situation: A colleague approaches you and asks your advice on how to improve attendance in a support group. What kinds of information will this chapter lead you to ask for? List the questions you will ask and discuss them with a small group. Discuss answers to these questions.
2. Reflect on the following possibility: You have a female client who has an alcohol problem. You have strongly urged her to attend AA, but she has not done so. What actions would you take with this client? Imagine the same situation with other clients and other self-help or support groups. What steps would you take?
3. Develop an interview schedule for assessing how a person has come to affiliate with a self-help association. What questions would you ask based on the material in Chapter 4?
4. Develop a schedule for interviewing a person who has dropped out of a self-help group after only a few meetings.

ASSIGNMENT

Select a small sample of members of a self-help or support group. Using an interview schedule based on the material in this chapter, interview them about the stages they perceived in making a commitment to attend this group. Do their experiences fit with the stages of the affiliation process described here?

VIDEO RESOURCES

(This is a partial list. Contact headquarters of any group to see if videos are available. The prices quoted here may have changed since this was published.)

1. Alcoholics Anonymous, AA World Services, P.O. Box 459, Grand Central Station, New York, NY 10163.

   Alcoholics Anonymous—An Inside View, 28 minutes, VHS $15.00
   It Sure Beats Sitting in a Cell, 17 minutes, VHS $15.00
   Young People and AA, 28 minutes, VHS $15.00
   Hope: Alcoholics Anonymous, 15 minutes, VHS $15.00
   AA—Rap With Us, 16 minutes, VHS $15.00

2. Al-Anon Family Groups, 1600 Corporate Landing Parkway, Virginia Beach, VA 23456

   Al-Anon Speaks for Itself, 15 minutes, VHS $25.00
   Alateen Tells It Like It Is—The Video, VHS $25.00
   Walk This Path Of Hope: Al-Anon in Institutions, VHS $25.00

3. The Compassionate Friends, P.O. Box 3596, Oak Brook, IL 60522-3696

   The Healing Path, VHS, Members $30.00; Professionals $45.00
   Dealing with the Death of A Child, 10 minutes, $10.00
   Banquet Speaker, Rev. Simon Stephens, 41 minutes, $15.00

4a. National Alliance for the Mentally Ill, 200 N. Glebe Road, Suite 1015, Arlington, VA 22203-3754.

   NAMI-An Oral History, 21 minutes, VHS $10.00

4b. Alliance for the Mentally Ill of Alabama, 6900 Sixth Avenue South, Suite B., Birmingham, AL 35212-1902; (205) 833-8336

   When Mental Illness Invades a Marriage, 30 minutes, VHS $15.00
   When Mental Illness Invades a Minority Family, 30 minutes, VHS $15.00
   Childhood Mental Illness: Truth, Needs and Family Effects, 30 minutes, VHS $15.00

5. Depressive and Manic Depressive Association, 730 N. Franklin, Suite 501, Chicago, IL 60610

   Life in Balance, 30 minutes, VHS $22.45

6. Gamblers Anonymous International Service Office, P.O. Box 17173, Los Angeles, CA 90017

   Even Up the Odds, VHS $14.95
   Big Steve, VHS $14.95

7. Jewish Alcoholics, Chemically Dependent Persons and Significant Others (JACS), 426 W. 58th St., New York, NY 10019; (212) 397-4197. E-mail: JACS@shamash.nysernet.org

   JACS, 28 minutes, VHS, Price unknown

8. Obsessive Compulsive Foundation, P.O. Box 70, Milford, CN 06460.

   The Touching Tree: A Story of a Child with OCD, 37 minutes, $49.95

9. Recovery, Inc., 802 N. Dearborn St., Chicago, IL 60610; (312) 337-5661.

   Hidden Lives, VHS $10.00

   Eleven 30-minute tapes of panel examples by Recovery members in California will soon be ready for distribution. Call Recovery, Inc.'s national headquarters for more information. Panels focus on problems of anger, fear, phobias, anxiety and depression.

10. Schizophrenics Anonymous, c/o Mental Health Association in Michigan, 15920 W. 12 Mile Road, Southfield, MI 48076.

    Joanne Verbanic Speaks on Schizophrenia and Schizophrenics Anonymous, 28 minutes, VHS Buy $22.00/Rent $6.00

    How to Start a Schizophrenics Anonymous Group, 48 minutes, VHS Buy $22.00/Rent $6.00

    Both Tapes: Buy $40.00/Rent $10.00

11. Mystic Fire Video, P.O. Box 2249, Livonia, MI 48151; 800-292-9001

    Circle of Recovery (group for African-American Men, a Bill Moyers PBS program). 58 minutes, $19.95

Chapter 5

LONG-TERM PARTICIPATION

"I went all the time; every night I was doing NA stuff. I went to nine meetings a week for two years because they told me it would get better if I did."
—Tuchman, 1995, p. 5.

Group affiliation happens in stages. After the first meeting, one may drop out, attend sporadically or regularly, or become immersed in the group, attending often and taking on leadership roles (Jurik, 1987; Klass, 1984-1985; Raiff, 1978; Rudy, 1986; Smith, 1991; Taylor, 1977). Regular but cursory attendance may be all that some long-term members desire and is typical in support groups that often meet only once per week. Other participants enter into the social world of the organization to such an extent that their presence creates and sustains that world for others. They may become absorbed within subgroups, active in leadership circles; some become consumed by the group and its activities (Rudy, 1986; Smith, 1991).

Examining and understanding how individuals assume regular and highly involved participation in self-help groups is important because more intense involvement results in greater goal achievement, and highly involved members are vital to sustaining independent self-help associations (Emrick, Tonigan, Montgomery, & Little, 1993; Galanter, 1988; Luke, Roberts, & Rappaport, 1993). As a community, the self-help association provides support, friendship, a sense of purpose, a societal role, a means of achieving personal change, and a new way of life. For the group to function as a community, members must remain involved; and some members must assume leadership. Research on member involvement reveals that recruiting and maintaining membership is the biggest and most stressful challenge self-help group leaders face (Chesler & Chesney, 1995; Meissen & Volk, 1995; Revenson & Cassel, 1991). This chapter will examine how self-help groups use helping strategies that match the needs of people ready for action and those wanting to maintain a program of recovery. It will also explore affiliation at later stages of involvement, examine peer leadership within self-help groups, and consider termination after long-term involvement.

READINESS AND
LONG-TERM PARTICIPATION

Chapter 4 reviewed the five change readiness levels proposed by Prochaska, Norcross, and DiClemente (1994): (a) precontemplation (when one does not see a need for change); (b) contemplation (thinking about change); (c) preparation (the beginning stage of taking action); (d) action (when great effort goes into change), and (e) maintenance (maintaining gains made in the change process). Appropriate strategies for helping someone change vary according to these stages. When one moves from contemplation to committed action, one becomes more regular in meeting attendance. Long-term participants in self-help groups are thus likely to be in either action or maintenance stages.

Cognitive/experiential processes work well for people in the contemplation stage of readiness, whereas people in the action and maintenance stages need behavioral processes that involve practice and performance. Prochaska, Norcross, and DiClemente (1994) consider the following processes most appropriate for persons in action and maintenance stages: (a) self-liberation (making a commitment to act); (b) countering (finding alternatives for problem behaviors); (c) environment control (avoiding stimuli that elicit the problem behavior); (d) reinforcement management (rewarding oneself or obtaining rewards from another source); and (e) helping relationships (being open and trusting with someone who cares).

Self-Liberation

Self-liberation means making a commitment to the change process. This is basic to the action phase of changing. The very act of showing up at a meeting week after week, or day after day, is a behavior requiring commitment. Newcomers are told to "just keep coming back." As an example, a member of Overeaters Anonymous (OA) writes:

> I started the program by doing everything I was supposed to do: abstaining, speaking, volunteering for service, writing and giving away my inventory, becoming a sponsor. I went to as many meetings as possible

and worked the steps to the best of my ability. It took me four months to begin to understand what I was doing. (OA, 1980, p. 67)

Countering

Countering means substituting a healthy response for an unhealthy one. One example is the Recovery practice of countering an insecure thought, such as expecting something bad to happen, with a secure thought—something bad will probably not happen. Abraham Low, Recovery's founder, believed that it is impossible to maintain two contradictory opinions at the same time. Thus, when a member catches him- or herself worrying, he or she learns to replace the worry with a secure thought. Another example is countering an undesirable action with a desirable action. A compulsive gambler might attend a Gamblers Anonymous meeting during the running of the Kentucky Derby instead of watching the race.

Environment Control

Environment control helps an individual avoid high-risk situations. Many groups sponsor meetings at high-risk times, times when the problem is acute. For example, gambling may take place on weekends, or during the football season, or during the World Series; the group provides an alternative to interaction with betting friends and gambling places. A member of Gamblers Anonymous illustrates environment control:

> I realized how tough it was for me to go a whole week without gambling between meetings, so I started a second meeting [of GA] on a Thursday night to break up the week in the middle. I called every member, every day for the first six months or so. I guess that you could say that I was a sponsor to everyone in the program, but in reality, it was my calling them that saved me. (G.A., 1984, p. 179)

Rewards

Rewards modify consequences. Recovery, Inc. uses rewards in the form of self and group endorsement for making an effort to apply will training, even when the effort fails. Action steps should be achievable so that rewards will be frequent. AA's founders realized this by translating the classic petition for "daily bread" into the slogan that became their program's first principle: "one day at a time." Members can say to themselves, "if I do not drink alcohol this one day, I have succeeded." AA participants in some locales also use a chip system to reward length of sobriety. A white chip can be gained by attending the first meeting. Other colors signify 30 days, 60 days and 1 year's abstinence and participation in AA.

Helping Relationships

Self-help and support groups offer a multitude of helping relationships. Potentially, a relationship of mutual help exists between every member and every other member. In some associations, special relationships, such as sponsorship, guarantee someone will make a commitment to being available whenever needed. An Overeaters Anonymous (OA) member writes:

> My travels have carried me far, but always I have found the hand of OA stretched out to me. And I in turn have reached out to those who needed me. There is no limit to what can be accomplished in and through the lives of people who partake of the fellowship of Overeaters Anonymous. I know that whatever my future brings, I will be brought again and again into contact with those who can be helped by my experience. And through these contacts, I will be allowed to continue my own progress on this magnificent journey. (OA, 1980, p. 164)

In these diverse ways, self-help and support groups provide the means to achieve hoped-for results for members. These can only be realized, however, if the member remains involved through and beyond the early stages of affiliation. In addition, members must be able to recycle; that is, drop out and return. Changers take two steps forward, one back, and then move forward again. The Overeaters Anonymous text provides one such example:

> When the weight was almost all off, I began to think to myself, "There, I've got this thing licked; OA is really great, it helped me lose and now I'm normal again." A painful year of progressive relapse followed. After I had regained about half the weight, I realized my experience did not make me a failure. Nor was the program a failure. I got out the Big Book and really read it. I committed myself to abstinence. . . . (OA, 1980, pp. 138-139)

Settings that arbitrarily restrict recycling in and out of them ignore the fact that this is a normal aspect of the change process and that the timelines around recycling vary a great deal from person to person.

As readiness progresses from contemplation, to preparation, to action, and then to maintenance, so too does the actual affiliation process progress from those first few tentative meetings, to regular, committed involvement. Next we look more fully at affiliation beyond the initial stages of hitting bottom and the first meeting to the stages of commitment, taking action, and helping others.

THEMES OF AFFILIATION

What are the forces that bind persons to groups for sustained periods, even attracting some to leadership positions? Five themes emerge from the research as guides to finding significant milestones in the latter stages of affiliation: (a) commitment to regular attendance; (b) *real* ownership of the problem; (c) identity transformation; (d) formation of dyadic relationships and (e) helping others (Klass, 1984-1985; Raiff, 1978; Rudy, 1986; Smith, 1991; Taylor, 1977).

Commitment to
Regular Attendance

A middle stage of affiliation, commitment to regular attendance, bridges the period between the first contact and later stages of more intense involvement. The regular meeting attender may not participate in any other aspect of the group's activities and may never do so. For example, a newcomer to Recovery, Inc. might attend weekly meetings, but not read the group's literature or practice its method between meetings. At some point, however, this person may experience a turning point that motivates him or her to increase group activity beyond attending meetings. It might be something small, such as reading the manual between meetings. It might be something interpersonal, such as socializing with another member. It might be something structural, such as taking on a leadership role. This commitment marks the beginning of what one researcher called the "working the program" stage (Taylor, 1977).

Acceptance of the Problem

As the new member continues to attend meetings of the group, he or she identifies with other members. Through recognition of the exact nature of the problem and recognition that one's experiences match those of others, there develops not only identification, but gradual ownership of the problem. Identification takes place on two levels: first, the new member recognizes his or her current self in the stories of more experienced members and begins to accept on a "gut" level the reality of his or her problem; and second, the recruit identifies with the desirable traits of those who have achieved what the recruit strives for. The words of a bereaved mother in The Compassionate Friends illustrates this:

For the first three or four meetings I just stored their words of hope and advice for later because I wasn't ready to accept them at the time. Then I noticed that June, another mother whose child was killed a month before mine, was beginning to heal. I wanted desperately to be like her. I didn't know what to do to make it any better, but decided I was going to try. (Klass, 1984-1985, p. 362)

If identification does not happen, the recruit may discontinue involvement, saying, as many do, "I'm not like them—I'm not a compulsive overeater" or "I cannot accept the loss of my child or share how I feel with others." But if the newcomer can identify with others, he or she begins to look forward to a new identity like others who have changed.

Identity Transformation

The result of taking action is the formation of a new identity as one who has mastered the situation. One consolidates that change by telling one's story. Rudy (1986) summed this up by stating that stories "provide a condensed version of the entire affiliation or conversion process" (p. 40). Stories contrast the "previous, unacceptable life style and identity with the newly found life style and identity and describe how anyone can make this transition" (p. 40). These stories also help the teller to internalize a clearer picture of his or her new self and the changes he or she has wrought. These words from a recovering addict illustrate this point:

The program of Narcotics Anonymous gave me an identity. I can now hold my head high and tell anyone, "Hi, my name is —. I'm an addict." Before I came to the program and was asked "Who are you?" I wouldn't answer because I had no idea what it really meant. I love the newly found me. I love getting to know me and getting to know other people who are like me. (N.A., 1987, p. 165)

Dyadic Relationships

Individuals who are less comfortable in groups need to relate to one person who will assist them to become integrated within the group. Trice (1957) found that recruits were more likely to continue with AA if they had close contact with other members soon after their initial encounter. In other groups also, forming a relationship with an older, wiser member may be vital to eventual commitment to the group. Persons referred to the Manic Depressive and Depressive Association of Detroit, for example, were more likely to attend the first meeting if they had been paired with a volunteer sponsor while still in treatment (Powell et al., 1995). In this controlled study, 56% of the experimental group, who were paired with sponsors, followed through with attending one or more meetings compared with only 15% of a control sample.

For people with high affiliation needs, social integration with a group comes easily. People who have low needs for group affiliation and are less outgoing find social integration with a group more difficult and less attractive (Smith, 1991). Smith described two types of AA member: the "sociable," who loves people and reacts positively to group situations, and the "individualist," who prefers individual activities and is uncomfortable in groups (p. 106). For the former, mere exposure to an attractive group can be enough to induce regular attendance. Response to the group is emotional and immediate. Smith quotes one sociable:

> The people have been the most important thing. When I was sick, they called . . . sent flowers . . . people came into my life through the fellowship and they have been like family. It took me many years to accept myself and the spiritual part of the program. But the people kept me going. (p. 118)

Individualists are more inclined to form specific relationships and their conversion to a new identity is more cognitive. They read the literature, think it through, and talk to another person about it. Smith (1993) quotes an individualist:

> I read the Book and started doing the Steps with my sponsor. I felt better . . . even though things were still kind of a mess in my life. . . I felt more spiritual, better about me. (p. 699)

Smith proposed that the social integration of persons with low affiliation need begins with a dyadic relationship followed by increased attendance, identification with others, more dyadic relationships, and finally, a sense of belonging and perception of need for the group (see Figure 5.1). In contrast, sociables often begin their group participation with the sense of belonging, not requiring the many steps in between before they become integrated.

Helping Others

Helping others represents the final stage of affiliation (Jurik, 1987; Klass, 1984-1985; Raiff, 1978; Rudy, 1986; Smith, 1991; Taylor, 1977). Klass observed that in The Compassionate Friends group, helping others represented "the way many parents find growth and meaning in the child's death" (p. 368). For some TCF members "helping others is a way of retaining a relationship with the dead child and a way of healing the self" (p. 356).

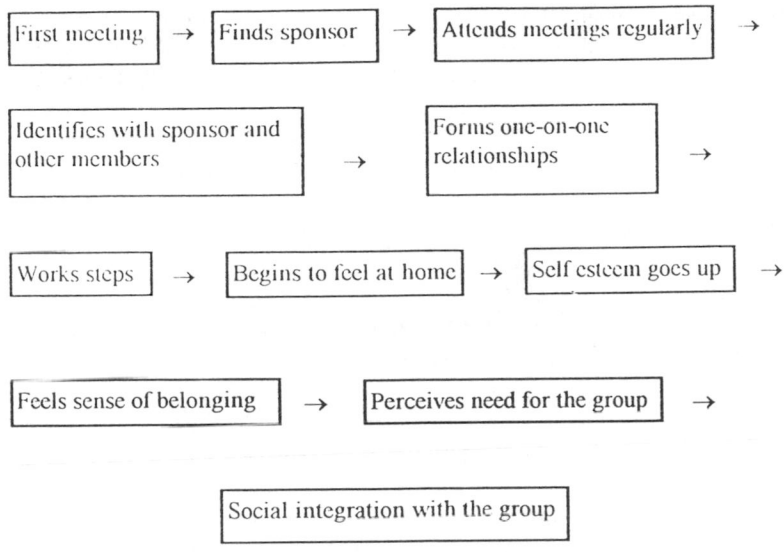

Figure 5.1. Pathway to Involvement by "Individualists"
Adapted from A. R. Smith (1993), The social construction of group dependency in Alcoholics Anonymous *Journal of Drug Issues, 23*, 689-704. Used with permission.

Reaching out to others can be a part of a self-help group at any point, but is usually recognized as something oldtimers do best. In AA and other Twelve-Step groups, this is usually referred to as "Twelfth-Step work." The last of the Twelve Steps states, "Having had a spiritual awakening as the result of these Steps, we tried to carry this message to alcoholics and to practice these principles in all our affairs" (AA, 1976, p. 60). This means extending oneself to others in many different ways, from the obvious ones of telling one's story in a meeting, talking to a potential new member, or participating in institutional meetings in hospitals, prisons, and the like, to the quieter ways in which even relative newcomers can gain a sense of helping—making coffee, putting out chairs, washing ashtrays, and other clean-up chores. Discovering one's ability to help other sufferers reinforces the sense that one's original hopes for recovery are being fulfilled.

Raiff (1978) labeled her final stage of affiliation with Recovery, Inc. as the "decision to volunteer" (p. 160). The two most frequent reasons members gave for becoming leaders were wanting to help others and using leadership as a form of "insurance" against relapse. Raiff quotes one interviewee:

I was helped when all other efforts were faltering. Through Recovery, I gained my mental health. I want to help make the method available to others. There is no other way other than volunteers such as myself. (p. 198)

Becoming a group's leader represents, perhaps, the most valuable gift a member can contribute. The next section examines nonprofessional peer leadership.

MEMBERS IN
LEADERSHIP ROLES

Leadership in self-help groups varies a great deal. For some groups, members assume leadership on a weekly rotating schedule, and all that is required is following a printed agenda. In others, the leader role demands much more. In the following section we will discuss how people assume leadership, variations in leader roles, and burnout among leaders.

Pathways to Leadership

Who is most likely to assume a leadership role? Raiff (1978) asked this question with regard to Recovery, Inc., an association that trains its member leaders. She found that two-thirds of the Recovery leadership had been volunteers in other types of community groups. When these leaders were asked for the original source of their decision to volunteer, 71% reported that they were recruited by their own group's leader. Only 14% had taken the initiative in volunteering.

Unlike the experience of leaders in Recovery, Inc., many heads of both Scoliosis Association and Candlelighter's groups became group leaders because they had founded their local chapter (Chesler & Chesney, 1995; Revenson & Cassel, 1991). The founder faces some typical pitfalls that can turn enthusiasm into a handicap. If the founder is able to develop new leadership and delegate tasks, the group gains by having a person with such initiative as its leader. On the other hand, Chesler and Chesney's (1995) studies revealed that founders sometimes performed so many of the leader tasks that they discouraged others from assuming responsibility. Founders often have to be helped to see that they must withdraw a little as the group matures.

Similarly, some groups develop a small clique of older members who take turns sharing leader tasks. This can be healthy for the group as long as the core group's ranks are open for others who want to lead; closed cliques, on the other hand, stimulate resentment and alienation among members. Small leadership cliques may need to be cautioned by the group's advisors to avoid giving such an impression.

Variations of Leadership

Recovery, Inc. and Twelve-Step group leaders face two extremes of stringency in leader roles. In Recovery, the leader must be present in all meetings and must know how to use the method of will training. Moreover, he or she must be able to involve the membership in giving examples of how they applied the method and then lead the group in discussion. Further, leaders must be able to socialize newcomers and set limits so that discussion does not drift off the topic. In addition, leaders' phone numbers are used as contact points and calls from the public come to them. The organization prepares its leaders by holding training meetings and by apprenticeship to a group leader. Apprentice leaders help the group leader to maintain discussion, take over leadership of meetings when the group leader is away, and gradually move into full leadership.

On the other hand, most Twelve Step meetings rotate the role of meeting chair. Typically rotation occurs weekly, but terms can be longer. Moreover, an agenda (usually written) is followed in each meeting. The bulk of the meeting is taken up with one of two or three basic programs: speakers who relate their story, discussion around a topic related to using the AA program, or discussion of one of the steps (step study group). Most groups require little facilitation because the meeting structures contributions in round-robin formation without cross talk. The chair's usual role is to announce each item of the agenda.

The individual who enjoys leadership in Recovery, Inc. is likely someone who enjoys positions of authority and is energetic, outgoing, and conscientious (Hogan, Curphy, & Hogan, 1994). Those who resist leader roles will fit more comfortably in the temporary, nonauthoritarian leadership roles of Twelve-Step fellowships. This is hypothetical, however, because leadership in self-help groups has not been investigated along these lines.

Many group leadership patterns fit somewhere in between the two extremes. For example, Chesler and Chesney (1995) found that Candlelighters' leaders used three basic styles. Some groups were all parent-led; some, both parent-led and professionally led; and others, completely professionally led. There were differences among them. Parent-led groups initiated a variety of activities, whereas professionally led groups tended to resemble a support-group model in that they focused primarily on members' emotions. Candlelighters group leaders assumed a relatively uncomplicated leadership role, but their terms lasted for longer periods than the rotated chair positions in Twelve-Step groups. Their roles tended to be either narrow or broad depending on the group and the ambitiousness of its agenda.

Burnout

Investigations of group leadership reveal that most leaders volunteer for this role out of a desire to help others (Chesler & Chesney, 1995; Meissen & Volk, 1995; Raiff, 1978; Revenson & Cassel, 1991). Too often, however, leadership was more a matter of performing less attractive jobs, such as recruiting new members, raising funds, and urging other members to accept leadership and service responsibilities. Leaders who shared their responsibility with a professional coleader often experienced role conflict. Others found themselves unclear about their role when they shared it with a professional.

Several ways of avoiding leader stress were suggested in this literature. Recruiting fresh leadership divides tasks among members and thus reduces the burden on a few. Moreover, assigning small tasks to newcomers, such as bringing refreshments and setting up the room, begins to prepare new leadership at an early stage of participation (Chesler & Chesney, 1995; Meissen & Volk, 1995; Raiff, 1978). How does a group find fresh leadership? Chesler & Chesney suggest leadership workshops that include lectures, group discussions, situational problem solving, role-play scenarios, and practice in leading sessions and using leadership skills (p. 134). This effort is crucial to the existence of self-help associations. New members are a self-help group's primary resource; being unable to sustain a steady membership represents a threat to its survival (Meissen & Volk, 1995).

Membership decline comes about not only as a failure of the group to attract new members, but also because the group may have helped members to succeed and thus to terminate participation. Although almost no research has focused on termination in self-help or support groups following long-term involvement, we turn to that subject and raise some of the questions surrounding it.

TERMINATION OF LONG-TERM INVOLVEMENT

Long-term participants may terminate for positive reasons, such as having reached a degree of success that makes the group unnecessary. But termination might also be due to such negative considerations as dislike of the group, its members, or the leader. Departure might also be due to changes, real or perceived, in the group itself. For example, leadership may be assumed by someone whose style conflicts with a member's expectations; the meeting time may become inconvenient; or the meeting place may change.

Since many self-help group members perceive a need for lifelong involvement, reasons why long-term members discontinue is of significant interest to group leaders and fellow members; but there is little published research on this question. An investigation of experiences in a variety of professionally led, open-ended groups indicated that it is typical for involvement to be brief (Galinsky & Schopler, 1985). Investigating this question with regard to Narcotics Anonymous (NA), Tuchman (1995) interviewed eight individuals who had attended four to nine meetings a week for between 2 and 7 years and who were now inactive.

Four (50%) indicated that they no longer found people in NA with enough maturity to assist them. Three others stated that they worked in the substance abuse field and therefore had been in meetings all day. In addition, these three were uncomfortable with meetings at which they encountered clients. Two people said they discontinued meeting attendance after feeling they had been judged and criticized during a meeting. Some of the interviewees complained that the presence of too many newcomers from treatment centers had spoiled the meetings because treatment "lingo" was replacing the principles of the Twelve-Step program and clouding its message. Despite the attendance fall-off, some of these respondents continued to be part of the broader NA network and still attended its social functions. Three of the interviewees felt guilty about discontinuing attendance and five said they missed the companionship and support of the NA fellowship. Only one person felt "okay" about not attending.

There are differences between the phenomena of recruits quitting the group before gaining what they came for and long-term members quitting because they have achieved their goals. More research is needed on both types of attrition. The latter reason may be a sign of group effectiveness; while the former, of group dysfunction. The following suggestions draw from what is known about long-term involvement and voluntary leadership of self-help and support groups.

IMPLICATIONS FOR PRACTITIONERS

Practitioners must be aware of the difference between early participation and later, longer-term involvement. Short-term participation starts the process of change, provides information, and supports people in crisis—all worthwhile goals and often all that is needed by the participant. Longer-term involvement is necessary, however, for the participant who needs to make a radical self-transformation, to maintain a radical change in lifestyle, and to endure long-term afflictions. Long-term involvement gives one an opportunity to give back, to help others, and to acquire leadership skills. Long-term attendance presents the participant with new avenues for achieving self-growth, increasing self-esteem, making a difference in society, and acquiring a sense of purpose. Members can be encouraged to remain involved in order to receive these rewards.

Relationships with sponsors can be very significant for some people. This is especially true for those who do not possess high affiliation needs and who experience discomfort in groups. Professionals can assist newcomers to find sponsors by linking them to such members within groups, and they can also encourage long-term participants to become sponsors.

Support group facilitators and self-help leaders should involve new members in small tasks to encourage their connectedness with the group. Furthermore, because identification with others in the group increases hope and provides role models, successful members should be encouraged to tell their stories and in so doing, explain how the group helped them.

Facilitators of support groups should understand the importance of activities outside of meetings. Meetings are only one of the ways self-help and support groups provide assistance. Practitioners must be aware that for some people, the group is a community; its members become the individual's social network, and the group's philosophy becomes a way of life (not an addiction to the group). Commitment and loyalty to a community is a sign of mental health, not a symptom of mental illness.

If the professional leader plans to gradually withdraw from the group so that it continues with peer leadership, the leader role must be streamlined and clarified. Leaders will be less likely to burn out and give up if their job can be structured to allow them to do what they want to do (helping others) and not just what no one else will do ("administrivia"). Helping the group to structure its leadership role in ways that can be learned quickly and easily rotated from one person to another will keep it going when the group becomes independent of the professional. The group will survive if many people are involved but will flounder if one person does everything.

Professionals who share leadership with a peer leader should note that this can result in role conflict for peer leaders. Pains should be taken to clarify the respective roles of each and to maintain open communication lest confusion occur.

Some participants move to highly intense levels of involvement in self-help and support groups; others drop out and move on with no apparent need for continuing their participation. It is important for professionals to recognize that either option is right for some and not for others. Intense participation requires a willingness to give of self for the sake of others, to continue spiritual growth by giving, and to reinforce one's own recovery. But some people move on and find fulfilling lives outside the self-help group. That choice should be questioned only if the person has a history of relapse or if the individuals have not achieved their original goals.

SUMMARY

This chapter has examined how self-help and support groups respond to succeeding levels of readiness. It has reviewed significant themes related to long-term attendance, including making a commitment, accepting the problem, identifying transformation, forming dyadic relationships, and helping others. Long-term participation is important because it helps people maintain changes and because it contributes to group longevity. Group leadership is one way in which veteran members can help others, the factor that most often motivates their willingness to serve.

DISCUSSION QUESTION

Imagine the following situation: You are a professional mental health worker and you have a client who has attended Gamblers Anonymous for 1 year and has not gambled in the past 9 months. This client has decided to stop attending GA because he thinks he has his gambling under control. Prior to attending GA, this person had been gambling for 20 years progressively sinking more in debt. What would you say to this person? In what stage of readiness is this client? Discuss this situation in a small group and decide what is likely to be the best approach with this person.

CLASSROOM EXERCISES

1. Develop an interview schedule for assessing how a person has become a long-term committed member of a self-help association. Can you determine the factors that made the individual become active and intensely involved in the organization? Use this interview schedule for interviewing long-term members in order to complete the assignment shown below.

2. Develop an interview schedule for assessing why some individuals have terminated participation in a self-help group after having once been intensely involved and members of the group's leadership.

ASSIGNMENTS

1. Locate a small sample of long-term self-help group members and interview them about reasons they have remained active in their group. Ask about their later stages of affiliation and about their contributions to the group's leadership. Assess what motivated these individuals to accept leadership positions. Assess whether they have "burned out" with the position, and if they have not, what seemed to prevent this. Write a brief paper discussing your findings.

2. As an alternative to assignment 1, locate a small sample of long-term group members who have stopped attending their group. Ask them about the intensity of their former participation and why they stopped. Write a brief paper discussing your findings.

PART 3

THE PRACTITIONER

Chapter 6

PROFESSIONAL ROLES
IN SUPPORT GROUPS

"It was the people in the group that were the most important and satisfying. The group leader was OK but wasn't as important as the group. We helped one another because we understood our mutual problems and feelings."
—A support group member, Glajchen & Magen, 1995

Support groups seem simple to construct and facilitate, but aspects of them can baffle a practitioner who lacks experience with such groups. The quotation above suggests that the group's facilitator is not very important, but this is not true at all. The support group facilitator's greatest challenge is to foster a sense of mutual aid so that the member thinks it is the group that is important and not the leader (Gitterman & Shulman, 1994). Here we will consider the basic steps in starting, facilitating, and consulting with a support group (self-help groups will be discussed in chapter 7). The chapter concludes with discussion of common problems found in facilitating or consulting with support groups.

Support groups are those that meet with the assistance of a professional or agency-based facilitator. They are usually small and often time-limited. The most important first step in developing a support group is to determine whether a substantial population in need of it exists. As a presenter in continuing education courses, I often hear the question, "What can I do if group members do not come to meetings?" This automatically raises a corresponding question, "Are you sure there is a real need for the group?" You can avoid some of the stress of low attendance if you first assess the number of persons who need and desire a support group. You may also consider whether a substantial number of the people that you want to serve have reached an action stage of readiness for group participation. But these considerations alone will not eliminate the problem of poor attendance, to which we shall return.

STARTING A GROUP

When starting a new group, the practitioner must decide on its size, determine membership criteria, find a meeting place, formulate a recruitment plan, and determine who will lead the group. The practitioner should be well-informed about support groups and ready to transmit his or her knowledge of them to the group's members. In addition, a professional facilitator should be knowledgeable about the problem the group will address. A group for pregnant teenagers requires understanding about pregnancy, about adolescence, and about some of the typical dilemmas faced by pregnant teens.

One of your first decisions will be whether the group you are forming will be an open-ended or closed group. Many, if not most, support groups are open-ended; that is, they constantly add new members as older members drop out or attend sporadically (Galinsky & Schopler, 1985). Before making too many decisions about such matters, an experienced practitioner will identify a core group of people who represent those for whom the group is intended and will obtain a commitment from them to help it begin. This core group should be involved in planning and deciding issues such as those listed above. Only if forming a core group is not possible, should you make these decisions on your own.

Size of the Group

Small groups typically include from 8 to 12 active members (Galinsky & Schopler, 1985). Fairchild (1995) described typical postpartum support groups that had from 2 to 8 members with an average of 5 at each meeting. If your group is to be a closed group (not open to newcomers or the general public), begin with more members than you want to have in attendance, because not all of your original group will be active, and there will be absences. An agency in Long Island with experience in forming support groups for people with AIDS, HIV-Positive individuals, and their families, recommends beginning with 20 members (Barouh, 1992). Of 20 potential members, you can expect that approximately 60% (12) will attend. If you plan a fixed and relatively short-term group, close the membership once the group begins to meet.

Support groups can involve more members than a typical therapy group, yet still operate with 4 or 5 members. If the group is to be advertised to the public, remain flexible about numbers. It may happen that either very few or very many may attend. If you have a core group, you can count on those members to attend in the first meeting and help recruits to become integrated and committed to participation.

Establishing Membership Criteria

Support groups depend upon having members with the same problem or concern. Lacking this kind of homogeneity, the group cannot be cohesive, establish its program, acquire new members, or extend experiential knowledge among members. Having the same focal concern is the essence of support groups; thus, this must be the first criterion for membership. Moreover, as you may recall from chapter 4, recruits will find a group into which they feel they fit more attractive. Reporting on cancer support groups, Glajchen and Magen (1995) found that it was necessary to form groups around specific types of cancer, even in the same stage of the illness. Less severely ill people objected to being in groups with later-stage cancer patients who faced imminent death.

Membership criteria, beyond the focal concern, may be decided by your agency, by you alone, or by you and your core group. Some groups limit membership to a particular agency population and include only the identified client or patient. Others open their membership to the public or to families and friends of the individual with the condition. Further, some groups encourage members to remain in the group indefinitely and to become the veterans who provide hope, stability, and wisdom to newcomers. Others terminate membership once the person leaves the agency or completes coping with the crisis caused by the focal concern. It is likely that groups with more open membership criteria will survive longer, grow larger, and have stronger and more independent leadership (Yoak & Chesler, 1985).

There is no one right way to determine membership characteristics beyond the rule about sharing the same concern, but for at least some of these issues you must decide on the criteria before the first meeting. If your group is open to the public and you do not first screen new members, some who are not qualified for inclusion may attend. This can be handled by stationing someone at the door to welcome newcomers and answer questions about the purpose of the group. Follow that strategy by announcing the purpose of the group at the beginning of each meeting and requesting that those who are unqualified meet with the facilitator after the meeting (when you will suggest other services to them). An alternative to this rather heavy-handed approach is to welcome everyone, but ask those who are not affected by the condition to remain silent. If these screening efforts are unsuccessful, you may have to take the unqualified person aside, explain the purpose of the group and ask them to withdraw. Obviously, the sooner you do this, the better. This is a very difficult thing to do because the individual may need to be in some kind of group, but it must be done for the sake of the group's long-term success.

Another way to handle moderate degrees of heterogeneity is to have some meetings or parts of meetings, such as those with an educational format, in common, then to divide the group into clusters for different kinds of members. For example, large Twelve-Step groups sometimes break into clusters for people focusing on different steps. One cluster may be for newcomers, another for working on the fourth step, and others on various topics of interest to the subgroup members. A cancer support group may divide over stage of illness or type of treatment.

Meeting Places

Typically, support groups meet in the sponsoring agency. A more neutral setting, however, may help the facilitator communicate nonverbally that the group is not the property of the agency, but belongs to the group members. On the other hand, when members themselves decide on the meeting place, they may prefer the sense of security and affiliation that comes with meeting in the agency. Groups often meet in churches. The group can meet in a private room of a local restaurant if the meeting is organized around having a meal. If the group is for persons who feel stigmatized by their condition, the meeting should probably not be held in a public place.

The meeting place should be accessible to potential members and offer them safety and convenience. It should be a comfortable and inviting place where those assembled will not be disturbed by other events. Organizers must determine how to deal with child care needs and set policy about children in the meeting. Once established, the meeting place should not change, particularly if the group is to be of the long-term open-ended variety. Members will drop in and out and must be able to count on the permanence of time and location.

Recruiting Members

White and Madara (1995) offer numerous suggestions for recruiting members. One way is distributing a flyer in locations frequented by members of the target population. Notices may be posted in public places. Contact clergy persons and other helping professionals who can make referrals. Talk to persons from similar support groups and ask what methods they found helpful. Inform local information and referral helplines about your group. Place notices in newsletters, church bulletins, and local newspapers. Give spot announcements to local radio stations, and be prepared to go on a speaking circuit to explain the program and the group.

Flyers and other communications should make clear the exact purpose of the group and what will take place in meetings. Before entering the group, new members may be screened for appropriateness for inclusion in the group and oriented to the group's purpose and norms (Galinsky & Schopler, 1985). A major fear of potential members is that they will be asked to speak about their problem before a group of strangers. Good publicity allays this fear. It may help to ask those interested to call you or a member of the core group before the actual meeting. Such an invitation allows the hesitant to test the setting and gives the facilitator an opportunity to prepare the pioneer members.

Leadership

As stated in the previous chapter, leadership may be member-only (without a professional leader or with a professional staff person who does not act as a leader but is in attendance), professional-only, or shared equally by a member and a professional. Two large studies of support groups for parents were able to contrast these patterns of leadership within the same national network (Cherniss & Cherniss, 1987; Yoak & Chesler, 1985). In one of the studies, 44% of groups for parents of high-risk newborns were parent led, 33% were professionally led, and 20% were led by both (Cherniss & Cherniss, 1987). In the other study (of Candlelighters groups for parents of children with cancer), 49% of the groups were led only by parents, 26% only by professionals, and 26% by parents and professionals sharing leadership (Yoak & Chesler, 1985).

Findings from both of these studies suggested that when professionals begin a group, they are likely to remain in control of it whether they want to or not. Professionally-directed groups were smaller, more limited in membership, did not reach out to newcomers to maintain the groups, and engaged in fewer group activities. Parent-led groups were more structured and more apt to retain parents after the infant left the hospital (first study) or after a child either died or recovered (second study). Yoak and Chesler found that groups with shared leadership were the largest, most long-lived, and most active. A follow-up study of those groups 10 years later showed the same pattern (Chesler & Chesney, 1995). These findings show how the decision about who is the leader can affect other facets of the group's life.

The American Self-Help Clearinghouse in New Jersey recommends that professionals think "shared leadership" from the beginning when establishing any group (Bernstein, n.d.). In addition, practitioners should share virtually every task with a member of the group. Leadership and other major tasks can be rotated periodically to avoid overwhelming one or two people and to allow members to gain group leadership skills. The Clearinghouse also suggests that the group meet in a neutral place rather than on the practitioner's turf. Chairs should be arranged so that members are seated in a circle, thus preventing one person's becoming the focus.

Advantages of coleadership are the mutual support leaders give one another and the complementary abilities that each brings to the role. The coleaders can model a mutually supportive relationship (Kostyk, Fuchs, Tabisz, & Jacyk, 1993). Peer leaders, by demonstrating the functions of leaders, may inspire others to assume leadership. Their bringing experiential knowledge to bear also shows members the value of what they can offer each other. The professional coleader brings organizational expertise, knowledge of the problem, and access to resources in addition to his or her group work skills.

FACILITATING THE GROUP

As the first meeting draws near, you and your core group, if you have one, must begin to plan the actual meeting—format, length and frequency of meetings, communication patterns, goals, facilitation techniques, stages of group development, and method of withdrawing from leadership.

Meeting Format

Kirschenbaum and Glaser (1978) suggest three possible formats for a support group. Format 1 is "each-one-teach-one," in which each member takes responsibility for sessions on a rotating basis and is responsible for setting up the entire meeting. Format 2, the structured model, offers a formal agenda with an opening, a program, and a closing. Format 3, the combination model, blends the first two. Parts of the meeting follow an established agenda, and others are spontaneously led by rotating leaders. White and Madara (1995) suggest the meeting format shown below:

Greet attendees at the door
Standard opening, statement of purpose
Introductions
Main program
Business
Formal closing
Refreshments

Regardless of the format chosen, members in most groups socialize before or after the meeting. Often this is accompanied by refreshments, usually something simple such as coffee, soft drinks, and donuts. Refreshments can reflect community norms. For example, in a posh Marin County, California group "two or three types of cheeses and crackers laid out, alongside a selection of chips and dips, freshly cut apples, carrots and celery sticks, grapes and strawberries, several types of cookies, a large selection of herbal and non-herbal teas, and freshly brewed caffeinated and decaffeinated coffee . . ." (Kaskutas, 1994, p. 5). For some populations, the refreshments can be a major motivating force. Some groups serve the refreshments before the meeting in order to stimulate early arrival and the opportunity to socialize with newcomers. It might be wise with other groups, however, to save refreshments until after the meeting in order to reward those who stay for its duration. In groups that serve people who are homeless or are otherwise impoverished, the food becomes a major attraction to otherwise reluctant recruits.

Length and Frequency of Meetings

You will also have to decide how long your meeting should last and how often to meet. Support groups may meet monthly, biweekly, weekly, or even more often. For people who are in serious crises, the more often the group meets, the better it can support its members. On the other hand, meeting more than once a week may be unfeasible and may reduce the average number of members in each meeting unless there is a strong demand for the group. Meetings may last for an hour, although an hour and a half is more typical. Because the pre- and post-socializing can take on much significance, one hour of formal meeting time may suffice.

Communication Pattern

Typically, support groups engage in free-floating communication, meaning that the discussion flows from one person to another in a spontaneous interchange sometimes referred to as "cross talk" or back and forth communication. Often, however, support group leaders favor a "round-robin" pattern that provides each member a turn to speak without direct responses across the circle (Barouh, 1992). In most groups, members can avoid verbal participation by stating "pass" when their turn comes. When demand for talk-time exceeds that available, some leaders divide the group time by the number of members and give each a fraction of total time in which to speak. Because monopolizers can be a problem in some groups, these methods are worth considering. It is important to help members discover that listening can be just as important, or more important, than talking. Some Twelve-Step groups use a saying, "Take the cotton out of your ears and put it in your mouth," to remind especially (but not only) newcomers that practicing the program should precede explaining it.

Goals for Facilitation

According to Wasserman and Danforth (1988), support-group facilitators aim for eight process goals: (a) information exchange, (b) an atmosphere of mutual support, (c) group cohesion, (d) increased coping and self-efficacy, (e) reduction of social isolation, (f) stress reduction, (g) an atmosphere of safety, and (h) reinforcement of members' positive activity in and outside the group.

Information exchange is one of the most important roles of the facilitator. He or she disseminates information about the problem condition, the available resources for help with it, and the methods of conducting the group's meetings. The facilitator also helps members to recognize the value of their own experiences and encourages them to speak of these experiences when it is comfortable for them to do so.

The goal of *mutual support* can be furthered by introducing the concept of mutual aid and demonstrating to group members how to use empathic responses and supportive comments. If the facilitator works with a cofacilitator, they can model empathy and support.

One way the facilitator enhances *group cohesion* is by emphasizing the members' similarities. He or she can also minimize social distance between him- or herself and the group's members by sharing a personal experience, by using first names, and by sharing tasks with members. The facilitator can encourage the use of decision making by consensus, in which all members come to a mutually acceptable agreement, and by not making arbitrary decisions for the group.

Coping and self-efficacy come from successful mastery of difficult situations. Members enhance one another's coping skills when they relate how they have coped in the past with the difficulties shared among them. Mutual sharing of this kind helps to maintain participation by seasoned members as well as newcomers. In this way, older members have the opportunity to help others, and newcomers benefit from the veterans' experience.

Reduction of social isolation can happen quite naturally when support group members meet. Many of those who choose to join a support group do so because they have either too small a support system or a system that does not comprehend what they are going through. The group fulfills the need to communicate with others who understand and who are not judgmental. The facilitator's intervention can be crucial in helping this process along. For example, in a group for military families affected by the Persian Gulf War, a woman told a story filled with sadness. Before she finished, during a pause, another member changed the subject.

> The coleader, recognizing what was happening, brought the group back to this young woman, interpreted the group's sudden shift away from her, and then helped the group to focus on helping her. Almost the entire group was in tears by the time she finished her story. . . . This incident marked a turning point for the group, proving to each member that the group could handle difficult and intense situations. Such trust was important because the potential existed for group members to experience the death of a loved one in the Gulf (Parker, Hutchinson, & Berry, 1995, p. 95)

Stress reduction is a primary goal in support groups. Professionals should be especially aware of this difference between support groups and groups designed for personal change. Anxiety in the latter group may mobilize readiness for change in treatment, but may stress unnecessarily those who are primarily in need of support. The facilitator can curtail factors that increase stress, whether those be self-induced or group-induced. Self-blame, for example, can be a self-induced stressor. A group-induced factor causing stress might be confrontation or disagreement among members; these should be minimized. Structured meeting formats help to reduce stress. Relaxing and fun activities are also stress reducers.

An extremely important goal for the group is *safety*. It may fall to the professional facilitator to initiate norms of safety in the first few meetings of the group. For example, he or she can give newcomers permission to not speak until they feel ready. Demands for self-disclosure should not be made. Differences should be tolerated as long as the participant meets minimum qualifications for attending the group. The facilitator should be ready to set limits on any behavior that threatens others. To avoid the necessity for doing this, the leader can reinforce norms of safety by stating them at the beginning of the meeting. For example, some leaders say at the beginning of meetings that the names of those seen in the group will not be divulged outside it and that personal confrontations are not acceptable.

A support group should *reinforce the positive and productive* activities of members. It is human nature to complain, but the group's focus must move quickly from members finding fault, to solutions that ease stress. As members gain seniority in their participation, their coping methods and successes should become the focus of meetings. As members become adept at thinking in terms of success, their self-esteem will rise. They may be unaware of the link, but the focus on what is wrong instead of what is right is depressing and damaging to self-esteem. Focusing on progress is empowering because it reminds the person that progress has been made and can continue.

Group Facilitation Skills

Toseland and Rivas (1995) summarize leadership skills used in working with small groups. Skills that facilitate group process include attending to members, responding, focusing the group's communication, guiding group interaction, and involving members in the communication pattern. The group worker uses a number of skills in assessing individual members and in assessing the group's progress and effectiveness.

Support group facilitation relies less on interpreting member interactions (appropriate in group therapy) and more on helping the group to become a supportive information system. Support groups do not stress member insight and change; they rather attempt to sustain functioning and ease burdens. The facilitator offers more support in the beginning of the group, gradually tapering off interventions once the group is underway. The facilitator may contribute as much before and after meetings as during them. He or she finds resources, consults with the member/leader or core group, obtains publicity, recruits new members, and interprets the group's purpose to colleagues.

Stages of Group Development

Leadership and facilitation skills should be matched to the developmental stage of the group. In the beginning stages of a support group, members attempt to discover their similarities in order to find common ground (Budman, 1975; Hermann, Cella, & Robinovitch, 1995). They seek information and alternative solutions to problems. It is important for the facilitator to encourage these processes. Furthermore, the facilitator will concentrate on establishing trust, helping the group establish norms and goals, and assisting it to develop structure.

The middle stage begins when members become more open to self examination, able to offer help to one another, and ready to search for the meaning in their experience. They explore new ways of coping. The more cohesive the group, the more self-examination will take place. Members establish bonds that reach beyond the group's meetings, and a mutual support network begins to form. Budman (1975) states that it is only in this phase that the mutual-aid system reaches maturity. The facilitator role is to develop content issues, help members share personal experiences, nurture the development of a core group, and maintain the group's momentum.

The final stage can be one of termination or a time for transition to independent existence. If the group officially ends, several outcomes are possible. The support group may continue unofficially, in which case it will likely begin to assume some of the characteristics of a self-help group. Members may also move on to existing self-help groups, may develop independent networks of friendship, obtain help from other formal helping systems, or continue infrequent meetings of the old support group.

At the point of termination, the facilitator may become more active, assisting the group to engage in such termination tasks as saying goodbye, evaluating progress, and making transitions to other services. It may be difficult for the members at this point to know whether they really want to continue the group on their own or whether they are simply sad to see the group meetings come to a close. The facilitator can help them to look carefully at the options and guide them in making a decision with which they can live.

Withdrawing From Leadership

If the group is not time-limited, peer leadership (among members) becomes stronger. For professional facilitators, this signals the potential for converting to a consultant role. This transition can be effected through three strategic moves by the practitioner: first, gradually becoming less active in the meetings he or she attends; second, not attending every meeting; and third, meeting with peer leaders for consultation outside the group's meeting time. For some groups, this eventual transition has been an early goal. For others, the practitioner remains in the leadership role. Either is an acceptable choice.

THE CONSULTANT ROLE

The role of the professional facilitator who is successful in empowering peer leadership will gradually devolve into that of a consultant. With already existing, more independent groups, the consultant role may be all that was expected from the beginning. Several authors have discussed the consultant role with a support or self-help group and provided models for offering such services, as well as for how to develop this relationship without coopting or otherwise weakening the essence of the mutual-help model (Auslander & Auslander, 1988; Powell, 1987; Silverman, 1978; Wollert, Knight, & Levy, 1980).

Consultation has been defined as an "interactional helping process in which an expert—the consultant—aids a second party—the consultee—to deal more effectively with work-related problems" (Kadushin, 1977). Silverman (1978) cautioned that the professional should proceed with consultation only if five criteria exist: (a) one receives an invitation to consult; (b) one maintains a collegial relationship with the consultee; (c) one recognizes the value system of the consultee; (d) one understands that he or she cannot tell the consultee how to use the information; and (e) one bears no responsibility in assuring that the advice is carried out. She advised further that, when consulting with members or leaders, one meet with more than one person from the group. This helps prevent the consultees from over-identifying with the consultant and assuming the role of junior professional.

Auslander and Auslander (1988) reported on a consultation experience in which the social worker consulted with support groups in a family service agency. Typical problems brought to the consultant were lack of group cohesion, inability to attract new members, lack of clear goals, discrepancy between the goals of newcomers and of regular attenders, and the mechanics of forming a group. On some occasions, the consultant linked the groups to concrete services, such as meeting room and copying facilities. On others, he facilitated linkages with agency services.

Wollert et al. (1980) described consulting with an affiliate of Make Today Count (a group for the terminally ill). The authors observed many meetings of this group that had the following problems: too few members, lack of cohesive format, too much focus on problems without solutions, and infrequent meetings. Other professionals had visited the group; however, their presence was more destructive than helpful in that they showed little respect for the group, and they attempted to practice their skills on members and criticized them without giving useful advice.

The consultation of Wollert and colleagues began with a nonevaluative, long-term approach in which they were careful to show respect for the group's right to accept or reject their inputs. They began by educating the group about the values and strengths of self-help groups. As a result of the consultation, the group made five changes that improved its functioning. These were (a) developing a more clearly defined purpose; (b) reordering the meeting format; (c) increasing the number of meetings; (d) rotating leadership in the meetings; and (e) adopting group discussion techniques more in line with those of a support or self-help group.

The experiences described by Wollert and his colleagues illustrate many of the typical needs of support groups. In the next section, we will continue to discuss some common problems often brought to those who consult with support group leaders and briefly address some solutions to those problems.

PROBLEMS ENCOUNTERED
IN SUPPORT GROUPS

Although most support groups have few problems, some difficulties can interfere with the workings of the group (Anderson & Shaw, 1994; Barouh, 1992; Kirschenbaum & Glaser, 1978; Meissen & Volk, 1995; Schopler & Galinsky, 1993; Wasow, 1986). Following are 12 common problems and suggestions as to how to deal with them.

1. Too Few Members and Absent Members

This is the most common complaint in support groups. Low attendance can have many sources, and until you discover the chief factor, it is difficult to solve. There are at least seven possible sources of low attendance:

- Time and place. Is the time convenient and can potential members get to the meeting? Is the place safe and familiar or is it in an unsafe area of town or an area unfamiliar to members? If so, can this be changed?
- Too few committed members. Support group members typically drop in and out and many are often absent. The group must have enough members to compensate for this attendance pattern.
- Lack of similarity among members. Do all share the same difficulty or are they in the group for different reasons? If the group is not homogenous, a redetermination of the group's goals and its membership criteria must be undertaken.
- Group safety. Are members fearful of exposure, of being made to speak before they are ready, or of being criticized? These fears must be allayed.
- Negativity. Members often complain without seeking constructive solutions. They must be redirected to engage in positive discussion.
- Participation is limited. Do a few members dominate the group? Limits must be placed so that all have opportunity for participation.
- Lack of child care. If the group serves primarily women, especially mothers or other primary child caretakers, having available child care is essential.

2. Dominating Members

Another common complaint concerns members who dominate the meeting. Reminders to the group that it is important for everyone to have a chance to speak may be sufficient to handle this problem. If not, more decisive action must be taken. Discussing this common group problem, Yalom (1995) cautioned group leaders not to expect the group to limit these members. It is a facilitator's (leader's, therapist's) responsibility to do this. The monopolizer typically has little awareness of his or her effect on the group and cannot be expected to achieve the ability to restrain this habit without intervention.

The facilitator should discuss this behavior privately with the monopolizer. Point out that the individual is missing valuable contributions from other group members because they are unable to contribute. Suggest that reducing vocal activity might become a private goal, that the individual choose very carefully what he or she will say and not say. Because monopolizers are sometimes very uncomfortable when they are not talking, the leader may need to help the person privately to gain insight into the reason for excessive talking. The monopolizer may leave the group. This outcome, though unfortunate, is preferable to losing several other group members because of their frustration with this person.

Another way to deal with overly talkative people in a support group is to structure the group by eliminating cross-talk and using the "go-around-the-room" pattern. You may have to state often that the time is limited and everyone should have a chance to speak. You can hope that eventually the group will adopt this limitation as a group norm. Going even further, you can divide up the total time the group meets and give each member a time limit. However, some dominators seem so utterly oblivious to the passage of time and their use of it that it may be necessary to not only give the member a time limit, but also to time the individual's contribution and announce when the time has elapsed.

3. Leader Burnout

As discussed in chapter 5, reasons for burnout include overwork, lack of clarity about group goals, role conflict with a coleader, and worries about recruitment of members. Furthermore, taking a leadership position solely because of obligation, without really wanting to do it, can lead to burnout. Solutions include delegating leadership functions to others, rotating leadership, and initiating role clarification. Membership recruitment should not be the responsibility solely of the leader; a recruitment committee might help. The leader may need to lower expectations for attendance or for other accomplishments. Unlike other groups with which professionals work, attendance in support groups is often spotty and successes difficult to measure.

4. Dilemmas About Group Composition

Support groups should be composed of people with the same basic problem, but that still allows for a great deal of heterogeneity. For example, should both family members and patients attend the same group? If the group is for families, should that include several generations, or should the group be divided by generation? Should people in early stages be combined with people in later stages of experiencing the problem? There is no one right answer to these questions. If the group attracts enough members, and if subgroups feel a need to separate, that is a workable solution. One might keep the group together for part of the meeting and separate it for another part. Keep in mind that there will be trade-offs if you do this. The various subgroups may have much to share with the others.

5. Bringing Unwelcome Others to Meetings

Lack of baby sitters can be a major problem for a support group, particularly one composed of parents. Agency facilitators may be in a position to arrange for child care and should do so as part of planning the group. It is almost impossible to sustain a satisfactory group with small children present. Older children are often capable of sitting quietly in a meeting, but this arrangement is fraught with difficulty. These children can hear and understand what is said. Participants may be unwilling to tell troubles or even reveal their membership in the presence of a child. Worries about violations of confidentiality multiply when school-age children are present.

Members may also wish to bring relatives, friends, or even pets to the meeting. Rules about who is welcome in the group need to spelled out very clearly at the inception of the group and with each newcomer on arrival. The group's facilitator must, however, be prepared to deal with the possible attendance of someone who does not meet the group's criteria. A useful procedure is to establish in advance with the group how to proceed if a visitor wants to attend. For example, students often attend such groups in order to learn more about them. Once a visitor policy is established, exceptions should be made only rarely. Once an uninvited outsider is admitted and allowed to remain in the meeting, others may violate this norm; members who are uncomfortable with such intrusions but do not wish to seem unfriendly may simply drop out of the group.

6. Anger and Conflict Expressed in the Group

As discussed in chapter 3, the social climate in support groups is typically low in anger and aggression. Moreover, the research on GROW, discussed in chapter 2, found that negative comments during meetings correlated with negative group evaluations by participants. This suggests that harmonious interaction should be established in a support group, with alternatives available if angry feelings arise. For example, angry feelings might entitle one to a private meeting with the leader. If anger is so pervasive that it continues to disrupt the group or takes inordinate time of the leader, the composition and goals of the group must be questioned. It is quite unusual for members of a support group to display anger and conflict. If the anger expressed has to do with societal or interpersonal injustice outside the group, the facilitator should attempt to focus on solutions and social action rather than on the anger.

7. Becoming Upset After the Meeting

Since most support groups avoid high levels of emotional intensity, being upset after a meeting usually occurs because of events outside the group. The group's leaders or other members may offer themselves as someone to confide in if a member's emotional state indicates a need for this. If, however, a particular member needs repeated help after meetings or relies too heavily on the practitioner or other group members, it may be that this person needs a therapist, a therapy group, or other services.

8. Too Few Minority Members

As discussed in chapter 4, people usually prefer groups in which they are not a minority, thus a majority European-American group will likely have difficulty retaining and attracting members of other races and ethnic groups. An obvious solution is to recruit several people of the same ethnic or racial group, so that individuals will not feel isolated in their first meeting. If the group is open-ended with little opportunity to choose members, the presence of coleaders of different races and cultures can also allay the minority person's feeling of isolation. In addition, special efforts to recruit others can promote the group in neighborhoods where minorities may be present. Literature about the group can depict members of varied racial or ethnic groups.

9. Intense Feelings Not Expressed in the Group

The question of whether support group members should be urged to express painful feelings in meetings is somewhat controversial (Wasow, 1986). On the one hand, facilitators are urged to minimize the expression of intense feelings in support groups. On the other hand, some clinicians think expression of feelings lessens their intensity and allows the person to obtain needed support. In general, support groups differ from therapy groups on this point. While expression of deep feelings may be necessary in a therapy group, it is common for support groups to remain more superficial. If a group's leader thinks that feelings of a member must be addressed, this can be done in a one-on-one session or by referring that person to a therapist. On the other hand, groups can be quite tolerant of occasional intense feelings of sadness during crises experienced by members. This kind of expression is not encouraged as much as it is taken in stride. But it is not recommended practice to prod for intense feelings in support groups. An effort to do so will inevitably frighten some members away from the group and possibly strain the group's capacity for support. Support groups work best when positive solutions and reframing cognitions are their focus.

10. Unwillingness to Risk in the Group

Some groups, in contrast, avoid dealing with any serious issue (Kirschenbaum & Glaser, 1978). They may do this by turning the group into a social session—talking about such things as last week's football game or the weather. Another type of low-risk activity is spending all the time talking about a problem without arriving at solutions. This problem must be recognized by the facilitator and the group gently reminded that solutions and coping methods should be addressed because this is the purpose of the group. Having a mixture of newcomers and experienced members in the group helps to deal with this problem.

11. Revelations of Criminal Behavior

In certain kinds of groups, the potential for revealing criminal or unethical behavior may arise. For example, facilitators of groups for grandparents raising grandchildren hear reports that an adult child has abused the grandchild. The facilitator must report the abuse. Another example is that members of AIDS/HIV support groups confess to having unsafe sex with persons they have not informed of the medical condition. If such confessions appear to be likely, it is a good idea to inform the group, in the beginning, of your legal and ethical requirements to protect confidentiality *and* the duty to warn others if a crime has been committed or is likely to be.

12. Abuse of Alcohol and/or Other Drugs

Groups should have clear norms about alcohol and drugs. Most groups do not tolerate drunken or drug-abusing behavior in meetings. The group's tolerance of any use, such as the odor of alcohol on one's breath or having alcohol in one's possession, should be clearly stated. These norms may vary depending on the extent that alcohol is a problem to the group's members. For example, the use of alcohol by AIDS patients can compromise their immune system; therefore, norms about alcohol use might be more strict for them than for other populations.

SUMMARY

In this chapter, the focus has been on facilitating support groups. Professional roles with support groups are more involved than with self-help groups. However, the initiator, facilitator, and consultant roles with support groups are quite different than the therapist role taken with a treatment group or the chairperson role taken with a task group. The practitioner who takes a leadership role with support groups sometimes shares the leader role with a nonprofessional member and works to move the group toward autonomy. When this happens, the professional role becomes that of consultant as the group matures and develops confidence on its own. The chapter identifies 12 common problems often found in support groups and offers suggestions on how to handle them.

The next chapter focuses on professional involvement with independent self-help groups. Roles discussed include linker, initiator, and researcher.

DISCUSSION QUESTIONS

1. Identify the advantages and disadvantages of sharing leadership in a support group.
2. How would you advise a group worker who facilitates a group in which none of the members is willing to accept a leadership role?
3. What would you suggest to a group facilitator faced with a situation in which one or two members dominate a group?
4. Identify some methods of increasing membership in a support group.

CLASSROOM EXERCISES

1. Form a group and identify a common problem among you. This could be something trivial like difficulty getting up in the morning, procrastination, or not doing well in one or more of your courses. Plan a support group by giving it a name, identifying a place for meetings, deciding who will be eligible for membership, and how you will recruit members. Establish a meeting format and decide upon a program for your first meeting. Report on your plans to the rest of the class.
2. Form a group and choose one person to role-play the facilitator role. Have that person role-play teaching the group the concepts of mutual aid, empowerment, and experiential knowledge.

3. In the same group, role-play a group discussion twice, once as a therapy group and once as a support group. Have the person playing the leader model appropriate but different responses for the two types of groups.
4. Form the class into subgroups. Each group should choose a facilitator and role-play one or more of the problems listed above. Allow members to take turns demonstrating how they would handle the situation.

ASSIGNMENT

Go to a meeting of a support group. Following the meeting, jot down the characteristics and actions of the individual or individuals who assumed leadership. Write a brief paper highlighting how this person demonstrated concepts and recommendations found in this chapter. Also discuss observations you have about problems noted in the group. Suggest possible changes the group might make to improve its effectiveness.

Chapter 7

PROFESSIONAL RELATIONSHIPS WITH SELF-HELP GROUPS

Professionals should remain "on tap, but not on top."
—Leonard Borman, 1980

Self-help groups have a different kind of relationship than do support groups and professional practitioners. In fact, this is one of the primary differences between the two kinds of group. Practitioner involvement with self-help groups is a more distant relationship. How distant it is depends on how established the group is, whether it is local or national in scope, the historic role of professionals within the group, and the nature of the group's program. Unlike the facilitator roles taken with support groups as discussed in the previous chapter, practitioner roles with self-help groups involve behind-the-scenes activities, such as linking clients with groups and giving moral support to leaders.

Schubert and Borkman's (1991) typology, discussed in chapter 1, shows professionals assuming active roles in hybrid groups (which meet some self-help criteria but combine that with professional sponsorship, facilitation, or leadership) and managed groups (self-help-type support groups sponsored by a professional organization). Professionals also play vital roles with independent self-help groups. Table 7.1 presents an overview of the typical roles of professionals with both self-help and support groups: (a) directive roles within the group; (b) facilitator roles within group; and (c) external linking roles and behind-the-scenes support. Chapter 6 discussed the first and second columns pertaining to directive and facilitating roles within support groups. This chapter deals with the last column, focusing on self-help groups. After a brief summary of the research on professional/self-help relationships, the chapter addresses linking clients

Table 7.1
Continuum of Professional/Mutual-Aid Involvement

Levels of Involvement	Directive Within Group	Facilitating Within Group	External Coordinative
Type of Group	New Group	Support Group Combination Self-Help and Support Group	Self-Help Group
Examples	Local Support Group	Some Alzheimer's groups; Hybrid groups like Parents Anonymous	Twelve-Step groups; Recovery, Inc.; Candlelighters; The Compassionate Friends
Professional Roles	Organizer; Facilitator; Consultant; Linker; Board member; Supporter	Facilitator; Consultant; Educator	Linker; Advocate within the professional community; Initiator (rare); Researcher
Professional Activities	Needs assessment; Initiates core group; Calls meetings; Trains leaders; Facilitates meetings; Interprets concepts; Consultation; Referrals	Refers to; Gives organizational advice; Assists group process; Trains leadership; Interprets program to others; Invites members to the agency	Observes meetings; Reads literature; Gives place to meet; Becomes a member; Displays literature; Escorts newcomers to first meeting; Links clients to temporary sponsors; Holds workshops and demonstration meetings; Action research.

with groups, initiating founding chapters or affiliates of self-help organizations, and researching self-help groups.

RESEARCH ON
PROFESSIONAL RELATIONSHIPS

Self-help groups represent an important community resource. For this reason, professional attitudes toward, awareness of, and use of them is of considerable interest to researchers. Professional indifference or hostility toward self-help groups could limit the number of persons referred to such groups and threaten their ability to maintain a vigorous membership. Much of the research on practitioner/self-help relationships deals with the attitudes, awareness, and appropriate roles of practitioners.

Attitudes

Most surveys of professionals reveal their positive attitudes toward self-help groups (L. F. Kurtz, 1990a). Still, some recent findings indicate that a certain proportion of professionals harbor apprehensions about self-help groups. One survey showed, for example, that 47% of graduate social work and psychology students think mental illness is an inappropriate problem for self-help groups (Meissen, Mason, & Gleason, 1991). Another survey of professionals in mental health programs found that they rated professionally led groups most helpful, support groups second most helpful, and mutual help (self-help) groups least helpful (Salzer, McFadden, & Rappaport, 1994).

A survey of self-help group members from 426 groups in California found them to be positive about professional services (Lotery & Jacobs, 1995). Reacting to a list of belief statements regarding professionals, 37% believed self-help groups were more helpful than professional mental health services, and 11% believed that professionals and self-helpers were too different to work together.

Stewart, Banks, Crossman, and Poel (1995) interviewed approximately equal numbers of self-help members (n=49) and professionals (n=47); they found that in addition to many positive kinds of interaction identified by both groups, there were a number of tensions and barriers to successful collaboration. These included negative attitudes, competition, ideological conflicts, and role ambiguity. The authors recommended strategies to achieve working partnerships: communication building, role and goal clarifying, trust building (most frequently mentioned by both groups), establishing credibility, and educating the public.

Lack of Information

Lack of information about, and awareness of, self-help groups has presented an even larger obstacle to their use. Self-help group leaders in Kansas told interviewers that lack of public awareness was their main problem (Meissen, Gleason, & Embree, 1991). In a survey of professionals in the mental health field, Kurtz, Mann, and Chambon (1987) found that only half linked clients to the four most available mental health groups: Recovery, Inc.; GROW; the Manic Depressive and Depressive Association; and Emotions Anonymous. The most common reason was lack of awareness of either the groups' existence or their programs.

Professional Roles

Although most professionals do not involve themselves with self-help groups of any kind, many, if not most, existing groups have contacts with professionals. Lotery and Jacobs (1995), investigating roles professionals played with the self-help and support groups, found that 83% of groups surveyed in California reported that one or more professionals had been involved with them in ways other than as regular group members. The highest ranking roles were referral source, speaker, consultant, coleader, and resource person. Medical groups reported the most involvement. Twelve-Step groups reported the least involvement of professionals in their professional roles, but the most involvement by professionals as members.

Stewart et al. (1995) compared professionals' and members' opinions about professional roles. Professionals identified the top five roles as referral source, empowerer, educator, helper, and facilitator. Self-help members agreed with them on the roles of referral source, educator, and helper, but very few endorsed the empowerer or facilitator roles.

Practitioner/Self-Help Relationships
in Other Countries

It is important to keep in mind that the research just cited is based on experience in North America. The published accounts we have about self-help in other parts of the world suggest that North American groups may be significantly more independent of professionals than those in other countries. A comparison of two North American associations with two Israeli ones, for example, found professional roles in the two countries to be quite different (Gidron & Chesler, 1995). In the American groups, the most common professional roles were referring new group members, providing information, referring members for special help, consulting with the group, and advocating for the group's existence. Least commonly reported were roles as trainers, agenda setters, activity planners, and supervisors. In contrast, the most common roles for professionals in Israel were leader, agenda setter, and activity planner.

We find something similar in Von Appen's (1995) description of self-help groups in Germany. Categorizing groups established under the auspices of the Ministry for Families and the Elderly in the Federal Republic into five types, she found that three—family counseling groups, groups for disabled persons funded by jobs programs, and self-help employment projects—have roles for professional staff. In the United States, these groups would not be identified as self-help groups.

Likewise, Oka (1995) describes how groups in Japan called themselves "self-help" but were really, in fact, professionally sponsored. The Japanese culture, as described by Oka, does not favor an egalitarian concept like "self-help." The Japanese are very respectful of hierarchy and of professionals, so that even if professionals try to promote egalitarian helping situations where fellow sufferers exchange mutual aid, the members insist that professionals assume leadership roles.

The research indicates that it is difficult to generalize about appropriate roles for professionals who interact with self-help groups. It is important to choose one's role carefully by being attentive to appropriateness for the particular group, sensitive to the timing of one's interaction, and aware of the attitudes one brings to the interaction. In spite of such cautions, a few generalizations are possible.

THE LINKER ROLE

As noted above, the role most often mentioned in surveys of professionals and self-help members is that of *linker* (sometimes referred to as "referral agent") (L. F. Kurtz, 1985; Kurtz, Mann, & Chambon, 1987; Lotery & Jacobs, 1995; Stewart et al., 1995). Theories of interorganizational relationships support the importance of the linking role as crucial in determining whether an organization will flourish in harmony with its environment, degenerate in ideological strife and hostile takeover, or fade due to indifference and neglect (Litwak & Meyer, 1966). Litwak and Meyer offer a "balance theory" that suggests appropriate coordinating activities designed to prevent either of the two extremes.

Balance Theory

To achieve productive interdependence, cooperating organizations must develop coordinating strategies that reduce conflict and promote the goals of both groups. Balance theory maintains that when coordinating activities between powerful organizations and primary groups such as self-help groups, the two must achieve a balance between independence and dependence. This is accomplished through strategic linking activities that reduce the threat of the stronger taking over the weaker. The formal organization must choose activities that allow the more vulnerable group freedom to maintain its different but complementary style.

Litwak and Meyer (1966) outlined several practices that are used to link primary and bureaucratic systems. Although some of their methods are unsuitable for linking professional and self-help groups, others do apply. One of these is the use of an intermediary voluntary organization in which representatives of both meet on common ground. Another commonly-used linking method is the "settlement-house approach" (p. 40) in which the large organization is linked to the smaller group by giving it a place to meet and by bringing together members of the formal organization and the smaller group for communication between them. In another approach, a "common messenger" (p. 41), who is a member of both the organization and the primary group, serves as an interpreter and go-between.

Linking Practices

Larger, more formal, and affluent organizations can easily overpower smaller, less organized groups. Because practitioners recognize the value of small, intimate community groups, we take special care not to overpower them. This value rises above all other aspects of professional involvement with self-help groups. We link our clients with self-help groups as well as we can without imposing ourselves and our methods. The following briefly discusses a series of linking actions that both respect and enhance self-help groups in the community, as well as further the goals of the professional organization.

Observation. The linking role may require attending meetings of the group to learn more about its program or about the particular group and how it functions. Lotery and Jacobs (1995) surveyed self-help group representatives and found that 92% believed it a good idea for professionals to sit in on meetings. Observation of local chapters of groups (in those that permit observers) allows the professional to gain a sense of who would best fit into the group. The way to arrange for this is to call the group's contact person to inquire whether it is open to non-member observers. Some groups—Recovery, Inc. is an example—are always open to visitors, whereas others, such as Al-Anon, are almost always closed. Closed groups, however, can poll their membership to ascertain if anyone would object to a one-time-only observation by a specific person. In groups that are not open to observation, other methods must be used to gain some knowledge about them.

Institutional Meetings. The linking role may include inviting a group to meet in the agency or having members come to the agency to simulate an informational meeting for potential recruits. Instruction for developing institution-based meetings can be found in AA's *Treatment Facilities Workbook* (AA, n.d.). Although this workbook was developed for Alcoholics Anonymous, the ideas and procedures it recommends can be generalized to other groups as well. It contains approximately 100 pages of suggestions, problem solving methods, ideas for appropriate methods of cooperating with such staff, and outlines for holding workshops for institutional staff. *Treatment Facilities Workbook* (and other material) can be obtained directly from AA (see resources list at the end of the chapter). Later in this section, an example of a project involving institutional meetings between Schizophrenics Anonymous and residential group homes for people with mental illness offers a glimpse of the factors that lead to both success and failure of this method.

Workshops. Formal educational events can be an effective method of encouraging linkages between human service professionals and community self-help groups. Inviting representatives of both to come together for a few hours or a day gives each group an opportunity to become personally acquainted and informed about the other's activities and beliefs.

Temporary Sponsors. Some professionals escort clients to their first meetings. Others link them to a kind of temporary sponsor or contact person, a veteran group member who gives the client information and takes him or her to a meeting. An intervention designed to use temporary sponsors to connect potential new members with the Manic Depressive and Depressive Association in Detroit resulted in 56% attendance at one meeting or more by individuals with a sponsor (Powell et al., 1995). In contrast, only 15% of the members of a control group, who were not connected with a sponsor, attended a meeting.

Literature Display. Literature published by self-help associations prominently displayed in the agency informs clients of the groups' existence, purpose, and meeting places. This smooths the recruitment process for potential members and lends credibility to groups. Most groups can provide pamphlets and brochures describing the organization and its activities. Some groups will also provide a rack on which to place these materials in waiting rooms. For example, racks can be ordered from AA World Services (see resources list).

Videos. Many groups sell videos that discuss the problem with which they are concerned as well as introduce their program. These can be ordered through the organization at prices much lower than videos purchased from for-profit organizations. (See list of video resources at the end of chapter 4.)

Example: Using Introductory Meetings in Group Homes

Researchers at the University of Michigan examined the process of linking potential recruits to an existing self-help association (Schizophrenics Anonymous) through the use of introductory meetings in four group homes for people with mental illness (Salem, Gant, & Campbell, 1996). The researchers' goals were to acquaint residents with the program of Schizophrenics Anonymous (SA), to give them an opportunity to feel comfortable attending and participating in SA meetings, and to inform them about the groups that met in nearby communities. Researchers and SA leaders hoped that because of these meetings, residents would continue participation with existing SA groups in the community.

Four teams composed of two SA leaders ran a series of six introductory SA meetings in four group homes. They also conducted pre- and post-project interviews with group home residents (N=44), SA leaders (N=8), and home managers and staff (N=42). After the project ended, they followed up with all residents to determine if any continued SA attendance.

Findings indicated that staff attitudes and whether members had been able to identify with the temporary groups' leaders most influenced whether the meetings became a successful or "working meeting" (as opposed to a "mixed" or "non-working" meeting). In the two homes that achieved working meetings, staff were positive and respectful, and they transported people to meetings. This was not the case with the other two homes, whose staff viewed the project as a nuisance and even actively interfered with the meetings by requiring residents to do other tasks during meeting time and openly expressing hostility about the meetings.

Members' identification with leaders emerged as an important ingredient of success. In groups with working meetings, members perceived that they had something in common with the SA leaders and that they shared similar problems, experiences, and basic demographic characteristics. Moreover, one of the leaders had once lived in the group home. The perception of similarity with leaders did not exist in the groups with mixed and non-working meetings. In one home, the leader had similar demographic characteristics, but residents did not think they had anything in common. In the other home, the residents were all young males and the leader was a middle-aged woman with whom they had nothing in common.

Severity of the group home members' illness also contributed to success or failure of the meeting. Observers noticed that residents in the least successful home experienced more severe symptoms and medication side effects than the residents in the other three homes.

Following the six introductory meetings, despite successful meetings in two of the homes, none of the residents continued involvement in SA. Follow-up interviews with staff revealed that, although there was some interest by residents in continuing meetings, the staff had discouraged it for various reasons—thinking that residents were not well enough or already attended another type of group. One manager discouraged a resident because she had a hearing defect.

This shows that special self-help meetings can be established for agency populations and that the outcome of these efforts can be at least initially successful. It also reveals some of the pitfalls in this practice and the importance of the involvement and attitudes of staff in making such an effort successful. Findings also point out the importance of newcomer identification with the group's members and leaders.

As discussed in chapter 4, the linking role can be crucial to affiliation with self-help groups. It is also critical to the life of the group; for without new members, the membership will dwindle. Linking the client to the group involves knowledge of the group's approach and meeting activities, ideological compatibility between the professional and the group, and an ability to measure the readiness level of the client for engagement in the group's program. The practitioner should at least accept the idea of group participation and refrain from discouraging it.

Next we turn to the topic of professional initiation of self-help groups. Helping create a self-help group differs from developing a support group, but can be a vital and crucial element of success for the fledgling group.

INITIATING SELF-HELP GROUPS

In general, we think that self-help groups are independent of professional services and that professionals can begin support groups, but not self-help groups. This assumption is only partially correct. When a small group of fellow sufferers comes together within an agency and is directed by a professional, it usually remains a support group. Some associations, however, begin as professionally directed groups, but then begin to assume characteristics of the self-help model. In other groups, professionals play important consultative and supportive roles for founding members of independent self-help groups. The following stories illustrate the efforts of professionals who, in very different ways, assisted the beginning of the two oldest North American self-help associations.

Recovery, Inc.

Abraham Low, the Chicago psychiatrist who began Recovery, Inc. in the 1930s, did not start out to build a self-help organization, although he was the first person to apply the term *self-help* to such a group (Low, 1943a; Rau & Rau, 1971).[1] Recovery, Inc., began as an outpatient group for Dr. Low's patients who were discharged to the community after treatment at the Illinois State Psychiatric Institute. His motive was to reduce relapse, and he thought it both effective and efficient to teach relapse prevention in groups, since the same methods applied to all patients. In addition, he found that older members reinforced his methods by testifying to their effectiveness.

The Illinois medical community, however, viewed Low's group work unfavorably. Their disapproval, sharpened by Low's efforts to organize the patients to influence passage of a reform of the mental health code, made him fearful for his reputation and his medical license to practice (Rau & Rau, 1971). Eventually, the medical community's lack of support led Low to abandon his group. However, the group continued to meet. Both surprised and heartened by their action, Dr. Low (1950) resumed his work with them and wrote the basic text, *Mental Health Through Will Training,* that today still forms the heart of Recovery's program. Within 10 years after his death in 1954, Recovery, Inc. had grown to 520 affiliated groups and close to 5,000 members (Recovery, Inc., 1993).

Alcoholics Anonymous

AA's story is a familiar one because of a recent television movie as well as numerous books on AA history, but the role professionals played in its founding has not been emphasized (AA, 1957; AA, 1984; E. Kurtz, 1979; Pittman, 1988). Unlike Recovery, Inc., AA's beginnings received ample professional support. Bill W., AA's New York cofounder, relied heavily on William Silkworth, his physician; Harry Tiebout, his psychiatrist; and two members of the clergy, Father Ed Dowling and Rev. Sam Shoemaker. AA's other cofounder, Akron-based Dr. Robert Holbrook Smith, was a physician himself. Although his speciality, proctology, is generally thought to have little to do with alcoholism, the ability to mention "Dr. Bob" as cofounder served as a cachet for many early AA members.

Dr. Silkworth repeatedly and patiently helped Bill W. to detoxify and accepted his rendering of his conversion experience during one of his hospitalizations, the experience that led Bill W. to found Alcoholics Anonymous. Dr. Harry Tiebout, described as the first psychiatrist to discover in AA a significant approach to the treatment of alcoholics, treated

Bill W. for psychological depression, and became an early member of AA's Board of Trustees (E. Kurtz, 1979). Rev. Edward Dowling, a Catholic priest, served as Bill W.'s spiritual sponsor for over 20 years. More importantly for AA's growth, Father Dowling helped to prevent opposition by the Catholic Church to Catholics' participation in AA. Dr. Sam Shoemaker, one of the earliest leaders of the Oxford Group, was a close friend of Bill W. and helped AA's founders develop its spiritual principles.

These stories reveal some of the possible roles that a professional might play in the founding of a self-help group. These roles may include inventing the method or program taught by the group, providing moral support for the initial core group, advising participants as a member of the board of directors, being a supporter and friend to the leadership, giving concrete assistance (such as a place to meet and a coffee pot), lending credibility to the group, helping to promote the group, helping the group to develop its own literature, and aiding its efforts to finance itself.

Founding Chapters of Existing Organizations

Perhaps the most common way of participating in the initiation of a local self-help group is to obtain materials from the offices of an existing national organization to help a group of potential members form a chapter affiliate. A variation of this practice can be found in the example of special groups of AA members. For example, professional staff members working with seriously mentally ill substance abusers have begun to establish special AA groups for the clients they serve who have both problems (Bond, McDonel, Miller, & Pensec, 1991; Kurtz, et al., 1995).

The Role of Self-Help Clearinghouses

There are self-help clearinghouses in 24 states, and national self-help clearinghouses in New Jersey, Pennsylvania, Massachusetts, and New York. (All North American clearinghouses, as well as those known in other countries, are listed in the appendix.) These clearinghouses have been established to provide information about the existence of all known groups to both group developers and potential members. Clearinghouse staff also consult with individuals who are starting, leading, or otherwise assisting self-help groups.

Self-help clearinghouses recommend that practitioners beginning a new group should seriously consider forming affiliates of national organizations (White & Madara, 1995). In other words, avoid "reinventing the wheel." To do this, check the *Self-Help Sourcebook,* published by the American Self-Help Clearinghouse in New Jersey, to find listings of groups for a myriad of difficulties and conditions. For the most up-to-date information, computer users with on-line access can consult with the directory available on the World Wide Web at http://www.cmhc.com/selfhelp/. Additional resources from this clearinghouse are listed and discussed in chapter 11. Some organizations list their main office and offer to provide information about specific locations over the phone. Most will provide a starter kit and guidelines for the formation of new groups and offer telephone consultation to their organizers. Some of the listings are for one-of-a-kind groups that can be used as a model for others.

If there is no exemplary model available for the problem you are dealing with or if you choose not to develop an affiliate group, a clearinghouse can help you to begin an entirely new type of group. The clearinghouse web site can also inform you of new groups that may be in the formation stage. Existing groups will consult over the phone and also provide you with printed materials that have been prepared by persons who have experience with organizing chapters of that association.

Much of what practitioners do with self-help groups can have a dual purpose of linking people to groups and helping the group to improve its operation. In the last 20 years, academics and practitioners have done research on many groups, and in so doing, have assisted them to improve aspects of their functioning. The next section will examine three approaches to research on self-help groups.

RESEARCH ON
SELF-HELP GROUPS

Researchers pursue three kinds of studies related to self-help groups: studies of participant outcome, investigations of group-level factors though ethnographic-qualitative methods, and participatory action research (Chesler, 1991; Levy, 1984; Powell, 1987). Although some groups, such as AA, have been investigated by hundreds of researchers, most groups have received very little scholarly attention. Moreover, when groups do receive systematic attention, the study often focuses on only one affiliate or chapter, rendering generalizations about the entire organization inappropriate. The paragraphs that follow discuss in turn, studies of outcome evaluation, research on groups as systems, and participatory action research.

Outcome Evaluation

Outcome studies seek to determine whether an intervention's stated goals are met. One problem with much of the extant research in this area, however, is that psychologically oriented researchers often regard self-help groups as a form of therapy and measure psychological symptom reduction. Since voluntary associations rarely aim to cure or alter psychological, behavioral, or medical conditions, they seldom see a need to measure such outcomes. As Borkman (1991) has pointed out, "There has been an over-emphasis on these groups as human services . . . and not enough attention is paid to them as fellowships that provide social support, alternative kin networks, or as new forms of communities of interest structured to suit mobile urban . . . life styles" (p. 645).

As discussed in chapter 1, outcome evaluations that employ rigorous, controlled designs are notoriously difficult to use with self-help groups. Occasionally associations ask to be evaluated, as did GROW International in 1981 (Rappaport et al., 1985), but this is rare. A common way of side-stepping group collaboration is to track clients referred from other treatment settings to the group. One of the problems with this approach is that this sample may be quite unlike the group's typical members.

Other factors that impair outcome evaluation include lack of membership records, anonymity of membership, inability of researchers to observe closely and record actual group processes, and inability to establish random assignment with experimental and control conditions (Levy, 1984). As Levy wrote, "given the fact that . . . attempts to manipulate groups experimentally might well destroy the very qualities of the phenomena in which we are interested, it would appear that well controlled, rigorous, experimental studies are virtually impossible" (p. 161).

As an example of how *not* to circumvent this difficulty, one group of researchers evaluated Alcoholics Anonymous by arranging for random assignment of chronic drunk offenders on probation to one of three treatment conditions: a psychiatrically oriented clinic, AA, and no treatment (Ditman, Crawford, Forgy, Moskowitz, & Macandrew, 1967). But as one researcher using meta-analysis has pointed out concerning this and other such studies:

> Because AA is intended to be a voluntary program open to persons with a desire to stop drinking, evaluating its effectiveness with persons who are required to attend and who do not necessarily want to stop drinking does not provide a fair test of its effectiveness. (McCrady & Delaney 1995, p. 173)

In another effort to undertake a clinical trial of the effectiveness of self-help, researchers at the University of Pittsburgh randomly assigned persons to groups in consumer drop-in centers financed by the mental health system (Kaufman, Schulberg, & Schooler, 1995). These groups were not true self-help groups, although they possessed characteristics of peer therapy. Disappointingly, however, the unwilling subjects randomly assigned to the drop-in center groups did not attend them, undermining the experimental aspects of the project. Unfortunately, despite these consistent failures, research funders continue to place a high priority on traditional experimental designs in which the group is regarded as a treatment intervention.

Research on Self-Help Groups as Systems

Levy (1984) argued that qualitative study using ethnographic methods is necessary to gain knowledge about the natural history of self-help and self-help group processes and to generate theoretical hypotheses for testing. He called for a general systems perspective that views self-help groups as component systems functioning within a larger system: "The effectiveness of a particular self-help group cannot be meaningfully studied apart from a consideration of the social and institutional context within which it operates" (Levy, 1984, p. 164). Mäkelä (1996) and Room (1993) have made similar appeals, insisting that AA be studied as a social movement that countered radical individualism in American society.

Maton (1993) followed Levy's suggestion and attempted to advance the perspective of self-help research by employing an ecological paradigm that calls for moving self-help group research beyond the level of individual analysis to group and community analysis (see Table 7.2). Viewing the self-help group as what it really is, a community organization, means that research can take a broader focus, examine groups more accurately, and produce more useful findings. This paradigm takes into account that individual investigation has its uses and provides a number of variables that can apply on the individual member level as well as on larger system levels.

Many advantages can be seen immediately. By using the group as the unit of analysis, random samples are more easily obtained. The complexity of real life, as it happens within group's internal and external environment, can be conceptualized and thus researched. The importance of group interaction variables, social climates, leadership, and countless other elements of group life can be captured and made part of the research design.

An example of a study focusing on group-level variables is an investigation of the National Alliance for the Mentally Ill (NAMI) affiliates in

Table 7.2

Mutual Help Group Research
Variables by Variable Domain and Level of Analysis

	Level of Analysis		
Variable Domain	*Individual*	*Group*	*Community*
Focal Problem	Duration, severity	Type, nature	Prevalence, incidence
Helping ideology	Personal belief system	Group ideology	Professional, lay beliefs
Climate	Personality, belonging	Leadership, cohesion	Professional, lay attitudes
Structure	Nature/number of role involvements	Role structure, order/organization	Community, human services
Helping mechanisms	Coping style, help provision, receipt	Types, frequency, effectiveness	Types, accessibility
Linkages	Social network, friendships	Affiliations, networks	Referral networks
Stressors	Life stress, group stress	Internal stress, systemic stress	Social problems
Resources	Psychological, social, tangible	Tangible, systemic supports	Human service budgets
Temporal	Length of time in group	Member turnover, age of group	Population stability
Demographic	Gender, age, SES, ethnicity	Composition, size	Composition, size
Well-being	Behavioral, emotional, physical	Viability, stability	Epidemiology, life quality
Subjective appraisal	Perceived benefit, satisfaction	Systemic appraisals	Appraisals of groups

SOURCE: Maton, K. I. (1993). Moving beyond the individual level of analysis in mutual help group research: An ecological paradigm. *Journal of Applied Behavioral Science, 29,* 272-286. Used with permission of the publisher.

Indiana (Perkins, LaFuze, & Van Dusen, 1995). Researchers obtained group climate and group effectiveness ratings from members and leaders of all NAMI affiliates in the state in order to determine the degree to which member demographics, group size, material resources, and social climate influenced perceived group effectiveness. Group effectiveness was defined as member satisfaction and member estimates of benefits received. Researchers found that social climate factors were more predictive of satisfaction with the group than other possible predictors (i.e., material resources, size of group, or members' demographic characteristics).

Participatory Action Research

In participatory action research, the investigator's role is first and foremost to help solve problems that the group itself identifies (Lavoie, 1984). In 1994, two colleagues and I participated in the first step of such a project. The three of us met over a weekend with the national board of directors of a large self-help association. On the first day, the board members presented subjects about which they wanted more information. These included practical issues such as how to maintain groups, how to increase the number of groups, and how to increase referrals from professionals. At the end of the first day, the consultants drew up a list of 16 research questions inspired by the day-long discussion. On the second day, the researchers presented the board members with the list, and the day was spent discussing how data answering these questions could be obtained. At this point, the researchers offered their services in assisting with this research.

Table 7.3 presents Chesler's (1991) comparison of conventional research with participatory action research. As the table shows, participatory action research objectives are to advance practical knowledge for the group rather than to advance academic knowledge. Such research involves the subjects in the research design and gives them control over the endeavor. Findings of the research help the group to improve.

Mark Chesler (personal communication, May 12, 1993; Chesler & Chesney, 1995) described the process of his participatory action research with Candlelighters as consisting of the following eight steps:

1. Decide on research objectives.
2. Select a sample.
3. Write to contacts in groups.
4. Visit each group in the sample. Interview members, conduct group interview, interview professional liaisons, observe meetings, gather records.
5. Listen to audiotapes of interviews, make notes, and code the interviews.
6. Send a summary of information gained to contact persons in groups for their feedback.
7. Organize and code the data. Theorize from the data.
8. Implement a change process based on data. These processes include workshops for leaders, articles for publication, papers to professional audiences, and setting of group policies.

Table 7.3

Comparison of Alternative Paradigms for Research and Action

	Conventional	*Participatory Action*
Goals	Advance academic knowledge; Evaluate services	Advance practical knowledge; Serve group goals; Strengthen and empower members
Methods	Linear from theory to data to results to use; Standardized measurement	Reflexive and cyclical from data to use and action to theory
Relationships with participants/groups	Researcher control; Objectivity through detachment	Participant co-control or participant control
Base of operations/funds	University/academy; Federal funds; Agency	Self-help group or community; Foundation funds
Research issues	Known ahead of time; Demonstrate group "effectiveness"; Compare with professional services	Evolving from experience in the field
Products and actions	Few or no actions; File research reports; Contribute to scientific literature; Test or advance theory	Participate in group improvements and system change; Generate theory; Write reports for public/academic audiences

Adapted from Chesler, M. A. (1991). Participatory action research with self-help groups: An alternative paradigm for inquiry and action. *American Journal of Community Psychology,, 19*(5), 757-768. Used with permission of the publisher and the author.

These research strategies, carried out in partnership with community self-help groups, make a contribution to consumers of social services and those who seek to generate consumer empowerment. Funds for supporting such research may be scarce; and carving out time for it requires dedication and generosity by practitioners wanting to assist a self-help group to succeed.

SUMMARY

Becoming informed about self-help organizations is the first obligation of the practitioner. Linking clients to them will be more successful when practitioners can knowledgeably discuss the group's activities, what its meetings are like, and what types of people attend them. Observing the group, reading its literature, attending workshops cosponsored by the group and the agency, watching videos published by the group, and informal social contacts are all ways of increasing such knowledge.

Linking people with self-help groups requires that the practitioner be well acquainted with the group and its members so as to be able, if necessary, to match referrals with temporary sponsors who can introduce them to the group and explain it to them. Other linking methods include use of institutional meetings, literature displays, and videos.

Practitioners can become familiar with the resources of the self-help clearinghouses located in 24 states and particularly with the American Self-Help Clearinghouse, which provides a national directory, computerized online services, and printed literature related to working with self-help groups. Rather than initiating entirely new self-help models, practitioners can assist core groups to implement chapters or affiliates of existing national organizations, where resources such as starter kits and telephone advice are available.

If outcome evaluations are pursued, researchers are encouraged to consider the group's objectives and to remain faithful to them when measuring outcomes, rather than importing measures of outcomes unrelated to the purpose of the group. In addition, researchers are encouraged to conceptualize the group as the unit of analysis and to pursue macro-level research rather than focusing on individual members and psychological measures. Last, but most important, practitioners and social scientists are encouraged to consider use of the participatory action research model described above.

This chapter has reviewed the roles that professionals may take on when working in conjunction with an independent self-help association. Unlike the coleader/facilitator role taken with support groups, the roles of linker, initiator, and researcher demand that the professional walk a narrow line between being too involved and being too indifferent to the self-help group with whom he or she interacts. There are subtle traps into which even a conscientious professional might fall. This could lead to an unintentional undermining of a self-help group's independence and special character— for example, referring recruits who do not fit the group's membership or who feel coerced into attending. There is also unintentional harm when the professional fails to refer clients (i.e., the group may die for lack of new members). Evaluating the group as though it were a clinical service, or imposing stringently "scientific" standards, represent subtle forms of sabotage. On the other hand, joining with the group to research itself can be an empowering activity for group members and of immense help to the group's ultimate survival.

The next three chapters will examine more closely three major categories of self-help groups: Twelve-Step fellowships; non-Twelve-Step, change-oriented groups; and supportive-educational groups. In these examples, the reader will be able to see illustrated the various categories of self-help and support. The final chapter discusses telephone and online groups.

NOTE

1. The probable first use of the term *self-help* occurred in 1859 in a book by Samuel Smiles, *Self-Help: With illustrations of conduct and perseverance*. London: John Murray.

DISCUSSION QUESTIONS

1. Identify and describe linking strategies with self-help groups keeping in mind the linking practices described by Litwak and Meyer.
2. Do you agree with Litwak and Meyer when they say that community primary groups and professional/bureaucratic organizations must achieve a balance between over- and under-involvement? Discuss how to implement this advice.
3. In small discussion groups, discuss the linking strategies in which you have engaged in your practice. Say whether you think these practices were intrusive or correctly placed at a midpoint between over- and under-involvement with the community group.
4. What are possible drawbacks to professionals' use of community primary groups?
5. Describe to others experiences you have had in working with self-help groups.

CLASSROOM EXERCISE

In a small group, decide that an imaginary or existing agency wants to increase participation in community self-help groups. Identify all the groups that you know about in the community that would be of potential benefit to your agency's consumers. Decide on an action plan that you think will result in increased use of, and client participation in, these groups. Also determine how you will measure participation to evaluate if your strategy was successful.

ASSIGNMENTS

1. Look up research reports on self-help groups and analyze them with an eye toward discerning whether the findings would be of use to the group studied, of no use but no harm, or potentially harmful to the organization. Discuss your findings in a brief paper.
2. Choose a group to which you belong or one to which you can gain access. Meet with some core members/leaders and discuss what kinds of information they would like to have about their group (examples could be member satisfaction, whether goals are met, why some newcomers do not come back, group climate). Develop and carry out an action research project, write up your findings, and share them with the group.

RESOURCES

1. AA World Services, Inc., Box 459, Grand Central Station, New York, New York 10163. Phone: (212) 870-3400; Fax: (212) 870-3137.

   Literature Display Racks, $17.00.
   Cooperation with the Professional Community Workbook, $15.20
   Correctional Facilities Workbook, $7.00
   Treatment Facilities Workbook, $17.30
2. White, B. J. & Madara, E. J. (Eds.). (1995). *The self-help sourcebook: Finding and forming mutual aid self-help groups,* 5th edition. American Self-Help Clearinghouse, Northwest Covenent Medical Center, 25 Pocono Road, Denville, NJ 07834-2995. Phone: (201) 625-7101. Price: $9.00.

PART 4

REPRESENTATIVE GROUPS

Chapter 8

TWELVE-STEP PROGRAMS

". . . a new therapy based on kinship in common suffering; one having vast potential for the myriad other ills of mankind."
—from the text of the Lasker Award, AA, 1957, p. 301

In 1935, two alcoholic men began what would become the largest mutual-help fellowship in the world—Alcoholics Anonymous (AA). Frank Riessman recently observed that the special significance of AA rested on two major factors: "its impact on mainstream human services . . ." and "its comprehensiveness, including the theoretical structure for interpreting the phenomenon of alcoholism and its intervention rationale, broad infrastructure of help, and remarkable organizational model" (Riessman & Carroll, 1995, p. 53). This chapter will explore the AA organizational model and the Twelve Steps and explain how this model applies to conditions other than alcoholism.

Most Twelve-Step fellowships follow the AA model. In the Schubert & Borkman (1991) organizational autonomy typology, they fit into the federated category because each individual group is autonomous. There are no leaders in Twelve-Step fellowships; meetings are chaired on a rotational basis. In the national offices, staff rotate so as not to assume too much authority over the services they administer. Twelve-Step fellowships are funded solely by member contributions and literature sales.

This chapter begins with Alcoholics Anonymous for two reasons: First, the lion's share of scholarly study and professional attention has been on AA, other Twelve-Step groups receiving comparatively little; and second, the Twelve-Step principles and philosophy were developed within AA, and

AA members remain the most consistent expositors and implementers of that way of life.

HISTORY OF
TWELVE-STEP FELLOWSHIPS

The Twelve-Step story began in the 1930s in the midst of the Great Depression following the stock market crash of 1929. In part due to over-optimism about Prohibition, alcoholics of that era rarely received treatment, and few recovered. Most citizens deemed problem drinking a moral failing, and alcoholics were either punished or ignored. Bill Wilson epitomized the stereotypical hopeless case. Unable to hold a job and with a wife distraught over his drinking, he was three times readmitted to a hospital where he dried out, but did not recover.

How Alcoholics Anonymous Began

AA's cofounders, Bill Wilson and Dr. Bob Smith, met each other in 1935 in Akron, Ohio. Both had sought help for their compulsive use of alcohol in the Oxford Group, a quasi-religious/spiritual movement of the 1920s and 1930s (E. Kurtz, 1979). Having found each other, the two sought out other problem drinkers to whom to tell their stories. When Bill W. returned to his home in New York City, he continued this practice, using what he had learned in his experience with Dr. Bob and recruiting other alcoholics to Oxford Group meetings.

In 1937, the New Yorkers abandoned the Oxford Group to become a separate entity (the Akronites followed suit in 1939). In formulating their program, members of the new fellowship drew from the spiritual principles of the Oxford Group, from William James's *Varieties of Religious Experience* (1902/1958), and from such books as Richard Peabody's *Common Sense of Drinking* (1931), filtering what they learned from these sources through their own experience (E. Kurtz, 1979; McCarthy, 1984; Pittman, 1988). Their ideas and stories were published in the book, *Alcoholics Anonymous* (AA, 1939/1976), the title of which soon became the name of the new fellowship.

AA has grown and diversified over the years. It is more international, and its literature has been translated into several languages. The numbers of women and younger members (under 40) have steadily increased, the percentages reported in 1992 being 35% and 51% respectively (AA, 1992). In 1995, AA reported 32,578 groups and 516,015 members outside of the United States and Canada (AA, 1995). Within the United States and

Canada, there were 58,084 groups and 1,307,803 members. This includes groups that list with the AA's General Service Office (which many do not do) and groups in correctional facilities (AA, 1996).

Proliferation of
Twelve-Step Fellowships

In the early 1940s, wives of the first AA members met with their husbands in AA meetings; later, auxiliary groups formed in various parts of the country (Al-Anon, 1966, 1986). By 1948, there were 87 separate auxiliaries for family members. Because this apparent linkage between AA and the unnamed wives' groups violated AA's tradition of nonaffiliation, AA's founder urged his wife to form a separate fellowship. Thus, Al-Anon formally began in 1951. In 1957, Alateen became another of the Al-Anon Family Groups (AFG). Today there are over 30,000 separate AFG chapters in 114 countries (Al-Anon, 1993; 1995).

In a similar situation, nonalcoholic drug users did not qualify for AA membership. Their presence in meetings violated the third and fifth traditions defining the desire to stop drinking alcohol as the requirement for membership and the group's single purpose of carrying its message to the alcoholic who still suffers (AA, 1952). Although not formalized under that name until 1953, Narcotics Anonymous (NA) began as early as 1947 in response to the specific needs of the users of drugs other than alcohol (Peyrot, 1985). According to most recent estimates, NA chapters number over 25,000 worldwide (White & Madara, 1995).

Well over a hundred groups make some use of the Twelve Steps; an unpublished list names 258 groups that have used the steps and/or the name "Anonymous"[1] The American Self-Help Clearinghouse issues a more current and verified list of 94 Twelve-Step Groups[2] Thus, it is impossible to mention all of them. Perhaps best known are the following: Overeaters Anonymous (OA) (10,000 groups); Gamblers Anonymous (GA) (1200 chapters); Emotions Anonymous (EA) (1350 chapters); and Families Anonymous (500 groups) (White & Madara, 1995). Also, although some associations that use the term *anonymous* are not Twelve-Step fellowships (e.g., Parents Anonymous, Schizophrenics Anonymous, and Homosexuals Anonymous), other fellowships adhere to a Twelve-Step philosophy but do not use the term *anonymous* in the title (e.g., Jewish Alcoholics, Chemically Dependent Persons & Significant Others [JACS]). The next section examines the Twelve- Step program itself. More information on groups that have adapted the steps or that use "anonymous" in their name but are not Twelve-Step groups can be found on the American Self-Help Clearinghouse list.

THE TWELVE-STEP PROGRAM

The Twelve-Step program revolves around the steps, but it is important to understand how each variant use of the steps defines the problem. Once the problem definition is clear, it is also necessary to grasp the goals of the fellowship. First, we look at the typical definition of the problem within a Twelve-Step group. Next we examine the original Twelve Steps and Twelve Traditions. Finally, we look at how Gamblers Anonymous and Narcotics Anonymous have adapted the Twelve-Step program in ways that differ from the original.

Defining the Problem

In most of the well-known fellowships, the problem is seen as entrapment in the use of a substance or behavior that produces feelings of euphoria or eliminates pain (usually both) but that gradually takes over one's life, resulting in negative consequences for the individual and others with whom he or she is involved (L. F. Kurtz, 1990b). The problem becomes so extreme that the sufferer, in striving for total control, loses all control of use of the substance or behavior.

One "hits bottom" when one realizes that one can no longer continue the obsessive use or behavior without suffering serious consequences. Within the Twelve-Step experience, this is the point at which the person admits powerlessness over the behavior, surrenders the struggle for control, and asks for help from a power greater than the self—a process contained in the first three of the Twelve Steps. Surrender is not an abdication of responsibility for self, but rather a letting go of unreasonable efforts to control what one cannot control. As the NA (1987) text states, "Surrender means not having to fight anymore. We accept our addiction and life the way it is. We become willing to do whatever is necessary to stay clean, even the things we don't like doing" (p. 21).

Overeaters Anonymous adapts the AA model for an overeating membership by defining addiction to be to a particular type of food (such as sugar) (Malenbaum, Herzog, Eisenthal, & Wyshak, 1988; Yeary, 1987). Abstinence is sought only for that specific food, which can vary according to each member's particular craving. Members believe that recovery from compulsive eating involves a lifelong effort to remain abstinent, which can be achieved through "working" the Twelve Steps and frequent consultations with sponsors. Members develop a food plan that defines the off-limits food. They go over their food intake with their food sponsors frequently, sometimes as often as daily. Members also "work" the Twelve

Steps and may have one or more additional sponsors for this aspect of their program.

The Twelve Steps

The groups that follow AA have changed the wording of the Twelve Steps very little (Al-Anon, 1966; EA, 1978; GA, 1984; NA, 1987; OA, 1980). OA's version (1980) is typical, in which the word *alcohol* is changed to *food* in Step 1 and *alcoholics* to *overeaters* in Step 12. The first three steps are recognizing powerlessness and turning one's life over to a power greater than the self; Steps 4 through 9 are action steps; the final three steps offer a maintenance program.

The Twelve Steps of Alcoholics Anonymous

1. We admitted we were powerless over alcohol—that our lives had become unmanageable.
2. Came to believe that a power greater than ourselves could restore us to sanity.
3. Made a decision to turn our will and lives over to the care of God as we understood Him.
4. Made a searching and fearless moral inventory of ourselves.
5. Admitted to God, to ourselves and to another human being the exact nature of our wrongs.
6. Were entirely ready to have God remove all these defects of character.
7. Humbly asked Him to remove our shortcomings.
8. Made a list of all persons we had harmed, and became willing to make amends to them all.
9. Made direct amends to such people wherever possible, except when to do so would injure them or others.
10. Continued to take personal inventory and when we were wrong promptly admitted it.
11. Sought through prayer and meditation to improve our conscious contact with God as we understood Him, praying only for knowledge of His will for us and the power to carry that out.
12. Having had a spiritual awakening as the result of these steps, we tried to carry this message to alcoholics, and to practice these principles in all our affairs. (AA World Services, 1952, pp. 5-9)

Members find that those who follow the path suggested by the steps eventually realize a spiritual awakening that leads to serenity. What are sometimes termed AA's "promises" exemplify some of what this means:

We are going to know a new freedom and a new happiness. We will not regret the past nor wish to shut the door on it. We will comprehend the word serenity and we will know peace. No matter how far down the scale we have gone, we will see how our experience can benefit others. That feeling of uselessness and self-pity will disappear. We will lose interest in selfish things and gain interest in our fellows. Self-seeking will slip away. Our whole attitude and outlook upon life will change. Fear of people and of economic insecurity will leave us. We will intuitively know how to handle situations which used to baffle us. We will suddenly realize that God is doing for us what we could not do for ourselves. (AA, 1976, pp. 83-84)

In all Twelve-Step fellowships, the objective is serenity, which is achieved by "working" the steps. Prominent in this process is learning to let go of those things that cannot be controlled and to be grateful for what one has. A simple slogan heard in a meeting conveys this message: "Contentment is wanting what you have, not having what you want." And finally, "Spirituality teaches us, or has taught most of us, how to deal with failure" (Kurtz & Ketcham, 1992, p. 1).

The Twelve Traditions

The Twelve Traditions emerged during the late 1940s as people from all parts of the country sent questions to AA's New York service office about how to conduct their newly formed groups. The answers, which were generally derived from similar experiences in other groups, evolved into the Twelve Traditions. Recent history suggests that the Traditions are as important to the groups as the practice of the Steps is to individual members. Groups that ignore their guidance tend to abandon the vocabulary of the Steps for the language of therapy (Flynn, 1994). Yet the Traditions themselves are not rigid, centralized policies. AA groups remain autonomous and adhere to the traditions out of respect and a belief that these 12 customs are what has kept AA alive over the past 60 years.

The Twelve Traditions of Alcoholics Anonymous

1. Our common welfare should come first; personal recovery depends upon AA unity.
2. For our group purpose there is but one ultimate authority—a loving God as He may express Himself in our group conscience. Our leaders are but trusted servants; they do not govern.
3. The only requirement for AA membership is a desire to stop drinking.
4. Each group should be autonomous except in matters affecting other groups or AA as a whole.
5. Each group has but one primary purpose to carry its message to the alcoholic who still suffers.

6. An AA group ought never endorse, finance, or lend the AA name to any related facility or outside enterprise, lest problems of money, property, and prestige divert us from our primary purpose.
7. Every AA group ought to be fully self-supporting, declining outside contributions.
8. Alcoholics Anonymous should remain forever non-professional, but our service centers may employ special workers.
9. AA, as such, ought never be organized; but we may create service boards or committees directly responsible to those they serve.
10. Alcoholics Anonymous has no opinion on outside issues; hence the AA name ought never be drawn into public controversy.
11. Our public relations policy is based on attraction rather than promotion; we need always maintain personal anonymity at the level of press, radio, and films.
12. Anonymity is the spiritual foundation of all our traditions, ever reminding us to place principles before personalities. (AA World Services, 1952, pp. 9-13)

Adapting AA

Little attention has focused on the way in which newer associations have adapted the AA program. Do Twelve-Step group members actually use the steps and traditions in the same way that alcoholics use those of AA? Gamblers Anonymous (GA) and Narcotics Anonymous (NA) serve as examples of how a Twelve-Step fellowship based on AA can modify the program in subtle but important ways.

GA officially began in 1957, although chapters were meeting earlier. GA is not large, listing only 1,200 chapters in 1995 (White & Madara, 1995); but it represents one of the early pioneers in adapting the AA program to help those with problems other than alcoholism. Browne's (1991; 1994) comparison of GA with AA revealed three significant differences. The first difference is that GA omitted God as the ultimate authority in its rendering of the second tradition. In AA the second tradition reads, "for our group purpose there is but one ultimate authority—a loving God as He may express Himself in our group conscience. Our leaders are but trusted servants; they do not govern." The second tradition in GA reads, "Our leaders are but trusted servants: they do not govern." As a result, Browne argued, political power and status occupy much of the GA group's attention (Browne, 1991, p. 194).

A second difference is in how GA groups define the problem. AA defines the *real* problem as self-centeredness, not as drinking. In GA, the problem is gambling. Within AA, program "oldtimers" maintain an emphasis on spiritual concerns of self versus other-centeredness, rather than on mere abstinence. In GA, once the gambling has ceased, many members see no reason to continue. Thus, GA remains a smaller organization with fewer "oldtimers" making their "experience, strength and hope" available to others.

A third difference is in the use of the steps. GA members tend not to use the steps as guides to a new life without gambling. Instead, their everyday focus is on page 17 of their "combo book," a short summary of the GA program. Page 17 gives a list of seven rules for recovery that cover such things as living one day at time, being patient, and so on. While these are all good advice, they are not the same as the Twelve Steps. Browne argues that only GA members who attend another Twelve-Step program and/or have a sponsor who attends another Twelve-Step program actually learn to practice the Steps and attain a "Twelve-step consciousness" (p. 199).

Browne's analysis offers a perspective on how differently similar world views can be interpreted and practiced. He believes that other Twelve-Step groups use the steps and traditions in a broader, more spiritually-focused manner than does GA. But do they? In-depth studies of other Twelve-Step programs should investigate this question more completely.

In a less systematic analysis, Gifford (1991) compares AA with NA, particularly with regard to NA's appropriateness for adolescents with dependence on chemicals. He contends that NA's focus on addiction, rather than on one class of drugs, makes it more adaptable for a polydrug-using adolescent population. Furthermore, its lack of slogans makes it more suitable for young people who are less able to think abstractly. NA's conception of itself as a "family" offers an unconditional acceptance that differs from the more adult-oriented AA program. NA members share a history of antisocial behavior, loneliness, social ostracism, insecurity, immaturity, and antiauthority tendencies beyond those typically experienced by adult alcoholics. The NA *Basic Text,* written in the 1970s, is easier for adolescents to identify with than the AA Big Book, much of which is still the original 1939 version. Gifford argues that AA, while a splendid resource for alcoholics, is far less appropriate than NA for adolescents.

Because Twelve-Step fellowships have no centralized authority, what they are remains very much a product of their assembled members. We turn, then, to an examination of the members of some of the larger Twelve-Step fellowships.

MEMBERSHIP

The profile of members in Alcoholics Anonymous has changed over time. Originally, AA was a nearly all-male fellowship; and it still retains its white, middle-class, middle-aged male image. Yet a 1992 survey of AA members revealed it to be 35% female, 51% under age 40 (AA, 1992). An international study found that the proportion of women among members of AA varied from 10% in Mexico, to 44% in Austria, and 50% in Switzerland (Mäkelä, 1993a). In all countries for which data are available, women seem to be overrepresented in AA compared to their share among heavy drinkers and clinical populations seeking treatment. Finnish sociologist Klaus Mäkelä (1993a) pointed out that because identification with older members is so important to the affiliation process, the demographic composition of AA in various parts of the world is highly dependent upon the characteristics of those who formed its original groups.

Although AA does not obtain figures by race, impressions are that a majority of North American AA members are European American. This is probably correct; however, at least one study (reviewed in chapter 4) indicated that the race of members in any AA group reflects the racial makeup of the particular locale in which that group meets (Humphreys, Mavis, & Stöfflemayr, 1995). Class representation in AA, as indicated by participants' occupation, is estimated to be about a third middle class (managerial, educational, medical, professional), a third working class (service worker, sales worker, laborer, clerical worker, transportation worker), and the rest either unemployed or not in the labor force (AA, 1992).

About a third of the membership in 1992 had been sober more than 5 years, a third sober less than 5 years but more than 1 year, and a third sober less than 1 year. Members' average attendance was 2.5 meetings per week and 63% had received professional treatment before AA participation.

A 1993 survey of Al-Anon Family Groups (Al-Anon, 1993) revealed that most were female and half were between the ages of 36 and 55. The largest percentage of Al-Anon members (41%) had been in the program more than 5 years. Sixty-nine percent were the spouses of alcoholics. Of Alateen members, 60% were female and 54% were under age 14. The largest percentage had been members more than one year. For most Alateens, the alcoholic in their life was a parent.

Al-Anon members attended an average of two meetings a week; Alateens an average of one meeting per week. Of Al-Anon members 60% and of Alateens 56% had received some form of counseling in addition to their Al-Anon Family Group participation. Over the years, the makeup of Al-Anon has become increasingly male, educated, currently married to an alcoholic, attending for a longer period, and working with a sponsor. Alateen membership has become increasingly made up of those whose mother is the alcoholic and of those whose alcoholic family member is in

AA. Like AA, Al-Anon and Alateen do not gather data on racial/ethnic identification.

OA members, according to a survey commissioned by them in 1992, were evenly divided across the age span from 18 to 55 years of age and were predominantly female (86%) (OA, 1992). The typical OA member attended 8 meetings per month, participated in OA an average of 4.3 years, and was 44 years of age. The largest proportion had attended OA less than a year (37%); 31% had attended 2 to 5 years, 17% 5 to less than 10 years, and 15% 10 or more years.

Illustrating how different individual group composition can be, a survey of one OA group's bulimic members in 1988 found them to be 95% single, with a mean age of 28. Their mean length of membership was 3 years and 2 months, and most attended meetings 5 times per week (Malenbaum, Herzog, Eisenthal, & Wyshak, 1988).

A 1977 survey of 150 members of Gamblers Anonymous (1984, p. 102) revealed that they were 96% male, a figure that does not reflect the proportion of gamblers who are female. The survey also indicated that a large majority of GA members were married, well-educated, and employed. Of those surveyed, 40% had seen a mental health professional before going to GA. The average member began gambling at age 17 and first attended GA at age 39.7. The author of this survey warned that it is unlikely that these characteristics could be generalized to all members of GA or to all who gamble. This study found that a large percentage of the members were Jewish, a finding that had been supported in other studies (Browne, 1994). Both Jews and Italians participate in GA in disproportionate numbers. Browne (1994) thought that the fact that these two ethnic groups are more casual in their religious beliefs, may be the basis of GA's secular approach to the Twelve Steps.

Little is known about the characteristics of participants in other Twelve-Step fellowships. Narcotics Anonymous, Families Anonymous, and Emotions Anonymous have not conducted surveys of their memberships; and published literature contains no descriptions of members of other fellowships.

RESEARCH ON
TWELVE-STEP FELLOWSHIPS

Although there exists a large body of literature on AA, much of which is empirical research, few studies have concentrated on the other Twelve-Step fellowships. This may be because AA is older and has a multitude of conveniently located groups. Also, once a body of research develops, it sows the seeds of further study. Furthermore, researchers are more interested in a group that is more populated by men than women (Cutter, 1985).

Studies of AA

E. Kurtz found 509 items of research on Alcoholics Anonymous between 1938 and 1995 (E. Kurtz, personal communication, January 26, 1996). Yet, the best published source covering research on AA, a meta-analysis by Chad Emrick and his associates (Emrick, Tonigan, Montgomery, & Little, 1993), stated, "Alcoholics Anonymous, one of the most widely used approaches to recovery in the United States, remains one of the least rigorously evaluated" (p. 42). The following summarizes the meta-analysis of outcome evaluations on AA by Emrick et al.(1993).

The meta-analysis covered quantitative research conducted and reported in the English language in published and unpublished sources. Its authors reported on the sample and research design characteristics, relationships between AA affiliation and personal characteristics of members, relationships between participation in AA activities and drinking behavior outcome, outcome when AA and professional treatment are combined, and relationship between AA attendance and improvement in areas other than drinking. Chapter 4 presents a review of their findings with regard to personal characteristics and AA affiliation. The two major findings related to personal factors were that (a) more serious drinking histories led to AA affiliation more often than less serious drinking; and (b) sociodemographic factors did not correlate with AA attendance.

Beyond these two findings, researchers found that certain practices within AA correlated with better outcomes (defined as abstinence). These included "having an AA sponsor, engaging in Twelfth-Step work, leading a meeting, and increasing one's degree of participation in the organization" (p. 54). Sponsoring someone else and working the last seven of the Twelve Steps was positively associated with better outcome. Participation in AA prior to treatment did not produce significant effects, but participation concurrent with and after treatment produced a modest positive effect on outcome. The authors concluded that successful members are more involved in AA and follow its behavioral guidelines more carefully than less successful ones (Emrick et al., 1993).

In examining outcomes other than drinking, Emrick and his colleagues found that AA involvement was correlated with employment, social/family/marital adjustment, having an active religious life, possessing a more internal locus of control, and having a better legal situation. A strong relationship was found between AA involvement and psychological adjustment. It is worth noting that this meta-analysis found no data to indicate

AA is harmful to its participants. Mäkelä (1993a) observed that four-fifths of the studies included in the analysis were based on inpatient or outpatient samples, that most were retrospective and were with people who had initially failed to attain success in AA. Investigations on more representative samples of members could have quite different results.

AA's diffusion over the globe invites multicultural research on the fellowship and its program. Results of the first broadly-based, multicultural, international research project are reviewed briefly here. Known as the International Collaborative Study of Alcoholics Anonymous (ICSAA), the project was headed by sociologist Klaus Mäkelä, who is based in Helsinki, Finland (Mäkelä, 1993a; 1993b; Mäkelä, 1996). The sociological approach of the ICSAA study contrasts with the more psychological, treatment-oriented studies analyzed by Emrick and his associates.

Mäkelä (1993a)began one chapter by stating that

> . . . the treatment evaluation perspective should . . . be complemented with a social movement perspective. Basic issues may remain the same, but the research questions are formulated differently. For example, the social movement perspective formulates its questions in terms of membership turnover rather than in terms of treatment efficacy. (p. 202)

The ICSAA analyzed AA as an international mutual-aid movement, studying how it adapted to diverse cultural surroundings (Mäkelä, 1996). Its authors used three conceptual frames: AA as social movement and social network; AA as a belief system; and AA as a system of interaction (Mäkelä, 1996). ICSAA researchers obtained data from eight countries: Austria, Finland, Iceland, Mexico, Poland, Sweden, Switzerland, and the United States. In these diverse countries, they found much variety among AA groups. Resisting the temptation to define "true AA" and to label divergent forms as adulterations, they illustrated the diversity of AA and described the main dimensions of variations within AA. Their studies explored membership composition, group variations, and the effects of non-AA influences, such as formal treatment.

One example of ICSAA's results is a depiction of an AA meeting as a series of "speech events." Mäkelä used conversation analysis to determine the "rules of speech" in a meeting. He found some 10 such rules operating in the Finnish groups observed:

1. Do not interrupt the person speaking.
2. Speak about your own experiences.
3. Speak as honestly as you can.

4. Do not speak about other people's private affairs.
5. Do not profess religious doctrines or lecture about scientific theories.
6. You may speak about your personal problems in applying the AA program, but do not attempt to refute the program.
7. Do not openly confront or challenge previous turns of talk.
8. Do not give direct advice to other members of AA.
9. Do not present causal explanations of the behavior of other AA members.
10. Do not present psychological interpretations of the behavior of other AA members. (Mäkelä, 1996, pp. 140-141)

Mäkelä pointed out that the second rule describes how AA members frame their contributions in self-narratives, reinforcing for participants the importance of applying the AA concepts to themselves. What happened when someone broke a rule? In Finland, as in the United States, that individual was not addressed directly, but later speakers indirectly mentioned the rule. Direct advice may have been given after the meeting.

Research On Other Twelve-Step Groups

One of the first studies of Al-Anon, by Bailey (1965), compared the wives of alcoholics who were members of Al-Anon with wives of alcoholics who were not. She found that Al-Anon members were more educated, more likely to be employed, and of higher socio-economic status than nonmembers. Nonmembers were more likely to suffer physical abuse than were members. Al-Anon members more often reported that they did not drink or seldom drank alcohol and were far more likely than nonmembers to see alcoholism as an illness. This survey was limited to New York State, but other studies have described their subjects similarly (Ablon, 1974; Gorman & Rooney, 1979).

Ablon's (1974) qualitative study of Al-Anon meetings described how sharing experiences and coping strategies educated members about the disease concept of alcoholism and other aspects of surviving with an alcoholic spouse. She found that wives who had resisted a therapist's effort to focus on their role in the spouse's drinking became willing, in the nonthreatening milieu of the Al-Anon group, to examine their own behavior.

Several researchers obtained self-reports related to outcome of Al-Anon membership (Cutter & Cutter, 1987; Gorman & Rooney, 1979; Humphreys, 1993; L. F. Kurtz, 1994). Cutter and Cutter (1987) found that adult children of alcoholic (ACoA) members of Al-Anon were less depressed, more assertive, and more accepting of themselves, as well as more realistic and more philosophical about the degree of responsibility they should assume than they had been before attending. Humphreys described how the worldviews of ACoA members changed within Al-Anon, in that members assumed more self-worth, became less willing to take responsibility for others, and developed a view of God as loving and parents as forgivable victims of a generational disease (Humphreys, 1993). L. F. Kurtz (1994) found that Al-Anon members were helped to deal with crises and claimed greater ability to value and assert themselves while also experiencing a sense of spiritual well-being. Gorman and Rooney's (1979) study of coping patterns found that Al-Anon members dropped ineffective coping behaviors (blaming, covering up the drinking, emotional outbursts) and acquired newer, more effective coping patterns, such as detachment and attending to their own needs.

Al-Anon membership also correlated with spousal improvement and AA participation, although a causal relationship cannot be claimed (Bailey, 1965; Coremblum & Fischer, 1975; Wright & Scott, 1978). In Bailey's survey, Al-Anon members' spouses were more likely to participate in AA than the spouses of non-Al-Anons. Wright and Scott found that when spouses (wives) attended Al-Anon in addition to getting professional treatment, husbands were more likely to report abstinence. Finally, joint participation in Al-Anon by the spouse and AA by the problem drinker correlated with improved marital relationships (Coremblum & Fischer, 1975).

Martin (1992) examined Al-Anon's history and literature to discover how that fellowship portrayed its ideal member and whether this image had changed over time. She found that the ideal of the selfless, detached, but serene wife that was dominant in the earlier works had been replaced by an image of one more emotionally resolved to repair psychological damage done by alcohol.

Of the few studies of NA, two examined outcomes of treatment and use of AA and NA after discharge from formal treatment programs (Alford, Koehler, & Leonard, 1991; Johnsen & Herringer, 1993). Both of these studies found that follow-up attendance at AA and NA produced better outcomes in terms of abstinence and social functioning. However, the investigators did not separate AA attendance from NA attendance; the two groups were treated by investigators as if they were the same program. Two recent studies, both in Great Britain, focused solely on NA (Christo & Franey, 1995; Christo & Sutton, 1994). One found that attendance at NA and abstinence from drug use reduced anxiety, although it was at least 3 years before these former addicts achieved anxiety levels as low as those of a nonaddicted comparison group (Christo & Sutton, 1994). A second study of NA attendance after discharge from treatment found that participation correlated with less drug use, although causality could not be claimed due to limitations in the research design (Christo & Franey, 1995). This investigation also found that spiritual beliefs, locus of control, and belief in the disease concept—all hypothesized to be predictors of outcome— actually made no difference in either abstinence levels or in frequency of NA attendance.

In 1992, Overeaters Anonymous commissioned the Gallup Organization to conduct a study of its members (OA, 1992). Researchers found that the main reason for attending was to lose weight. Of the respondents, 30% had achieved what they considered to be a comfortable weight, and 50% of those had maintained it for 2 or more years. The average (mean) weight lost was 40.8 pounds. When asked what had changed most for them, 41% said that their emotional/mental health had changed most since attending OA, and 30% replied that their spiritual life had changed most. Ninety-four percent reported that their self-esteem was either higher or much higher since joining OA. A majority reported improvements in all aspects of their lives, including emotional, spiritual, family, physical health, social life, physical activity, job performance, job satisfaction, and finances. In addition to participation in OA, members exercised and many received psychotherapy; thus improvements cannot be attributed solely to OA participation.

A survey of *Glamour Magazine* subscribers with eating disorders found their participation in OA (investigators did not report intensity of involvement) to be more harmful than helpful (Yager, Landsverk, & Edelstein, 1989). A later survey of a different sample of OA participants by one of the same investigators found that roughly half were satisfied and half were dissatisfied with the results of participation in OA (again, no report of intensity of involvement) (Rorty, Yager, & Rossotto, 1993). In contrast, another nonrandom survey of bulimic members who averaged attendance at 5 meetings per week found over 50% had been abstinent from specified foods since the first month of participation (Malenbaum, et al., 1988).

IMPLICATIONS FOR PRACTITIONERS

As AA spreads throughout the world, and as women, minorities, young people, and diverse socio-economic groups overcome alcohol problems, AA membership becomes more representative of the entire heavy-drinking population. Demographic characteristics are not the critical factor in whether one will or will not participate in AA or other Twelve-Step groups. It is thus important to recognize that any person may benefit from AA, regardless of race, gender, or ethnicity. However, as pointed out in chapter 4, the individual's readiness for participation is a crucial factor in whether such involvement will be beneficial. Thus coercive measures to induce group participation are unlikely to be fruitful and might even spoil the possibility that a person will return to the group when ready. On the other hand, the findings of Emrick et al. (1993) indicate that more intense participation leads to better outcomes. Once the individual has become ready for group attendance, encouraging frequent encounters with the group or its members is recommended.

The ICSAA studies provide perspectives on AA as a community-based, worldwide social movement. Specific practice implications can be drawn from investigation of interaction patterns. For example, understanding the intimate workings of group process, such as Mäkelä's "rules of speech," can help prepare potential recruits for participation or can aid discussions with clients about their AA involvement. Understanding a group's rules of speech can help both casual observers and nonparticipants gain a more accurate picture of what does and does not happen in AA meetings. Awareness of these rules can also allay practitioners' concerns about client vulnerability in a group, by sketching the boundaries that make the group a safe place for the individual. This information can help a practitioner learn how feedback, although not given in cross-talk, can and does come forth in the gradual and nonconfrontive turns taken by subsequent speakers.

Studies of groups in other countries and cultures highlight the tremendous diversity and variation among Twelve-Step fellowships around the world. Educated professionals, aware of the danger of stereotypical generalizations, should also realize that throughout the United States and the world, the AA program has been widely adapted. The Steps and Traditions remain the same, but these can be interpreted differently; moreover, meeting format, service roles, and meeting content can differ. In addition, the composition of the group may be quite different from one group to another. This, of course, is also true for Twelve-Step programs other than AA. Thus, it is important to help an individual who has been referred to a Twelve-Step program find a group where he or she can feel comfortable.

Twelve-Step groups typically set goals beyond those of abstinence; however, the case of GA reveals that such groups vary in their interpretation of Twelve-Step principles. In preparing someone for participation in AA, it is important to realize that the fellowship can assist the individual with problems other than alcohol. In GA, on the other hand, recovering gamblers may need assistance beyond that of the fellowship to address problems other than gambling.

In today's climate of opinion, it is important to understand the meaning of "surrender" within Twelve-Step programs. Surrender does not mean taking on a sick role or refusing responsibility; it does mean letting go of belief in one's own omnipotence and asking for help. The recruit is expected to end his or her futile effort to recover alone, but also to see that only he or she can initiate the recovery process. In a phrase more common, but not necessarily more true in the 1930s than today, "You alone can do it, but you cannot do it alone." This is an important point that practitioners must help their recovering clients grasp.

For practitioners whose clients use Twelve-Step programs as an adjunct to treatment, an understanding of the Twelve Traditions is essential. It is especially important to understand the principles of nonaffiliation and singleness of purpose (AA is only for alcoholics, OA for overeaters). Since little is known about Twelve-Step programs other than AA and Al-Anon, practitioners should attempt to obtain information about them directly from their members and avoid assuming that the AA model has been exactly imitated.

SUMMARY AND CONCLUSION

This chapter has reviewed the story of AA's beginning and the later development of Twelve-Step groups for families and for people with other problematic conditions. We examined the Twelve-Step philosophy, the goals of the fellowship, and the Twelve Traditions. Demographic characteristics of members in some of the best-known fellowships were examined and reviewed.

The next chapter examines two programs that are change-oriented, but do not use the Twelve Steps or follow the Twelve Traditions. These groups have long and very different histories, which may be contrasted with the groups just discussed.

NOTES

1. I obtained this list from John D.S. in Long Beach, CA at the AA Central Office on East Coast Pacific Highway, Long Beach, CA 90803 or contact Charles Bishop, 46 Eureka Ave., Wheeling, WV 26003; 304-242-2937.

2. Available from Ed Madara, American Self-Help Clearinghouse, Northwest Covenant Healthcare System, Denville, NJ, 07834.

ASSIGNMENT

Obtain literature or interview members of a Twelve-Step fellowship other than AA and define their understanding of the focal problem, the cause of the problem, and the means to recovery. Report the findings of your study in writing.

Chapter 9

OTHER CHANGE-ORIENTED ASSOCIATIONS

> How nice it is now to go through daily life taking an average view of the trivialities that continuously cross my path. I just bungle along, fumbling and stumbling here and there in a most average way.
> —Member of Recovery, Inc., Krezman, 1985

Many people experience anxiety, depression, and fatigue but cannot be diagnosed as having one specific type of ailment. Some groups—Recovery, Inc. is one of them—offer a method of dealing with rather general concerns. Other groups are more disease-specific (e.g., the Depressive Manic Depressive Association or Schizophrenics Anonymous). Recovery, Inc., profiled in this chapter, teaches a method that helps individuals reduce anxiety, tension, and inappropriate anger.

Some people experience a variety of concerns over parenting. They may have injured a child through excessive discipline or have fears of doing so. Or they as children may have experienced abusive treatment from parents. Parents Anonymous helps them deal with such concerns. Like many self-help groups, Parents Anonymous grew out of the frustration of a mother unable to find the help she needed from professionals.

Both of these associations represent groups that fall within the behavior-change category discussed in Chapter 1. Members want to reduce tension and conflict, to improve their relationships with children, or to cope with difficulties related to growing up in an abusive home. Recovery, Inc. groups fall into the category that Schubert and Borkman (1991) labeled the "affiliated" type because they are authorized and regulated by their national organization. Parents Anonymous groups represent the "hybrid" category in Schubert and Borkman's typology because ideally each group has both peer leaders and professional facilitators; both professionals and peers exercise leadership in the national organization as well.

For each of the groups, the following text will (a) offer a general discussion of the group, (b) tell of its founding, (c) describe its program, (d) examine its membership characteristics, and (e) summarize research on the group.

RECOVERY, INC.:
A PROGRAM OF WILL TRAINING

With the single exception of Alcoholics Anonymous (AA), Recovery, Inc. is the oldest extant therapeutic mutual-help association in the United States. Recovery currently lists 777 groups throughout North America, Great Britain, and Israel (Recovery, Inc., 1995). "Its purpose is to help prevent relapses in former mental patients and to forestall chronicity in nervous patients" (Recovery, Inc., n.d., p. 1). Any adult can participate in Recovery, but most who do so experience anxiety, mood swings, interpersonal problems, and other mental or emotional concerns. Recovery leaders come from among the membership; the association disqualifies professionals from group leadership, even when they attend meetings as members. Participants pay no fees, but make voluntary contributions at meetings. Recovery is supported by a combination of "free-will offerings," optional member dues, end-of-year donations, and literature sales. Foundation grants occasionally support special projects (S. Sachs, personal communication, January 29, 1996).

History of Recovery, Inc.

Recovery's story begins in the 1930s when Dr. Abraham Low, a Chicago psychiatrist working at Illinois State Psychiatric Institute, began groups for former patients as a way of sustaining their recovery after hospitalization (Rau & Rau, 1971). He intended that these groups would help patients continue to apply his methods. In addition, in the beginning, he encouraged members to advocate for changes in social policies related to the state mental health code. Officially begun in 1937, the organization was named Recovery, Inc. soon after.

As discussed in chapter 7, Recovery's political focus ended in 1941, when Dr. Low's initially successful efforts to change state mental health statutes aroused extreme opposition in the medical community. When the medical community rallied against him and Recovery, Dr. Low decided to disband the group. For a year, he did nothing to keep the organization going, but his patients refused to give up and asked Dr. Low to teach *them* how to impart his will-training method to others.

In 1942, Dr. Low began training members to lead groups in their homes. At the time, for patients to be able to help one another was unheard of; and Dr. Low was as surprised as anyone that this effort succeeded. Following this difficult period, when he saw that the groups could go on without him, Dr. Low began collecting examples from members' presentations of how the method helped them, using their examples to embellish his lectures. Out of this came his text, *Mental Health Through Will-Training,* published in 1950. Also, mindful of the needs of families, Dr. Low had written *Lectures to Relatives of Former Patients* (Low, 1943), still in print as *Peace Versus Power in the Family: Domestic Discord and Emotional Distress* (Low, 1967). After Low's death in 1954, Recovery continued as a completely member-run self-help association. Its vigorous life over the past 60 years is a testament to Dr. Low's well-conceived program. Group facilitators are trained by local area leaders, although occasionally a leader trainer is sent out from the Chicago headquarters. Group leaders train assistants, who may later become group leaders themselves.

Recovery, Inc. reached its numerical peak in the early 1970s with 7,578 members in 1972 and 1,021 groups in 1975 (Recovery, Inc., 1993). In 1995, of Recovery's 777 groups, 743 were in North America (including Canada and Puerto Rico), 34 were in Ireland, Wales, England, and Israel (Recovery, Inc., 1995).

Program: Will Training

Recovery's method teaches members that their daily problems often stem from angry or fearful temper and that to counteract the symptoms created by temper, the member must learn to "spot" it. Low defined *temper* as defeatist thoughts that produce symptoms such as depression, inhibitions, somatic complaints, and useless quarrels. Individuals who experience *angry temper* tell themselves they have been wronged, which provokes indignation, impatience, and similar reactions. Individuals who experience *fearful temper* think they may be or do wrong, with resulting shame, guilt, and withdrawal. The "symptomatic idiom" (using words that exaggerate the significance of experience) and "temperamental lingo" (vocabulary that reinforces temperamental reactions) intensify defeatist thoughts (Low, 1950, pp. 19-20). Low taught that people cannot control their feelings and sensations, but they can control their thoughts and impulses. Recovery training first helps them to differentiate between thoughts, impulses, and sensations and, second, to learn to control thoughts and impulses.

Using this method, Recovery members "spot" the onset of a temperamental reaction, a process referred to as "working oneself up," and quickly apply "trigger spotting"—naming what is going on—after which they blunt the reaction through use of one or more of Recovery's cognitive/behavioral principles. Low encouraged members to see success in every effort to apply the method. One did not have to experience a perfectly positive outcome with every effort to spot, but should endorse (praise) oneself for making the effort.

Members learn that something may be "distressing but not dangerous" (Low, 1950, p. 92); they learn to be "group-minded versus self-minded" (p. 158) and to resist "temperamental deadlocks" (p. 41). A depressed person learns to "move the muscles" to do what he or she fears to do. The program cautions members not to feel "exceptional" and to strive instead to be "average." Members learn to imagine what an average, cultured person will do and then to "wear the mask" of an average, cultured person.

In the meeting itself, members read from Low's book, give panel presentations describing the use of the method, and engage in mutual aid after the completion of panel presentations. Under the leader's direction, participants are not allowed to deviate from the prescribed format or to complain or be disruptive. Following each panel presentation, members spot on the example, speaking to the leader about aspects of the program they think relate to it. Cross talk is not allowed at this point. Later, in the mutual-aid session, participants further discuss presentations in a more informal back-and-forth manner.

Members

Researchers have surveyed Recovery members on three occasions: Grosz (1972) in 1970; Raiff (1978), who studied Recovery leaders a few years later; and Galanter (1988), who surveyed members in the mid 1980s. All drew their findings from national or international samples. Raiff limited her sample to group and area leaders. Table 9.1 shows demographic trends from 1970 to the 1980s and a comparison between regular members and the leaders in Raiff's sample.

Characteristics of Recovery members have been stable over the years. They are predominantly female, middle-aged, and married. The membership is primarily European American. Employed members have increased from under 50% to over 50%. The biggest change is in educational attainment, the proportion with some college experience having risen from 22% to 65%. In terms of psychiatric condition, Recovery members in the 1988 survey reported that 52% of the recent members and 49% of the leaders had been hospitalized for a psychiatric problem. Most of the

Table 9.1

Recovery Membership Demographics 1972-1988

	Grosz, 1972 Members	Raiff, 1978 Leaders	Galanter, 1988 Members
Male	27%	28%	23%
Female	73%	72%	72%
Age 35-65	82%	84%	Most
European American	–	–	87%
Employed	42%	56%	59%
High School or less	61%	51%	–
College	22%	47%	65%
Married	72%	74%	67%
Single	15%	9%	–
Sep/div/wid	13%	6%	–

members (91%) and of the leaders (89%), had used psychotropic medications at some time in the past.

Research on Recovery, Inc.

Raiff, in a 1978 study, examined the leadership characteristics and training procedures of the Recovery organization. She also measured outcomes using a variety of health indicators, including use of mental-health services and mental status self-reports. She found that Recovery members who were leaders showed improvement on hospital recidivism as well as reduced use of medical resources (physicians, medications). Members were more satisfied with their health and less worried about it than they were before participation. In addition, the quality of life satisfaction of Recovery leaders was similar to that of the general population (Raiff, 1978; 1984).

Galanter's 1988 study surveyed a random sample of leaders and members of Recovery's 211 North American administrative areas. He found statistically significant differences between prior and current adjustment and prior and current feelings of well-being. He found that 59% were working for pay after Recovery involvement, whereas only 41% had been working prior to involvement. Intensity of involvement was positively correlated with improvement, and the more involved leaders were more likely than shorter-term members to have terminated professional psychotherapy.

The next section describes Parents Anonymous (PA), a self-help organization that is more professionalized than Recovery, Inc. Yet PA began with the efforts of a mother who needed help, but found none available.

PARENTS ANONYMOUS

The Parents Anonymous mission is (a) to help parents learn how to discipline and care for their children without being abusive and (b) to help those who were abused as children. In addition, PA seeks to establish programs that prevent child abuse through public education. In 1994, PA served 15,000 parents and 9,200 children in 2,247 groups in the United States (PA, 1995a). PA groups are led by both professionals and parent members (PA, 1995a). Both peer leaders and professional facilitators are PA-trained volunteers. Parents Anonymous receives funds from financial and in-kind contributions, United Way, private foundations and corporations, special fundraising events, and government grants on local, state, and national levels (PA, 1995a).

History of Parents Anonymous

Founders Jolly K., a potentially abusive parent, and Leonard Lieber, social worker, met in 1970 in a California mental health clinic where Jolly K. sought help for herself because she was afraid she would abuse her children (Fritz, 1989; Lieber, 1983; PA, 1995a). Her efforts to obtain help were frustrated when she found that the child guidance clinic to which she applied required a 6-month wait before an initial appointment. At that time, there were few or no services for families with child abuse concerns.

Eventually, Jolly K. met Leonard Lieber, a therapist in a publicly supported mental health clinic. After several months of therapy, Jolly complained that the short appointments with him were not helping her. When Lieber asked her what she would do instead, she replied, "I'd form my own organization. I'd find other women like myself who are having abuse problems, and together with your help we'd find ways to help each other" (Fritz, 1989, p. 314). Lieber replied that this was an excellent idea and asked what she would call the organization. She replied, "Mothers Anonymous" (p. 314). Thus began what would later become Parents Anonymous.

The first brochure for the new group, "Mothers Anonymous" was printed in 1971 (Fritz, 1989). In 1973, Jolly K. testified about child abuse in Congressional hearings that ultimately led to passage of groundbreaking federal child abuse legislation: The Child Abuse Prevention and Treatment Act of 1973 (PA, 1995a). This legislation created the National Center on Child Abuse and Neglect, which has provided funds to support child abuse treatment and prevention programs throughout the United States (PA, 1995a, p. 1). Parents Anonymous subsequently received 12 years of uninterrupted federal funding and became a national service delivery system and an adjunct to Child Protective Services (Fritz, 1989).

In the 25 years since its founding, and in addition to its original groups for parents, PA has initiated groups for incarcerated parents, for children, for battered and homeless women, and for adults sexually abused as children. Today there are PA groups in almost all of the states and in many foreign countries; however, an informal search for groups in Michigan indicated that the number of PA groups has declined due to current cuts in federal funds. Cursory investigation indicates, in addition, that there are groups for parents in Michigan that use the PA name but are not affiliated with PA, and others that are PA groups but have not renewed their PA affiliation and use another name.

Parents Anonymous Program

Parents Anonymous "is a voluntary association without formal affiliation with any other agency; there are no eligibility criteria and there is no screening for admission" to its groups (Moore, 1983, p. 586). Despite its name, PA is not a Twelve-Step program; and although it is a self-help organization, it does use volunteer professional facilitators—social workers, teachers, health care givers, pastoral counselors, and student interns (PA, 1995a). These facilitators receive training from the organization on the use of the PA model, policies, and procedures. Parents share leadership in PA (coleading groups, acting as spokespersons, planning, serving on boards, training, and participating in advocacy).

During meetings, parents receive education as well as emotional support and learn skills for better parenting. Lieber (1983) indicates that the group experience consists of a weekly 2-hour meeting that deals with effective parenting and here-and-now issues related to it. Members are not required to give identifying information nor are they required to speak at meetings. Parents may exchange phone numbers. PA sponsors use many types of therapeutic techniques as well as educational aids such as Parent Effectiveness Training. There is no one clearly articulated method used in all PA groups.

PA operates much like a professional human services organization. Its literature refers to its "direct services" and "telephone counseling" and to the organization as a "national child abuse prevention program" (PA, 1995a). Despite the resemblance to professional services, PA retains some of its self-help philosophy. The 2000 weekly groups remain free to participants and meet in community settings such as churches, shelters, and schools.

Parents Anonymous illustrates how varied the goals of some self-help groups can be (Powell, 1987). Some members are not active abusers, others may be concerned with child neglect rather than physical abuse, and still others may regard their problem as one of emotional abuse. PA's 1994 Database Survey shows that in any given week, "1,064 groups served parents (47.4%); 360 groups served adults other than parents (16%); 539 groups served children (24%); and 284 were child care groups (12.6%)" (PA, 1995a, p. 3). There are 97 groups for incarcerated parents in 10 states, 9 groups serving those who are homeless, and 43 groups for teen parents. Among the parents' groups, there are specialized groups for substance abusing parents, minority populations, and adults abused as children (PA, 1993).

In addition to its groups, PA designs training materials, conducts workshops and conferences, and provides consultation. It maintains a national clearinghouse for making referrals to parents, professionals, and the general public. Parent members of PA compose an integral part of the association's leadership. They lead groups, train professionals, and speak out publicly about PA and about child abuse (PA, n.d.).

PA Members

A national sample of PA members in the 1980s indicated they are 83% female, with a mean age of 29 (Post-Kammer, 1988). Over half of the membership is married, and the mean number of children per member in the national sample is 2.6. Of the sample, 7% reported an income over $20,000, and 47% reported an income under $10,000. A 1988 study of members in Milwaukee found that more of the members were female than male, the mean age was higher than the national figures, income levels were higher, and there were slightly fewer children per member (2.4). There were more single people and fewer separated or married people than in the national sample. Ethnically, 71% were European American, 13% were African American, and the rest were from other racial or ethnic groups. In the Milwaukee sample, 21% of the members reported engaging in sexual abuse, 60% reported acts of verbal abuse, 44% reported episodes of physical abuse, 38% indicated they engaged in emotional abuse, and 9% reported instances of physical neglect. Seventy-one percent of the individuals in the sample reported that they were themselves abused as children (Post-Kammer, 1988).

Research on Parents Anonymous

PA's effectiveness has been examined in four research projects (Cohn, 1979; Hunka, O'Toole, & O'Toole, 1985; Post-Kammer, 1988; Powell, 1979). Powell (1979) interviewed 30 PA members, asking them to tell about their experiences in PA and to compare the effects of PA with those of professional services. PA members expressed opinions that were placed into seven categories:

1. PA is relevant to what parents need
2. PA offers important support
3. PA satisfies a need to be cared for
4. PA reinforces professional service
5. PA takes the parent's concerns more seriously than do other helping resources
6. PA is accessible and non-threatening
7. PA is limited in scope

In some instances, parents spoke more favorably about PA than professional services; in others, PA was seen as complementary to professional service. The final category represents awareness that professional service is needed for those requiring individual psychotherapy. Powell cautioned readers not to have unrealistic expectations of PA, such as, for example, expecting the group to monitor continued abuse.

Shortly after PA's 1970s debut, the Office of Child Development and Rehabilitation Service of the U.S. Department of Health, Education, and Welfare funded a project to develop and test alternative strategies for treating abusive and neglectful parents (Cohn, 1979). The studies conducted by this project found that clients receiving "lay" services, which included Parents Anonymous, reported reduction of abuse (53%) more frequently than clients not receiving these services (42%) (Cohn, 1979). The authors also pointed out that Parents Anonymous and other lay services were more cost-effective than professional services.

A research project in the 1980s utilized a theory of the etiology of child abuse to assess the effectiveness of PA (Kempe & Helfer as cited by Hunka et al., 1985). The dependent variables used in this study included social isolation, self-esteem, dependency needs, impulsiveness, passivity, attitude toward the child, knowledge of child development, problem-solving ability, ability to cope with stress, and child management. Eighteen members of two PA groups completed pre- and post-test measures. Findings indicated that significant positive change following approximately 4 months of participation in PA occurred on all 10 variables (Hunka et al., 1985). In this study, subjects ranked increased self-esteem as their greatest gain from participation; second came their ability to cope with the stresses of parenting. Other large changes included decreased social isolation and greater confidence in the availability of adequate social supports. The latter two outcomes reflected a sense of having exchanged overdependency on their children for healthier ways of meeting needs for companionship.

A study of PA in Milwaukee obtained data from members of three types of groups: groups for parents who abused children sexually, groups for parents who were physically abusive, and groups for elderly adults abused by their adult children (Post-Kammer, 1988). More than 80% of the parents reported that they had improved their ability to cope with stress. Daily verbal abuse dropped from 29% to 5% and physical abuse from 18% to 3%. Parents reported improvement in self-concept and understanding of their children. Length of membership in PA correlated with better understanding of children (Post-Kammer, 1988).

IMPLICATIONS FOR PRACTITIONERS

Recovery, Inc. represents an ideal resource for people who suffer from anxiety, depression, fears, and anger. Once participants become oriented to the language of the group, its method can easily be used by members. At present, the Recovery leadership is seeking ways to expand the number of groups and members. Professionals' recognition of Recovery will assist in preserving this association for others who need it. Videotapes for orienting potential newcomers and others will soon be available from the national Recovery headquarters. Practitioners can acquire these tapes by contacting Recovery in Chicago (312-337-5661; also see video resources list at the end of chapter 4). Members are also available to visit agencies and classrooms to explain the method.

Parents Anonymous is also an under-used resource. Practitioners who work with parents and children can contact the PA headquarters in Claremont, California (909-621-6184) to learn more about its varied services. Parents Anonymous groups also welcome students as sponsors of local groups as part of internships and field practicums.

SUMMARY

These two organizations, Recovery, Inc., and Parents Anonymous, present contrasts in evolution and in maintenance of the self-help ethos. Recovery began as a professional service and later converted to a self-help association, just the reverse of what one would expect. It is hypothesized that this happened because the Recovery method could be taught relatively easily to nonprofessional peer helpers. Recovery's wariness of professionals, which is surely greater than that of Parents Anonymous, may stem in part from the way in which Dr. Low was treated by members of his own profession. On the other hand, PA began and has continued as a hybrid organization that depended both on peer helpers and professionals.

Recovery, Inc. offers multiple methods of helping. Participants in each meeting (a) listen to reading by members of a brief lecture written by Dr. Low, (b) discuss or simply listen to four or five members describe instances of using the Recovery method, and (c) share in mutual support and refreshments. Meetings are open to anyone who thinks he or she may have a problem with mental illness of any kind and are free (contributions are requested but not required). This imaginative, successful, and long-lived program, although fully affordable for virtually anyone and applicable to almost any emotional problem, has not become well known to the majority of mental health professionals or to the general public (Lee, 1995). Its name, *Recovery*, leads many to confuse it with recovery from alcohol or drug abuse. In response to the declining number of groups, Recovery's national board of directors has launched a major effort to increase the number of groups and members and to reach out to professionals (S. Sachs, personal communication, January 29, 1996).

Parents Anonymous is an example of a mutual self-help association with a role for volunteer professional facilitators within the local groups. Although the organization has expanded the kind of services it provides and has become more professionalized as a social service organization, it retains some of its earlier commitment to mutual aid by peer helpers. PA must contend with the confusion created by use of the "anonymous" in its name, leading some to think that it is a Twelve-Step program. To compound this confusion, local groups for families have occasionally used the name "Parents Anonymous" (some are Twelve-Step groups) but have no connection to the national PA organization.

Professional services to local PA groups remain voluntary and unpaid, although many of the professionals receive released time from their social agencies to perform this service (PA, 1995a). The question of whether the mutual aid aspects of PA have been diluted by the participation of professionals and the formalization and expansion of the organization, however, has yet to be addressed by researchers.

These organizations participate quite differently in efforts to change public policy. When it first began, Recovery saw its role as both service and public advocacy; but an early unfortunate experience with advocacy in the political arena turned the organization away from further efforts along these lines. PA addresses policy issues, but does this primarily at the national level. The next chapter looks at supportive-educational associations in which three of the four carry out some public policy-change activities.

CLASSROOM EXERCISE

Both Recovery, Inc. and Parents Anonymous have experienced a decline in numbers of groups. In a small discussion group, imagine yourselves as consultants and devise a recommended plan for increasing the number of these groups in your community. Be sure to keep in mind the self-help ethos when developing the plan.

Chapter 10

SUPPORTIVE-EDUCATIONAL GROUPS

"The group with which I am working gives me something positive to do. I feel I am helping someone down the road and changing things in a positive manner."
—Member of Candlelighters, in Chesler & Chesney, 1995, p. 3

Many self-help associations confine their activities to supportive and educational goals. They have been placed in the self-help rather than the support group category because they limit leadership to those who have the problem or condition (peers) and they are larger and more organizationally independent of professional organizations.

Some of these associations include advocacy as a part of their mission. In addition to their support and education functions, these self-help groups and organizations also advocate for social change, such as improved government services, increased research dollars, and public acceptance of stigmatizing conditions. Typically, national-level offices devote more resources to advocacy, whereas local groups provide support and information to members. Three of the organizations examined in this chapter advocate for public policy change: The National Alliance for the Mentally Ill (NAMI), Candlelighters Childhood Cancer Foundation (CCCF), and the Alzheimer's and Related Disorders Association (ADRDA). The latter, however, carries out its educational and public policy activities in the larger, more professionalized association. The Compassionate Friends (TCF), the fourth organization discussed, is a support organization for parents who have lost a child; TCF has no explicit public policy or social change goals and represents most clearly the supportive kind of self-help group.

The groups profiled in this chapter fall into three of the Schubert & Borkman (1991) organizational autonomy categories: CCCF represents the federated type (local chapters are completely independent of the national organization); NAMI and TCF fall into the affiliated category (chapter affiliates receive directions from a national organization); and ADRDA represents the managed type because its groups often meet in social service settings and are subordinate to the larger association's more formal and professional operation, although this varies from one locale to another. Many, but not all of the ADRDA groups, resemble professionally-facilitated support groups.

All of these groups have another major feature in common: Participants are usually members of a family in which someone has an illness or, in the case of TCF, has died. For each of these four groups, the text includes: (a) a general description; (b) a brief history of the group's founding; (c) a discussion of its program; (d) a description of members; and (e) a summary of the research on the group.

THE NATIONAL ALLIANCE
FOR THE MENTALLY ILL

NAMI's mission is "to eradicate mental illness and improve the quality of life of those affected by these diseases" (NAMI, 1995a). Its goals include dissemination of information about mental illness, improved public understanding of the biological basis of mental illness, incorporation of current research on treatment of persons with mental illness, and allocation of increased government resources for research and treatment (NAMI, 1995a). NAMI defines "self-help" as the support and education part of its program, separate from its advocacy activities. Three main elements of self-help—emotional support, self-education, and practical advice—remain chiefly the function of local affiliates (Howe & Howe, 1987).

NAMI's 13-member National Board of Directors is elected by the membership. State and local groups are relatively autonomous from the national office; however, the central office requires locals to meet standards and certifies them when they comply. Only members who are primary consumers (patients) or their families are eligible to serve in the leadership structure of NAMI, although professionals occasionally serve in paid staff positions. NAMI's primary sources of funds are dues and contributions from members; less than 2% of its funding comes from the government (NAMI, 1995a).

History of NAMI

NAMI was formed in September 1979 in Madison, Wisconsin, when a group of families of persons with mental illness, calling itself the Alliance for the Mentally Ill, hosted a conference to which they invited other groups of families (Howe & Howe, 1987; NAMI, 1995a). Almost 300 people, representing family groups from 29 states and Canada, registered. Three types of local groups came together in Madison: "(1) independents: 34 groups that had been organized by the relatives of patients; (2) affiliates: 20 groups that were affiliated with state mental health associations and one that was affiliated with a mental health center; and (3) Huxley groups: 16 groups that were associated with the American Schizophrenia Association, a division of the Huxley Institute for Biosocial Research" (Hatfield, 1981, p. 409).

The idea of a national organization caught fire, and on that September 1979 weekend, representatives from these groups agreed on a name, purpose, and funding mechanisms. They drafted bylaws and selected a steering committee, creating the National Alliance for the Mentally Ill. Tax-exempt status was soon achieved, and in 1982 NAMI opened an office in Washington, D.C. (Howe & Howe, 1987; NAMI, 1995a). Six years later the organization had grown to over 600 groups, and a new affiliate was added every 10 working hours (3.7 new groups per week).

In 1988, NAMI began the NAMI Children and Adolescent Council (NAMI CAN), which advocates on behalf of children with brain disorders, including "affective disorders, bipolar and unipolar depression, anxiety disorders, schizophrenia and schizo-affective disorders, obsessive compulsive disorder, attention-deficit hyperactivity disorder, Tourette's syndrome, autism and pervasive developmental disability disorder, as well as other disorders characterized by demonstrable brain malfunctions" (Howe, 1995, p. 2).

Numerous professionals have assisted NAMI through writing about it and serving as staff or as consultants to the national board of directors. Some of these professionals were also in families with persons who have mental illnesses; many have served in the leadership of NAMI. One of the best known of these supportive professionals is Agnes Hatfield, a professor of education and author of numerous books on families of those with mental illness. Another is E. Fuller Torrey, a psychiatrist, researcher, and author of books and research reports on serious mental illness including *Surviving Schizophrenia: A Family Manual* (1995). Torrey has led the effort to recognize mental illness as a disease like any other physical illness.

Program

"NAMI is a grassroots, self-help support and advocacy organization of families and friends of people with serious mental illness, and those persons themselves" (NAMI, 1995a). A bimonthly newsletter, the *NAMI Advocate,* disseminates news of public policy, new research, legal progress, and literature reviews. Most state and local chapters also distribute newsletters detailing local policy and the group's advocacy activities related to local issues. Members form delegations to lobby in state legislatures, while in the national office a full-time director lobbies in Congress. NAMI pressures Congress for funds for schizophrenia research and combats the stigma of mental illness through public education.

NAMI members believe that "severe mental illnesses are biologically-based brain disorders that can profoundly disrupt a person's ability to think, feel, and relate to others and to their environment" (NAMI, 1993, p. 2). They believe that too many resources have gone to mental health programs that focus primarily on milder forms of emotional distress and too little has been allocated to research and treatment for more serious brain dysfunctions. For this reason, they do not use the term "mental health," preferring the term "mental illness" in referring to the focus of their activity. They advocate for research on the brain and for community-based supports for mentally-ill people who have problems with independent living (Howe & Howe, 1987).

Members

NAMI's membership is open to anyone who wants to join, but parents of adult patients form its largest membership category. In 1995, the organization had approximately 1,000 affiliated chapters throughout North America with contacts in 24 foreign countries. It listed over 130,000 active members throughout all 50 states (NAMI, 1995a). A 1990 national survey of NAMI members found that 80% were parents of a mentally ill individual; 50% of those parents were 65 or older (Jenson, n.d.). Typically, members were women, well-educated, and employed in professional or managerial occupations. Most were European American.

The member of the family with mental illness was most typically diagnosed as having schizophrenia (64%). Eighteen percent were diagnosed with major depression or schizo-affective disorder, and 15% with manic-depression. These family members' ages were between 30 and 44. Most lived in the community, and most had at least a high school diploma.

Over 70% of the adult children represented in the national sample received income assistance in the form of Social Security Disability Insurance and Supplemental Security Income or both (Jenson, n.d.). Other sources offered similar descriptions of the NAMI parent-members' children; that is, they were chiefly male, with an average age in the 30s, diagnosed as schizophrenic, and had attained at least a high school education (Bouricius, Kersten, Nagy, McCartney, & Stein, 1994; Hatfield, Coursey, & Slaughter, 1994; Kurtz, 1994; Medvene & Krauss, 1985; NAMI, 1995b; Perkins, Lafuze, & Van Dusen, 1995; Skinner, Steinwachs, & Kasper, 1992; Uttaro & Mechanic, 1994). Analogous surveys in four countries (Netherlands, Great Britain, Spain, and Germany) have reported similar findings (Schene & Wijngaarden, 1995).

Research on NAMI

Research on NAMI has focused on helping processes (Kurtz, 1994; Medvene & Krause, 1989; Medvene, 1990), service needs of members' mentally ill relatives (Skinner et al., 1992; Uttaro & Mechanic, 1994), costs and benefits of membership (Bouricius et al., 1994; Norton, Wandersman, & Goldman, 1993), and group effectiveness (Perkins et al., 1995).

Researchers have found that the supportive/educational processes in NAMI groups effect changes in members' understanding of mental illness. Members learn to reframe it as a brain disease rather than a behavior disorder, which removes from well members the guilt and self-blame they felt when they believed they caused or contributed to the illness (Kurtz, 1994; Medvene, 1990; Medvene & Krauss, 1989). When they join with other members, they become more self confident, able to assert themselves, and able to cope with crises (Bouricius et al., 1994; Kurtz, 1994; Norton, Wandersman, & Goldman, 1993). One study found that the most motivating feature of NAMI membership was the opportunity to advocate for better care for their ill members (Bouricius et al., 1994).

A 1992 investigation of service needs and preferences experienced by families identified six categories: crisis management (experienced by 71% of the sample), community living skills (70%), establishing friendships and social relationships (62%), finding productive activities (62%), illness management (57%), and basic self-care (22%) (Skinner et al., 1992; Steinwachs, Kasper, & Skinner, 1992). Aging caregivers expressed concern over the prospect of not being able to provide care in the future.

NAMI is widely considered to be "one of the most powerful and effective caregivers' organizations in the country" (Riessman & Carroll, 1995, p. 113). The organization's local groups are able to offer considerable support and information to their members while also advocating for societal change. Researchers investigating NAMI have broadened the scope of their study to include more than the psychological outcomes that often typify self-help research.

To assess group effectiveness, Perkins et al. (1995) examined the relationship between member characteristics, social climate, and group assets (membership, funds) and members' satisfaction with the group. They found that neither member demographics nor group assets predicted their perception of the effectiveness of NAMI groups. Social climate assessments, however, revealed that groups rated as highly supportive, with stable leadership and high order and organization ratings, were seen as more beneficial than groups lacking these characteristics.

THE CANDLELIGHTERS CHILDHOOD CANCER FOUNDATION

"The Candlelighters Childhood Cancer Foundation (CCCF) is an international organization providing support, education, and advocacy programs for families of children with cancer, survivors of childhood cancer, and the medical and psychosocial professionals who treat them" (CCCF, 1995a, p. 2). In 1995, the organization listed over 400 groups and 40,000 members. The national office of CCCF provides information and other resources for chapters throughout the world but has no official connection beyond resource provision with the local groups. Local groups are led by either parent members, professionals, or both. Groups charge no fees. The organization's largest source of funding is the American Cancer Society (42%). The remainder comes from grants and individual contributions.

History of Candlelighters

Candlelighters began in Washington, D.C., in 1970 when 35 families began meeting in the basement classroom of the old Children's Hospital (CCCF, n.d.a). Grace Powers Monaco, a parent and an attorney, led the early organizing effort. By 1975, this small group had grown to 22 groups nationally. In 1977, the organization began collaborating with the National Cancer Institute (NCI) to develop literature; in 1978 it hired its first paid staff member and hosted its first national conference attended by members of 100 groups from 42 states.

In 1981, CCCF established affiliation and funding agreements with the American Cancer Society, Inc., which provides literature and other resources (CCCF, n.d.a). In 1984, the official name of the association became "The Candlelighters Childhood Cancer Foundation." In 1990, CCCF initiated two new endeavors, the Survivors of Childhood Cancer Program and the Ombudsman Program. In 1994, the CCCF moved from Washington, D.C., to Bethesda, Maryland. Members celebrated its 25th Anniversary Conference in Crystal City, Virginia, in July 1995 (CCCF, n.d.a).

Program

Parent support groups associated with the CCCF focus on five kinds of activities to help families with childhood cancer: (a) information and education; (b) sharing and emotional support; (c) social and friendship activities; (d) fundraising; (e) making changes in the system of care through meeting with staff, working with schools, and advocating for insurance coverage (Chesney, Rounds, & Chesler, 1989, p. 127-128).

Emotional support, information and education, fund raising for organizational maintenance, social events, and informal contacts among parents are the central activities of most groups. Advocacy for change in the medical system and visiting families in the hospital are less common activities. Groups vary greatly with regard to activities and meeting structure (Chesney et al., 1989).

CCCF's Ombudsman Program provides consultation by attorneys on such things as health insurance and employment discrimination. A one-on-one casework approach provides support and facilitates problem solving (CCCF, n.d.b). These may be problems such as resolving unpaid health insurance claims, ironing out difficulties over the child's education, obtaining second medical opinions, helping with government benefits, and securing vocational rehabilitation services (CCCF, 1995b).

CCCF lobbies at local, state, and national levels to achieve goals such as increasing funds allocated to research and clinical application of that research (Monaco, 1993). It targets school systems and sensitizes them to the special needs of children with cancer. The organization has supported passage of federal legislation such as the 1990 Americans with Disabilities Act and the 1995 Family and Medical Leave Act. The Ombudsman Program advocates for members who face violations in these types of laws.

Members

Groups are open and include parents and others who are concerned with childhood cancer. Members in Chesler and Chesney's (1995) studies (see below) were between 35 and 40 years old, married and female, with modest family incomes. When compared with parents who were not members, they were more likely to be college-educated, and their children were more likely to have been diagnosed less recently. Few African Americans, Latinos, or Asian Americans were found in CCCF groups across the country, except in cities where there are high concentrations of these groups.

When compared with parents who did not join a group, members differed mainly in that they received less practical support from the medical system. Members' reasons for joining were to receive information, gain support and affirmation, and learn coping skills. Major reasons for not joining were (a) lack of time and energy; (b) a pattern of coping with stress in private, rather than with others; (c) feeling that the group will increase stress, be too emotional, or give misinformation. Other reasons hypothesized, but not supported by interviews with non-members were lack of information about the group, inconvenience of location, poor organization in some groups, and irrelevant activities.

Research on Candlelighters

In the late 1970s, researchers began studies of childhood cancer, which led to a study of 50 CCCF local groups in the early 1980s (Chesler & Chesney, 1995). After 10 years, researchers recontacted the groups, thus giving a perspective over time of leadership and other organizational events.

Because of its variety of leadership styles (parent, professional, shared), investigators had an opportunity to compare and contrast these styles (Chesler & Chesney, 1995; Yoak & Chesler, 1985). Parents lead groups differently than professionals do. For example, many professionally led groups were smaller, less formally organized, and sponsored fewer activities than parent-led groups. Moreover, professionally led groups were more focused on emotional needs and seldom stressed other kinds of needs or encouraged members to challenge the health system. Furthermore, they were more likely to limit membership to those with living children than did members in groups with shared leadership or with parent leaders. Groups with shared leadership (parents and professionals) had the greatest longevity. A follow-up study with many of the same groups 10 years later found little changed, although 9 of the original 50 groups had ceased to exist (Chesler & Chesney, 1995).

This investigation also examined factors that may increase the value of a group to its members (Chesler & Chesney, 1995; Chesney et al., 1989). Members most valued groups in which there was an active, involved core group capable of bestowing adequate support and help to them. Members also highly valued groups in which professionals from the medical facility involved themselves by serving as a link to the facility and its services.

Members were relatively indifferent to frequency and variety of group activities, social activities, characteristics of other members, meeting sites, and accessibility of the group. Marginal and potential members, on the other hand, were more sensitive to convenience and accessibility. Both members and non-members were asked if "being a private person" figured in the extent to which they used the group. Wanting to keep things "private" was not a factor in members' participation, but for nonmembers it was given as the second most important reason for nonparticipation.

Another aspect of the study explored the activist potential of the groups (Chesney & Chesler, 1993). Researchers found that members were much more likely than non-members to engage in activism. Individuals whose coping styles included active coping rather than passive coping were also more likely to have experienced positive changes in willingness to take action (Chesney & Chesler, 1993).

Much of what researchers have learned about Candlelighters is consistent with findings from other studies of self-help groups (i.e., demographic characteristics do not differentiate members from non-members, members who participate become more assertive and self confident, and members value help, support and education more than other activities of the group). Furthermore, people who did not feel comfortable speaking about their problems among strangers were less likely to use the Candlelighters groups, a finding shared with researchers of other associations (see chapter 4). Like NAMI members, CCCF members evidence desire and motivation to join with others in activist roles within the community.

THE ALZHEIMER'S DISEASE AND RELATED DISORDERS ASSOCIATION (ADRDA)

Headquartered in Chicago, the ADRDA is the oldest and largest national voluntary health organization dedicated to research for the cause and prevention of Alzheimer's Disease (ADRDA, 1993). It seeks to educate victims and their families, professional caregivers, and the general public. The Association also advocates for government funding for research and services to victims of the disease, raises money for research and services, and provides a national network of chapters.

The Alzheimer's Association chapter-network consists of more than 221 local chapters, more than 2,000 support groups and 35,000 volunteers nationwide (ADRDA, 1993). The chapters provide a variety of local services including meetings, newsletters, helplines, and speakers' bureaus. In addition, some chapters provide respite care, day care, and case management. Professionals, mainly social workers and nurses, staff approximately half of the affiliated chapters and either lead or colead many of the support groups. Affiliated chapters meet standards drawn up by the national association. Each chapter receives funding from a variety of sources, which can include member donations, corporate gifts and foundation grants, special events, memorials, and government grants (D. Wilkins, personal communication, November 13, 1995).

History of the Alzheimer's Association

Soon after the establishment of the National Institute on Aging (NIA) in 1974, its first director, Robert Butler, identified the need for a public constituency for Alzheimer's Disease (AD) and related disorders (Fox, 1989). Robert Katzman, a neurologist, had worked for years to bring such a constituency about. His 1970s research on AD had sharpened awareness of the illness as a discreet disease entity, which was eventually recognized as the fourth leading cause of death in the United States. With Butler's support, Robert Katzman and Leonard Wolin, a New York attorney, founded the Alzheimer's Disease Society in the late 1970s (Pollen, 1993).

Publicizing the illness was key to the growth of the new society. In 1977, Roberta Glaze Custer of Minneapolis allowed her story of caring for her Alzheimer's afflicted husband to appear in the *Minneapolis Star and Tribune*. After the Associated Press picked up the story, the publicity brought contacts with grassroots groups for caregivers and interested others throughout the country (Fox, 1989; Pollen, 1993). Scientists had started some groups as a means of advocating for an increase in biomedical research; others were founded by families whose relatives had AD or related disorders. On October 29, 1979, representatives of seven such groups met in Washington, D.C., and laid the foundation for the national organization.

A key ingredient in the growth of the organization was finding someone to head it. That person was Jerome Stone, a Chicago businessman whose wife had suffered from AD (Pollen, 1993). The new organization's name later changed to the Alzheimer's Disease and Related Disorders Association (ADRDA), although it is usually referred to as the Alzheimer's Association. The ADRDA held its first National Board meeting on December 4, 1979. Goals were outlined as "coordination, education, family support, research for disease prevention, public policy, advocacy, organizational development, and fundraising" (Fox, 1989, p. 84). Interest in the disease and the association swelled after a *Dear Abby* column in 1980 discussed it. The organization received between 30,000 and 40,000 letters in response to this column (Fox, 1989).

By the early 1980s, the ADRDA had emerged as a visible and viable advocacy organization. Throughout the 1980s, ADRDA spokespersons testified on a variety of issues before the U.S. House of Representatives. This kept the disease and the issues in the public consciousness and resulted in increased funds for research. By 1986, the association counted 125 affiliates in 44 states. By 1995, the number of affiliated groups had grown to over 200, with representation in every state.

The ADRDA has grown beyond what is generally viewed as a self-help association. Instead, it is a formal, professional organization with a strong record of volunteer involvement, particularly in the leadership of support groups. Because the focus of this book is self-help and support, only the ADRDA support groups will be discussed with regard to program, members, and research.

Support Group Program

The Alzheimer's Association has spearheaded the formation of the most rapidly growing mutual support group network for AD and is the largest single sponsor of support groups for the relatives of those afflicted with AD in the United States (ADRDA, 1995; Molinari, Nelson, Shekelle, & Crothers, 1994). Unlike many other, independently formed support groups for AD, Alzheimer's Association groups are made available to all caregivers for as long as they are needed (Gonyea, 1989).

An ADRDA brochure states,

> The purpose of an Alzheimer's Association support group is to offer families support and information that is specific to dementia. Some Alzheimer's Association Chapters have support groups especially for adolescents, male spouses, adult children caring for a parent, family members of nursing home residents, or widows and widowers. Some Chapters also have a special orientation for family members of a newly-diagnosed patient. (ADRDA, 1990, n.p.)

The number of participants in a meeting varies depending on the format (ADRDA, 1990). Educational groups are larger than support groups, which ideally have 6-12 members. Meetings are held monthly or bimonthly in a hospital, church, library, nursing home or senior center, or in members' homes. In the past, support groups have been for caregivers only. More recently, support groups for Alzheimer's patients have been initiated and are spreading among ADRDA chapters (Carey, Griffin, & Hastings, 1992). A typical meeting agenda consists of informal exchange of problems and ideas, formal education, a guest speaker, and information and referral.

Members

Surveys of ADRDA group members find they resemble caregivers for victims of other diseases. They are mostly women (wives or daughters), with a median age of 60 (Gonyea, 1989; Gonyea & Silverstein, 1991; Molinari et al., 1994; Wright, Lund, Pett, & Caserta, 1987). In Gonyea's Massachusetts sample, 56% were wives caring for husbands; most were European American. Three-quarters of the adult children were women caring for mothers or mothers-in-law. Thirty-two percent of the caregivers were employed full time. The largest number (52%) of patients were in the final stages of the disease and about half were residing in nursing homes. In Molinari et al.'s sample, composed of 95 attendees in 21 groups located in Houston, Texas, most were adult children of the patient (49%); 39% were spouses.

Research on the ADRDA

Although the Alzheimer's Association has been the primary impetus for the development of AD support groups, little research has been focused on them (Molinari et al., 1994). One study investigating why nonattenders do not participate discovered several reasons for this: lack of awareness of groups, failure of medical personnel to recommend them, not wanting to share feelings or hear the depressing truth about later stages of the illness, logistical problems of finding care for the ill person, transportation, location, and meeting time (Gonyea, 1989; Molinari et al., 1994; Wasow, 1986; Wright et al., 1987). Those with larger families were less inclined to attend than caregivers with fewer family supports, suggesting that those with more natural support had less need for a group (Wright et al., 1987).

A study of African-American and Hispanic nonattenders hypothesized a need for more ethnic-specific support groups (Henderson, Gutierrez-Mayka, Garcia, & Boyd, 1993). Subsequently, groups with racially or ethnically compatible facilitators, in ethnic neighborhoods and churches, and in Spanish for Hispanic members had good attendance.

Most often mentioned as benefits of attending the Alzheimer's support groups were the information and support received (Gonyea, 1989; Gonyea & Silverstein, 1991; Wright et al., 1987). Other benefits included the realization that others had the same experiences, friendship and camaraderie, learning ways of coping with stress, and improved awareness and use of community resources.

Research on ADRDA support groups reveals several guidelines for practitioners:

1. Medical and social service personnel should recommend the groups to caregivers.
2. There is a need to involve families whose patients are in earlier stages of the illness and to separate members according to stage of illness.
3. Health providers need to allocate financial resources to provide logistical supports such as transportation, respite care, and convenient meeting locations.
4. Utilizing facilitators who reflect the primary ethnic/racial population of the community being served should increase participation by people of color.

The three associations just discussed are very similar in that they all offer support, information, and advocacy. Advocacy is approached somewhat diversely in these groups. NAMI engages in grassroots mobilization of its membership around state and national policy issues. The ADRDA engages in more professionalized efforts to influence policy at a national level. CCCF promotes social policy nationally and engages in individualized advocacy at the local level.

The next association to be considered, The Compassionate Friends (TCF), illustrates a self-help organization that devotes most of its energy to support and experiential knowledge about coping with the death of a child. Its mission is exquisitely supportive; its members suffer from possibly the most intense kind of grief known to humankind—grief over death of a child.

THE COMPASSIONATE FRIENDS

The Compassionate Friends(TCF) states that its purposes are "to support and aid parents in the positive resolution of the grief experienced upon the death of their child, and to foster the physical and emotional health of bereaved parents and siblings" (TCF, 1993, p. 2). TCF is open to all parents who have experienced the death of a child, and it charges no dues or fees. The leadership, both national and local, comes from parents. There are no professional facilitators. Groups conform to national bylaws and guidelines. They must receive permission to use the TCF logo and must apply to the national headquarters to become a formal affiliate (Davidson,

1979). The association currently lists 675 chapters in the United States with additional chapters in Great Britain (White & Madara, 1995). The association depends on voluntary contributions from individuals at both the local and national levels (TCF, 1993).

History of the Compassionate Friends

The first meeting of the Society of Compassionate Friends occurred in Coventry, England, in January 1969, with six members in attendance (Davidson, 1979). One of its founders, Rev. Simon Stephens, the Assistant to the Chaplain in the Warwichshire Hospital, though not a bereaved parent, facilitated development of the association along with two recently bereaved families (TCF, 1993). From its beginning, the group restricted membership to bereaved parents. One year after its first meeting, the society became a national organization with chapters throughout England.

Stephens described the problems of many bereaved parents in his book *Death Comes Home* (1972), a significant inspiration and tool for TCF. Following its publication, Stephens promoted the organization in speeches and media appearances. An article on his work appeared in the United States in *Time* magazine in the spring of 1971; and in 1972, Stephens visited the United States. Soon after, the first U.S. chapter held meetings in Miami; and by fall of 1972, the new American organization of TCF began to serve as a clearinghouse (Davidson, 1979, p. 82).

The organization held its first U.S. national convention in Chicago in 1977. The convention's planning led to the emergence of national leadership through the work of the Hinsdale, Illinois, chapter. The Chicago convention saw the ratification of bylaws, elections, formation of a national newsletter committee, and the opening of a national office in Oak Brook, Illinois. Primary functions of the newly-established national office were twofold: receiving and answering letters from bereaved parents and interested professionals, and developing new chapters.

Program

The TCF mission statement reads as follows:

The Compassionate Friends is a mutual assistance self-help organization offering friendship and understanding to bereaved parents and siblings.

The primary purpose is to assist them in the positive resolution of the grief experienced upon the death of a child and to support their efforts to achieve physical and emotional health. The secondary purpose is to provide information and education about bereaved parents and siblings.

The objective is to help those in their community, including family, friends, employers, co-workers and professionals, to be supportive.(TCF, 1993, p. 5)

TCF adheres to seven principles for bereaved parents and six principles for bereaved siblings (TCF, 1991). These principles are

For Bereaved Parents

1. TCF offers friendship and understanding to bereaved parents.
2. TCF believes that bereaved parents can help each other toward a positive resolution of their grief.
3. TCF reaches out to all bereaved parents across artificial barriers of religion, race, economic class, or ethnic group.
4. TCF understands that every bereaved parent has individual needs and rights.
5. TCF helps bereaved parents primarily through local chapters.
6. TCF chapters belong to their members.
7. TCF chapters are coordinated nationally to extend help to each other and to individual bereaved parents everywhere (p. 1-3).

For Bereaved Siblings

1. TCF recognizes that siblings are an integral part of the family unit.
2. TCF offers friendship and understanding to bereaved siblings.
3. TCF believes bereaved siblings can help each other toward a positive resolution of their grief.
4. TCF reaches out to all bereaved siblings regardless of religion, race, economic class, or ethnic group.
5. TCF understands that all sibling members have individual needs and rights.
6. TCF recognizes that the term "bereaved sibling" encompasses all age groups. (TCF, 1991, p. 3)

Sherman (1979) describes typical Chicago Area chapter meetings of TCF. There are two types of meetings: afternoon coffees and evening meetings. Groups hold meetings in a community facility, such as a room at the YWCA, church hall, lounge in a hospital, or town hall. They begin with a standard introduction in which all those present give their name, the name and age of their dead child, and a brief description of the circumstances surrounding the child's death. After that, the program consists of either a presentation by a guest speaker or open discussion focusing on a particular issue of the grieving process. Typical subjects include medical or legal questions, marital strife, loneliness, guilt, and suicidal feelings. After the formal meeting, members remain and gather in small, informal discussion groups, often consisting of parents who had lost a child through similar circumstances.

Although the ideology of TCF was not formally articulated at the time of Sherman's study, his work offers a useful conceptualization of the group's philosophy as it has emerged more explicitly since his investigation (Sherman, 1979). The organization's overriding tenet is that the bereaved person experiences normal grief. Within this context, the group teaches methods of coping with denial, anger, guilt, marital strain, neglect of surviving children, isolation, and alienation due to the insensitivity of others. The group accomplishes these goals by providing times to grieve, opportunity to display mementos, and encouragement to visit the child's grave. It routinizes an introduction in which parents convey in each meeting the details of their child's death.

TCF also provides educational materials. It stresses activity to enhance the sense of being in control, decreases isolation by encouraging involvement in TCF, and discourages judgments of others who do not understand how bereaved parents feel. TCF specifically works to salvage the parents' marriage, for example, by emphasizing the importance of understanding that grieving styles may be incompatible. Stressing the importance of marital harmony, TCF presses for involvement by both parents; members openly discuss marital conflict in meetings. It counsels parents not to neglect or overprotect other children in the family and not to overidealize the lost child. The group encourages bereaved parents to break the "conspiracy of silence" by teaching friends and neighbors that it is okay to talk about the dead child.

Members

In a 1978 survey of 18 TCF chapters, most members (70%) were women and most (88%) were married (Videka-Sherman, 1982). Their average age was 41.2 years with a range of 21-67. They were middle-class, well-educated (27% were college graduates), and all but 5% were either homemakers or employed. A more recent study of TCF members found them to be similar to those described by Videka-Sherman, middle-aged, European-American (98%), middle-income, and well-educated (45% had at least one college degree). The largest percentage were Protestant (Wheeler, 1990).

Videka-Sherman and Lieberman (1985) found that bereaved parents who joined TCF were more distressed at the time of their joining than were those who did not join. These members ranked "to talk with others who had the same experience" as the most important reason for joining. This reason was followed by "to learn how other bereaved parents cope with problems, to share thoughts and feelings about the loss of my child, and to get relief from things or feelings that are troubling me" (Videka-Sherman,

1990, p. 160). "To get psychological help" was a reason for joining for the fewest respondents (10%), although many of the benefits most described were, in fact, psychological in nature.

Research on the Compassionate Friends

Videka-Sherman (1982) questioned whether increased involvement in TCF was associated with patterns of change in levels of depression or in self-assessment of personal change after the death of a child. She found psychological adjustment as measured by an open-ended "change in self" question associated with levels of involvement. More highly involved parents experienced more interpersonal changes, changes in beliefs about what is important in life, and changes in experiencing the self as resilient and strong. Increased involvement, however, did not correlate with reduced depression. Nevertheless, members rated themselves as deriving subjectively determined benefits; that is, they felt freer to express feelings, felt more in control of their lives, were more self-confident, were happier, and were less isolated.

Klass's study of TCF produced insights into the process of affiliation with groups (Klass, 1984-1985) (see chapter 4). His findings suggest that participants make three discrete key decisions as they join with the group: (a) the decision to attend, (b) the decision to affiliate, and (c) the decision to help others.

TCF possesses a rich organizational history, which has been well-documented. Thus it serves as a model for other self-help associations of the supportive-educational type. Its commitment to parent leadership and independence from professional organizations evidences strong adherence to the self-help ethos. Moreover, its commitment to giving back what one has gained rather than graduating from the group helps the association maintain itself without external supports.

IMPLICATIONS FOR PRACTITIONERS

Three of these organizations began with the assistance of professionals: Fuller Torrey, a physician, assisted the beginning of NAMI; Robert Butler and Robert Katzman, physicians, helped begin the ADRDA; and Simon Stephens, a clergyman, helped to begin TCF. These organizational stories illustrate how professional practitioners can assist with beginning a self-help association.

Research on these associations provides clear evidence of what is important to families that have chronically and seriously ill members. They need support, education, and helpful direction about how to cope. They want professional advice, consultation, and access to resources. They want someone to serve as a liaison to the medical bureaucracy. They also want to change policy, change the medical system, and change public perceptions of the illness with which they struggle. Practitioners can offer concrete assistance in each of these areas.

SUMMARY

These four self-help associations are alike in many ways, as we have just reviewed: They primarily serve family members; they all began organizing groups in the 1970s; and they have all grown rapidly, with off-shoots in most of the states and contacts in other countries. Three of the four associations have a social change focus.

There are hundreds more similar associations that serve families and patients who endure a vast array of physical and mental illnesses (White & Madara, 1995). With their existing or potential advocacy capability, these groups in coalition could exert a positive force on the seemingly out-of-control entrepreneurial health care industry—a force that no other organized effort in the United States has been able to muster.

DISCUSSION QUESTION

What are the elements of these four associations that you would want your colleagues to know about? If you were going to do staff training on any or all of these four associations, how would you structure the event?

CLASSROOM EXERCISE

Identify the steps involved in beginning a supportive-educational self-help association. Pick a problem suffered by a significant number of people and plan a first meeting. Write a mission statement and a list of goals. Role-play the first meeting.

Chapter 11

TELEPHONE SUPPORT
AND ON-LINE SELF HELP

> Hope. These phone calls are hope. I look forward to it. When that phone rings
> and I answer it, and they say, "This is your conference call," I'm happy. I'm
> like, O.K., well, here come my girls. I get to talk to my buddies.
> —An HIV-infected mother, in Wiener, Spencer, Davidson, & Fair, 1993

Technological progress has brought the world closer together in many
ways: International phone calls are clearer and more affordable; electronic
mail (e-mail) can be even faster and cheaper than the telephone if one
possesses the tools and skills to use it. Persons whose medical condition or
place of residence makes face-to-face communication with fellow sufferers
impossible find that the telephone and the computer can put them in touch
with comrades for the purpose of mutual aid. This chapter will briefly spell
out the fundamentals of using the telephone and computer for self help and
support.

TELEPHONE SUPPORT GROUPS

Literature on telephone support reveals that most telephone support
groups serve people who have debilitating diseases that make communication and travel to meeting places difficult (Rittner & Hammons, 1992;
Romness, Bruce, & Smith-Wilson, 1992; Stein, Rothman, & Nakanishi,
1993; Trang & Urbano, 1993). People in need often live in rural areas where
distance makes travel to meeting places too strenuous or caregiving duties
too demanding to allow meetings away from home (Meier, Galinsky, &
Rounds, 1995; Rounds, Galinsky, & Stevens, 1991) This section will

describe the mechanics of using the telephone for support groups; the typical composition of such groups; issues related to structure, format, and content; and some typical problems that may need attention.

Mechanics of Conference Calling

Telephone support groups use conference calling. There are several types of conference calls, and information about available options should be obtained from a carrier's conference call operator. The steps in setting up and facilitating a conference call begin with composing the group and forming a group contract with all members (discussed below). The mechanics are as follows:

1. Predetermine the time and day of the call with group members beforehand.
2. Call the telephone company business office and request a conference call operator (MCI # is 800-475-4700). You should do this no less than 15 minutes before the call. Inform the operator who is to be billed for the call.
3. Give the operator a list of numbers and the exact time of the call, and then hang up. As facilitator, you may want to ask the operator to make you the first person called so that you can greet other members of the group as they come on the line. Because it takes a few minutes for the operator to connect all callers, you should help those already connected to make small talk during this period (Bertcher, 1994; Stein et al., 1993)

Conference calling costs vary considerably. Bertcher (personal communication, December 15, 1995) advised that it is possible to pay less than $75.00 for a one-hour call with six group members and two facilitators, but this may take some shopping around. Romness et al. (1992) reported that Multiple Sclerosis groups of up to 10 members met by telephone for an average of $150 an hour. Wiener et al. (1993) gave the cost of a conference call as $.49 per minute per person with an additional set up charge of $3.50 through AT&T Tel-conferencing. In November 1995, MCI quoted a rate of $.47 per minute per connection during the week and $.25 per minute per connection on weekends. Costs can be spread among the members or billed to one number depending on type of call. Most such groups meet for 1 hour to 1 hour and 15 minutes.

Stein et al. (1993) recommended that practitioners who will be involved in telephone support prepare for it by simulating a conference call among colleagues in order to gain comfort with this method of contact. Bertcher (1994) advises that it is very important for all parties in the group to be able to be free at the time of the call and that all members must be able to participate every time it meets.

Group Composition

Because the nature of a conference call limits conversational cues, and to assure an opportunity for all to participate, experienced leaders suggest that the groups be quite small, from 3 to 5 in number (Rittner & Hammons, 1992). Others, however, have included up to 10 or 12 members (Bertcher, personal communication, December 15, 1995; Romness et al., 1992). Most groups close membership (i.e., the leaders do not add new members once the group begins). Some practitioners report that age similarity, as well as problem correspondence, is important; most groups described in the literature were highly homogeneous (Rittner & Hammons, 1992; Rounds, Galinsky, & Stevens, 1991; Stein et al., 1993; Wiener et al., 1993). Group members with incapacitating illnesses must also be assessed for ability to hold the phone, for verbal and cognitive skills, and for willingness to commit themselves to the process for the time period. Some group leaders recommend amplifiers or speaker phones for those who are unable to hold the phone and for comfort (Bertcher, 1994); others recommend against using speaker phones in favor of an inexpensive shoulder apparatus that holds the phone in place (Stein et al., 1993).

Structure and Content

The typical duration of closed, short term groups is 6 to 12 weeks, although Romness et al. (1992) report that multiple sclerosis groups have continued for years. Most groups described in the recent literature met weekly for a limited time period (Meier et al., 1995; Rittner & Hammons, 1992). A group for late-stage AIDS patients for whom memory and cognitive loss were problems required more frequent meetings (Rittner & Hammons, 1992). One author recommended a meeting period of 1 month (Wiener et al., 1993), another recommended 10 weeks (Stein et al., 1993), and yet another (Bertcher, personal communication, December 15, 1995) reports that government-funded telephone social clubs of the remotely rural elderly in Australia have met for years with no set termination date.

A group may be structured and topic-centered or unstructured and spontaneous, depending on the desires of the members and, at least initially, the approach of the professional who organized it. For AIDS patients and caregivers, typical themes were confidentiality, philosophical and religious issues related to dying, how and what to tell people, safe sex, overprotection by family and friends, funeral arrangements, and the meaning of life and death. Late stage AIDS patients revealed their anticipated date of death, and for them this was a core subject. Feelings about isolation and losses are typical discussion topics (Meier et al., 1995; Rittner & Hammons, 1992).

The first meeting of the group should include a discussion of its purpose, ground rules for the meetings, and introductions by all members. The purpose may be to accomplish a task, but more often the goals are supportive and social. Some groups exchange phone numbers, addresses, and pictures in the beginning; others do so at termination; and some never do so. By the second meeting, there should be some discussion of termination. At a later meeting, but not the last one, termination should again be raised for discussion.

Problems and Special Issues

Telephone group leaders should make efforts to help members hold down background noise during the time of the call and to disable or ignore call waiting during the meeting time. Talking while someone else is speaking is even more disruptive in a telephone conference call than in face-to-face situations, and a wise leader may contract with the group that reminders about this will be respected rather than resented. Interruptions can be minimized by setting the expectation that each time anyone speaks, he or she identify who is talking: "This is Harvey. Now I think . . . "

A typical group problem is members who monopolize the group's time; another is members who say nothing. Bertcher (1994) recommends that the facilitator have a list of the members at hand and, as each speaks, place a checkmark next to that individual's name. If one member talks a lot and another not at all, the facilitator may invite the nontalker to contribute. One helpful method of clarifying expectations is to create a written contract to be signed by each member before the group actually begins. This contract specifies the times, dates, dos-and-don'ts, charges if any, and names of the group's facilitators.

The telephone conference call offers great potential for practitioners, especially those who work with severely physically disabled individuals or those who inhabit areas of low population density. Another alternative, when face-to-face meeting is impossible, is to use the computer in much the same way as the telephone is used. The next section will address the ways in which computers have entered the self-help/support group scene.

ON-LINE GROUPS

The personal computer is another tool for overcoming some of the traditional barriers to group participation: no local group available, lack of transportation or time for travel, rarity of the condition, limitations of severe physical disability (Adam & Hoehne, 1989; Weinberg, Uken,

Schmale, & Adamek, 1995). Though far less common than telephones, home computers meet a greater variety of needs, making it possible for people to connect in new ways, not only in simultaneous participation, but in discussion threads that almost take on the form of a self-help group in slow motion. On-line participatory comments can be thoughtfully prepared off-line before being posted and thus are "often richer than real-time meeting exchanges" (Madara, 1995). Seizing on these advantages, a bare decade into the era of general on-line access, over a thousand self-help and support groups connect people with one another in this way.

The modem-equipped computer can also be a source of education about disabilities, providing information to both sufferers and interested professionals. A frequently forgotten population, homebound caregivers, can use a computer to find both prompt support and specific information (Brennan, Moore, & Smyth, 1991). Nor is the use of this new technology limited to the young, as Furlong (1989) details in her study, "An Electronic Community for Older Adults: The SeniorNet Network." But technology is a two-edged tool, and even more than in the case of the telephone, the personal computer can both help and hinder group process. The rest of this chapter will briefly address these potentials, noting both the advantages and the drawbacks of on-line groups.

Types of On-Line Groups and Access

Usenet, e-mail, bulletin boards, chat rooms, Internet Relay Chat (IRC), the World Wide Web, MOOs, and MUDs—by the time this is published, there are sure to be even more methods of electronic communication. First, then, we will provide a general overview; after that, some specific suggestions to help the reader help clients.

On-line resources can be accessed by anyone who has the necessary hardware (computer and modem) and software (a communications program and access), without the intervention of a social worker or other professional (Finn & Lavitt, 1994; Madara, 1993). Professionals can also use on-line communication to establish closed support groups with defined populations and to set agendas. These resemble the telephone conference except that messages can be posted any time of the day or night and as often as one desires (Weinberg, Schmale, et al., 1995; Finn, 1995).

Helping professionals may connect to on-line networks to obtain up-to-date information about available groups (as well as about other organizations and resources). In an increasingly common format, the Illinois Self-Help Center uses the World Wide Web to offer a model example of a local referral net plus connections ("links") to broader information sources. (As of this date, the web-literate may find this resource at http://www.prairienet.org/community/health/selfhelp/homepage.html.)

Some of the groups mentioned in this book (e.g., NAMI) maintain formal information resources on-line. Other groups, such as the Alzheimer's Association, offer World Wide Web homepages that provide hypertext links to an immense variety of literature and other resources. ("Hypertext" refers to highlighted words or images that, when chosen by keyboard arrow or mouse-click, connect directly with another resource without the necessity of typing in or even knowing its address.) Still other groups, such as Alcoholics Anonymous, have, in addition to an officially provided homepage, information furnished unofficially and informally by members.

Accessing Existing
Self-Help Conferences

Assuming that one has a modem-equipped computer and communications software, there are four main ways to connect with on-line resources. In order of likely preference and availability as of mid-1996, these are

1. commercial services (e.g., CompuServe, America Online), which will usually include "chat rooms" as well as "bulletin boards" and may offer wide Internet access or access to the World Wide Web or both;
2. direct access to the World Wide Web, via commercial Internet service providers or bundled software offered by manufacturers such as IBM or Microsoft;
3. internet access via institutional on-line service—employer, school, military;
4. direct dial-in connection to individual private Bulletin Board Systems (BBSs).

Bulletin Board Systems have been around the longest, and access to them is also offered by free services that make available hundreds of free BBSs that operate through international exchanges such as Fidonet. A person connects to all of these services in the same way, by modem-dialing a telephone number; but each Bulletin Board has its own telephone number rather than being reached through a service or provider. Most introductory pages, the first one to appear on your computer screen, are well laid out and offer clear instructions on how to access the choices available.

There are hundreds of BBSs focused on health issues. Because Bulletin Boards come and go, and telephone numbers change, it is most convenient to request a list of some 300 health-related BBSs from Ed Del Grosso, P.O.

Box 632, Collegeville, PA 19426. The mailed list costs $5.00; it can be downloaded free of charge from the Black Bag BBS at 610/454-7396.

On-line forums, however accessed, have three capabilities: message boards, database libraries, and conversational live-conferencing (White & Madara, 1995). Although BBSs are useful as message boards and information centers, little actual dialogue takes place on them. The commercial services carry many on-line forums adapted to conversational interchange. In each forum, one applies for membership and then can exchange electronic mail messages with all members as well as with specific individuals. For example, CompuServe provides access to the Diabetes Forum (over 18,000 members in 1994). The Self-Help Sourcebook (White & Madara, 1995; available on-line at http://www.cmhc.com/Selfhelp/) includes information on how to access some of the groups and how to obtain information about others.

Another way to connect with an on-line self-help group is through the World Wide Web using a net browser such as Netscape. This is especially useful if you do not know the name or BBS telephone number of a group for your situation. Using the browser, you can click on key words ["links"] and follow paths leading to the information you want. Although Web search tools and index lists change rapidly, with new and more powerful ones always appearing, at the time of this writing, Alta Vista,© accessed at http://www.altavista.digital.com, and Yahoo!®, accessed at http://www.yahoo.com, are among the most useful.

Of more direct help, the homepage of the American Self-Help Clearinghouse, when it came on line in mid-1996, offered links to over 800 self-help groups. Many people also find useful "Dr. John M. Grohol's Psychology and Support Groups Newspointer." And the *Argus/University of Michigan Clearinghouse for Subject-Oriented Internet Resource Guides* contains a "Guide to Internet Resources on Emotional Support: Physical Loss, Chronic Illness, and Bereavement" that offers comprehensive, yet compactly presented, information. The table of contents to this guide and the URLs of these and other resources are reproduced at the conclusion of this chapter.

Participating in Groups in Progress

Most groups operate via LISTSERVs, server-machines that send messages to a list of people who sign onto them because of a shared interest. There are both "open" and "moderated" lists. Anyone can subscribe to an open list by sending a SUBSCRIBE command to the LISTSERV address, a simple process explained in any elementary Internet guide as well as in the *Argus/University of Michigan Guide,* which also contains LISTSERV addresses for the groups that use this format. Participating in a moderated group requires gaining access to the group through its moderator, whose e-mail address may be published with the LISTSERV address, as in the Argus/University of Michigan Guide.

Although resources exist such as IRC ("Internet Relay Chat," which allows simultaneous on-screen communication), live participation in groups generally requires subscribing to a commercial service. Live conferencing takes place in "chat" mode. Some forums hold moderated "meetings" at specified times. These meetings, announced through the message board, are established by a moderator who acts as an on-line group leader. For example, the Health and Fitness Forum on CompuServe hosts weekly meetings of many Twelve-Step groups. Some of these live groups are limited to those who have preregistered; others are open to anyone. Several on-line Alcoholics Anonymous and other Twelve-Step groups hold such meetings, which can be found by following links from "Substance Abuse" in PsychWeb (http://www.gasou.edu/psychweb/resource/selfhelp.htm).

Although some conferences and LISTSERVS are "closed," in that they require application and acceptance to be admitted or put on the mailing list, it is generally possible to read the messages posted in most forums without participating. This is known as "lurking." One may lurk in live meetings, but one's presence is generally known, and the moderator may acknowledge it by asking for comment. Lurking on LISTSERVs and e-mail is easier and does not hold the risk of being asked to participate. Although researchers have been examining interactions on e-mail by lurking and downloading messages for analysis for some time (Finn & Lavitt, 1994; Salem, Bogat, & Reid, 1996), questions have recently been raised about the ethics of this practice (King, 1996). Salem et al.(1996) offer a concise footnote explaining the reasoning behind their own method. Anyone interested in following this discussion, as well as others related to research, is urged to subscribe to the SLFHLP-L list by sending the message <SUBSCRIBE SLFHLP-L yourfirstname yoursurname> to <listserv@listserv.utoronto.ca>. If you have any questions about the technicalities of using this discussion group, contact the list administrator at SLFHLP-L-REQUEST@listserv.utoronto.ca.

Little research has been published about on-line self-help groups, although several studies are in progress. Weinberg, et al. (1995) found several of Yalom's therapeutic factors present in a computer support group for victims of breast cancer. Salem et al. (1996) summarize other research in setting the context for their content analysis of two random, nonconsecutive weeks' postings to a newsgroup for persons suffering from depression.

An earlier report (Finn & Lavitt, 1994) presented findings based on analysis of one month's messages from five groups for survivors of sexual abuse. This study examined gender interaction patterns and group processes. Salem et al. focused on gender participation and message content. Both studies found evidence that although the on-line communications challenged some stereotypes, groups tended to reflect norms similar to those of face-to-face groups. Finn and Lavitt, who studied different conferences, noted that the abuse conferences differed on who participated. Some allowed participation by perpetrators of abuse, others did not. Members of cults and similar enthusiasts were not welcome in the conferences. One conference discouraged, but did not bar, nonsurvivor professionals.

Protocols and Customs of On-Line Groups

The absence not only of face-to-face presence, but even of tone of voice, means that on-line communication diminishes the ability to convey emotion as well as certain forms of humor. Users have therefore devised work-arounds, ways to overcome this. Most common is the para-language of "smileys" and abbreviations.

Emotions on the Net (and Other Shortcuts)

Although booklets on the subject have been published by the more (and less) imaginative, we will be content to offer a basic list of fundamental "Smileys," also called "emoticons":

:-)	basic happy smiley
;-)	winky smiley
>;–>	devilish winky smiley
:-(	sad, sorry smiley
:-o	oh,oh smiley
:-I	non-committal smiley
>:-@	angry smiley
:-P	Nyahhh . . . smiley

In addition, to save space and rest fingers, an accepted list of abbreviations, or Net-Lingo has evolved. Some common abbreviations found in mail notices are the following:

FWIW	=	for what it's worth
GOK	=	God only knows

HHOK	=	Ha, ha,—only kidding
HHOS	=	Ha, ha—only serious
IMHO	=	In my humble opinion
LOL	=	Laughing out loud
OTOH	=	On the other hand
BTW	=	By the way
YHGTBK	=	You have got to be kidding
ROTFL	=	Rolling on the floor laughing

Specific "netiquette" rules—such as that the use of all capital letters is akin to raucous shouting—supplement the usual norms about what topics may be discussed, the use of profanity, and the degree to which members can discuss "off topics" issues. Conflictual responses — "flaming"— violate an on-line social norm. Although informal group social pressures usually suffice, such norms can also be enforced by the group's moderator. If after repeated warnings a member continues to violate norms, it is possible to eliminate that person's participation.

Self-help forums have proliferated in the last several years. They exist on private, commercial, and public networks in such a constant state of flux that all will have a new reality by the time this book is published. They can be quite large, as suggested by the 1994 membership of over 18,000 in the Diabetes Forum. But computer-based groups may also be quite small, with closed membership and more traditional leadership.

Weinberg et al. (1995), for example, set up a private bulletin board for a support group of six breast-cancer patients and one leader. The group was to last for three months, its purpose announced as discussing member concerns about their medical situation or personal issues related to their illness. Members were encouraged to use the bulletin board regularly and to check for messages "every day or so" (p.50). After one month, the group's leader, deeming that some members had participated too seldom, telephoned them to encourage more frequent use of the group, an intervention that proved effective. In general, in discussing their medical situations, members avoided offering advice or factual information, concentrating instead on supportive exchanges.

Advantages Of and
Dangers In On-Line Self-Help

On-line self-help participation has several advantages beyond the obvious one of accessibility by people unable to travel to community groups. One can participate in most groups anonymously. E-mail can be sent or received at any time of the day and night, as and when one needs or wants to communicate. It can take place in the home, where the setting is likely to be more comfortable. Exchanges can be interrupted by other tasks without affecting the quality of the communication. On-line self-help groups do not require oral fluency, although individuals have to be able to express themselves in writing and be able to type on a keyboard. (There are exceptional technologies for some who are physically unable to do so.) For people with rare conditions, computers and telephones may be the only way currently available to contact scattered others who share that condition. For example, in 1995 there were no community groups for veterans with Persian Gulf Syndrome, but there were Friday night meetings for this population on America Online (White & Madara, 1995).

On-line communication is even more egalitarian than face-to-face community self help (White & Madara, 1995). One's clothes, car, appearance, age, race, accent, gender, and social status are invisible. Some limitations of the technology, such as the expression of emotions, can be overcome with the creative use of keyboard signals. The availability of many members can diffuse dependency needs so as not to overburden a few individuals.

In addition to providing information, social support, and shared experience, on-line groups can organize advocacy for disabled populations (Brennan, Ripich, & Moore, 1991; Brennan, Moore, & Smythe, 1991; Furlong, 1989; Gustafson et al., 1993; Peterson & Rippey, 1992). They can convey a group's ideology, implicitly as well as explicitly. They also facilitate research and consumer feedback through the analysis of messages, although the ethics of who, how, what, when, where, and under what conditions to do so have not yet been sufficiently studied.

Finally, for professionals, the way in which self help on-line takes the form of a "group in slow motion" (Madara, 1995) opens new educational horizons. Student facilitators, for example, can review messages with a supervisor before posting responses, thus benefiting from closer exposure to concrete reality in learning about group process (Weinberg, Schmale, Uken, & Wessel, 1995).

There are, of course, also disadvantages. Glitches in new software and the occasional erratic performance of telephone-line technology can strain the patience of people already emotionally stressed. High cost and the need for technical skills can restrict access to on-line groups by low-income and less-educated individuals. There are relatively simple ways to compensate for some of these, at least in part—for example, by having public terminals available in places such as post offices and public libraries, especially in low-income communities.

But there are other, less obvious, and possibly more perilous disadvantages. A person in crisis may post a cry for help that will be ignored by an anonymous mass of subscribers. Finn and Lavitt (1994), who analyzed on-line groups for sexual abuse survivors, speculated that personal stories revealed on-line may be too superficial to evoke genuine empathy. Further, group moderators are not regulated or trained. Through ignorance or malice, false information may be posted (Gilbert, 1996). In addition, members could be victimized by lurkers bent on exploitation. If it is more difficult to assess wealth and status electronically, it is also more difficult to judge honesty. An emotionally vulnerable population may be at special peril here. Information theorists point to research suggesting that correspondents tend to risk levels of intimacy far more rapidly on-line than in face-to-face relationships (King, 1994; Leslie 1994). Finally, on-line communications lack guarantees of privacy. Indexer programs, for example, can search, list, and make publicly available virtually any message to a Usenet group. Both professionals and consumers need to keep in mind that anything typed at a computer keyboard may become public knowledge. This added vulnerability decreases the likelihood that on-line groups will ever replace face-to-face gatherings.

IMPLICATIONS
FOR PRACTITIONERS

The application of computer technology to self-help and support groups is so new that little is known about the outcome and processes of on-line groups. What is obvious is that the rapid growth of this medium in a few short years makes the development of community self help over the previous 20 years seem minuscule in comparison. The technological revolution is running at top speed, and practitioners are racing to catch up with it. For those who wish to explore on their own more extensively, we conclude this chapter by pointing to three different resources:

1. Those searching for self-help resources via the World Wide Web will find a rich and well-linked means of access in the homepage of Ed Madara's New Jersey-based American Self-Help Clearinghouse: http://www.cmhc.com/selfhelp/.

2. Among print resources, by far the most thorough, as well as the most recent, is Dr. Tom Ferguson's (1996) *Health Online: How to Go Online to Find Health Information, Support Forums, and Self-Help Communities in Cyberspace* (Addison-Wesley 1996).

3. Those interested in the nature and future of on-line communities will find thought-provoking Howard Rheingold's (1993) *The Virtual Community,*

which, if accessed on-line, at http://www.well.com/user/hlr, links also to the further musings of a stimulating thinker.

But for most already overburdened human service professionals, perhaps the wisest course is to realize that there are information professionals who can apply their expertise to the service of ours. Obtaining such help need not be costly or necessitate an adventure into the esoteric innards of the world of microprocessors. Virtually every public library has, or soon will have, at least one staff member trained to help professionals make use of the information afforded by the new electronic techonolgies.

CONCLUSION

This chapter on telephone and on-line groups brings us to the conclusion of this book. It is fitting that this work end by acknowledging a new beginning—the rise of technologically-enhanced self help and support. In another 10 years, researchers and academics will likely meet with practitioners to assess the significance of support and self help in the electronic community. Meanwhile, practitioners should begin and continue to experiment with telephone support and on-line self help. Researchers must find ethical ways to examine self help in these contexts and to disseminate knowledge about how these resources might be used, the dangers inherent in them, and methods for making them available to everyone who can benefit from them.

DISCUSSION QUESTION

Discuss the ethics of lurking, especially by researchers. How can process research take place on on-line without violating the rights of the individuals who use on-line systems?

GROUP EXERCISE

In a small group, decide that you represent a group of practitioners who plan to develop a telephone or an on-line support group. Identify a population to target and develop a plan for implementing your support group. Identify each of the steps you must take to see the group in progress.

ASSIGNMENTS

1. Identify a problem situation that you or someone you know is presently encountering. Log on to your computer and modem (or one available to students in the university) and access Internet, the World Wide Web, or a Bulletin Board system. Obtain information about a group that deals with your problem. Describe the process you went through to get this information in a short paper along with copies of material you retrieved from the group. If possible, become part of an electronic mail exchange and exchange messages with members of the group. Report your efforts in class discussion.

2. Seek out the electronic information specialist in your local public library. Make an appointment with him or her and ask for help in finding an appropriate group for some particular client, real or imagined. Explore and evaluate how much help of this kind may be available to you in the future from this source.

HELPFUL HINTS

Computer resources and resource availability change weekly, even daily. Most standard indexes and search engines are not well designed for purposes such as those of persons interested in self-help and support groups. Thus, here are some practical suggestions that seem likely to stand the test of time:

1. If you have a telephone number or address, electronic or otherwise, of some group or service, and you have difficulty contacting it, check with Ed Madara at the American Self-Help Clearinghouse, St. Clares-Riverside Medical Center, Denville, NJ 07834; FAX 201/625-8848; or by e-mail to EdMadara@aol.com. A listing of resources is also available on line from this source at http://www.cmhc.com/selfhelp/.

2. If you wish to explore whether a group exists for some condition or situation, and the American Self-Help Clearinghouse is not of help, check the Argus/University of Michigan's Clearinghouse for Subject-Oriented Internet Emotional Support Guide at:
   http://asa.ugl.lib.umich.edu/chdocs/support/emotion.html.

3. Those interested in more exploring on their own may usefully begin with two World Wide Web addresses:

   – The PSYCHWEB list "Psychology Self-help Resources on the Internet" at http://www.gasou.edu/psychweb/resource/selfhelp.htm

- "Dr. John M. Grohol's Mental Health Page" at
  http://www.coil.com/7Egrohol/

Although no assurances are possible concerning either the continued existence or continued usefulness of these sources, what succeeds them will likely be richer rather than poorer in resources.

To facilitate familiarization with the range of resources available on line, a portion of the Table of Contents of the ASCII version of the Argus/University of Michigan Clearinghouse for Subject-Oriented Internet Resource Guide's list of Internet Emotional Support Resources is reproduced below. Devised and maintained by professional librarians, this resource seems more likely than many others to be maintained in up-to-date fashion with accurate information.

Argus/University of Michigan Clearinghouse Guide: Internet Emotional Support Resources: http://asa.ugl.lib.umich.edu/chdocs/support/emotion.html

Table Of Contents

1.0 Introduction
2.0 General Physical Loss, Chronic Illness, and Bereavement Resources
    2.1 Griefnet
    2.2 Regional Resource Directories
    2.3 Caregiver Information
    2.4 Other Guides
3.0 Physical Loss Resources
    3.1 General Disability Resources
    3.2 Amputation
    3.3 Blindness
    3.4 Deafness
    3.5 Facial Disfigurement
    3.6 Organ Transplants
    3.7 Traumatic Brain Injury
4.0 Chronic Illness Resources
    4.1 General Chronic Illness Resources
    4.2 AIDS / HIV
    4.3 Alzheimer's Disease
    4.4 Arthritis
    4.5 Autism
    4.6 Autoimmune Disorders - General
    4.7 Brain Tumors

Appendix

SELF-HELP CLEARINGHOUSES

U.S. Self-Help Clearinghouses

ARIZONA

Rainy Day People, P.O. Box 472, Scottsdale, AZ 85252. Call 800-352-3792 (in AZ) or (602) 231-0868.

ARKANSAS

Helpline, P.O. Box 9028, Jonesboro, AR 72403-9028. Call (501) 932-5555.

CALIFORNIA

Mental Health Association, 8912 Volunteer Lane, Suite 210, Sacramento, CA 95826-3221. Call (916) 368-3100; FAX: (916) 368-3104.

Mental Health Association of Yolo County, P.O. Box 447, Davis, CA 95617. Call (916) 756-8181.

Self-Help Connection, c/o Mental Health Association of San Diego County, 1202 Morena Blvd., Suite 203, San Diego, CA 92110. Call (619) 543-0412.

Self-Help Line of Mental Health Center, c/o Mental Health Association, 2398 Pine St., San Francisco, CA 94115. Call (415) 772-4357; FAX: (415) 921-1911.

Friends Network, 800 Scenic Dr., Modesto, CA 95350. Call (209) 558-7454.

CONNECTICUT

Connecticut Self-Help/Mutual Support Network, Consultation Center, 389 Whitney Ave., New Haven, CT 06511. Call (203) 624-6982; FAX: (203) 562-6355.

ILLINOIS

Self-Help Center, Mental Health Association in Illinois, 150 N. Wacker Dr., Suite 900, Chicago, IL 60606. Call (708) 291-0085 (group information); (312) 368-9070.

Self-Help Center, c/o Family Service, 405 S. State St., Champaign, IL 61820-5196. Call (217) 352-0099; FAX: (217) 352-9512; TDD: (217) 352-0160.

Macon County Support Group Network, Macon County Health Dept., 1221 E. Condit, Decatur, IL 62521. Call (217) 429-HELP.

Illinois Self-Help Center, Wright College, 3400 North Austin, Room 244, Chicago, IL 60634. Call (312) 481-8837; FAX: (312) 481-8903.

INDIANA - SEE MICHIGAN

IOWA

Iowa Pilot Parents Self-Help Clearinghouse, Iowa Pilot Parents, Inc., 33 N. 12th St., P.O. Box 1151, Fort Dodge, IA 50501. Call (515) 576-5870; 800-952-4777 (Iowa); FAX: (515) 576-8209.

KANSAS

Self-Help Network of Kansas, Wichita State University, Box 34, 1845 Fairmount, Wichita, KS 67260-0034. Call 800-445-0116 (in KS), or (316) 689-3843 (day); FAX: (316) 689-3086.

MASSACHUSETTS

Massachusetts Clearinghouse of Mutual Help Groups, University of Massachusetts, Massachusetts Cooperative Extension System, Dept. of Consumer Studies, 113 Skinner Hall, Amherst, MA 01003. Call (413) 545-2313; FAX: (413) 545-4410.

MARYLAND - SEE WASHINGTON, DC

MICHIGAN

Michigan Self-Help Clearinghouse, 106 W. Allegan, Suite 300, Lansing, MI 48933-1706. Call (517) 484-7373 or 800-777-5556 (in MI only); FAX: (517) 484-7373.

Center For Self-Help, c/o Riverwood Center, P.O. Box 547, Benton Harbor, MI 49023-0547. Call 800-336-0341 (in MI); (616) 925-0594; FAX: (616) 925-0070. (Serves Northwest Indiana).

MISSOURI

Mental Health Assn. of Kansas City, 7611 State Line Rd., Suite 230, Kansas City, MO 64114. Call (816) 822-7272 (24 hr. helpline); (Admin): (816) 822-7100; FAX: (816) 822-2388.

St. Louis Self-Help Clearinghouse, c/o Mental Health Assn. of Greater St. Louis, 1905 S. Grand, St. Louis, MO 63104. Call (314) 773-1399.

NEBRASKA

Nebraska Self-Help Information Services, c/o Barbara Fox, 1601 Euclid Ave., Lincoln, NE 68502. Call (402) 476-9668.

NEW HAMPSHIRE

New Hampshire HELPLINE, 2 Industrial Park Dr., Concord, NH 03301. Call 800-852-3388 (in NH) or (603) 225-9000; TDD/FAX: (603) 225-4033.

NEW JERSEY

New Jersey Self-Help Clearinghouse, Northwest Covenant Medical Center, 25 Pocono Rd., Denville, NJ 07834. Call (201) 625-7101; FAX: (201) 625-8848; TDD: (201) 625 9053.

NEW YORK

New York Self-Help Center, 120 West 57th St., New York, NY 10019. Call (212) 586-5770; FAX: (212) 956-1652.

Westchester Self-Help Clearinghouse, 456 North St., White Plains, NY 10605. Call (914) 949-0788 ext. 237 (voice mail); FAX: (914) 948-3783. (Can give statewide information).

Brooklyn Self-Help Clearinghouse, 30 Third Ave., Brooklyn, NY 11217. Call (718) 875-1420 and ask for "Brooklyn Self-Help Clearinghouse."

NORTH CAROLINA

SupportWorks Self-Help Clearinghouse, 1018 E. Blvd., Suite 5, Charlotte, NC 28203-5779. Call (704) 331-9500 (group information); (704) 377-2055 (Director); or FAX: (704) 332-2127.

NORTH DAKOTA

Hot Line, P.O. Box 447, Fargo, ND 58107-0447. Call (701) 235-SEEK.

OHIO

Greater Dayton Self-Help Clearinghouse, Family Service Association, 184 Salem Ave., Dayton, OH 45406. Call (513) 225-3004; FAX: (513) 222-3710; TDD: (513) 222-7921.

The Greater Toledo Self-Help Network, Harbor Behavioral Health Care, 123 22nd St., Toledo, OH 43624. Call Jodi Carter (419) 241-6191; FAX: (419) 255-5623.

OREGON

Northwest Regional Self-Help Clearinghouse, 619 S.W. 11 St., Room 300, Portland, OR 97205. Call (503) 222-5555 (Information & Referral); FAX: (503) 226-9385; (503) 226-9360 (Admin).

PENNSYLVANIA

Self Help Group Network of the Pittsburgh Area, 1323 Forbes Ave., Suite 200, Pittsburgh, PA 15219. Call (412) 261-5363; FAX: (412) 471-2722.

Shine, 528 Spruce St., Suite 420, Scranton, PA 18503. Call (717) 961-1234; FAX: (717) 348-5816.

SOUTH CAROLINA

Midland Area Support Group Network, Lexington Medical Center, 2720 Sunset Blvd., W. Columbia, SC 29169. Call (803) 791-2800 (information and referral); FAX: (803) 791-2299.

TENNESSEE

Mental Health Association of Greater Knoxville, 6712 Kingston Pike, Suite 203, Knoxville, TN 37919. Call (423) 584-9125 (Voice/FAX).

Self-Help Clearinghouse, Mental Health Assn., 2400 Poplar Ave., Suite 410, Memphis, TN 38112. Call (901) 323-8485; FAX: (901) 323-0858.

TEXAS

Dallas Self-Help Clearinghouse, Mental Health Assn. of Greater Dallas, 2929 Carlisle, Suite 350, Dallas, TX 75204. Call (214) 871-2420; FAX: (214) 954-0611.

Houston Area Self-Help Clearinghouse. Attn: Cheryl Amoroso, Mental Health Assn. in Houston and Harris County, 2211 Norfolk, Suite 810, Houston, TX 77098. Call (713) 523-8963(admin.) or (713) 522-5161 (information and referral); FAX: (713) 522-0698.

Mental Health Information Center, Mental Health Assn. in Greater San Antonio, 901 NE Loop 410, Suite 704, San Antonio, TX 78209. Call (210) 826-2288; FAX: (210) 826-9587.

Self-Help Clearinghouse for Tarrant County, MHA of Tarrant County, 3136 W. 4th St., Fort Worth, TX 76107-2113. Call (817) 335-5405; FAX: (817) 334-0025.

Texas Self-Help Clearinghouse, Mental Health Assn. in Texas, 8401 Shoal Creek Blvd., Austin, TX 78757. Call (512) 454-3706; FAX: (512) 454-3725.

UTAH

Utah Information and Referral Center, 1025 S. 700 West, Salt Lake City, UT 84104. Call Charles White (801) 978-3333.

VIRGINIA - SEE WASHINGTON, DC

WASHINGTON - SEE OREGON

WASHINGTON, DC

Self-Help Clearinghouse of Greater Washington, c/o MHA of Northern Virginia, 7630 Little River Turnpike, Suite 206, Annandale, VA 22003. Call (703) 941-5465; FAX: (703) 642-0803.

NATIONAL

American Self-Help Clearinghouse, Northwest Covenant Medical Center, 25 Pocono Rd., Denville, NJ 07834. Call (201) 625-7101; FAX: (201) 625-8848; TDD: (201) 625-9053.

National Self-Help Clearinghouse, CUNY, Graduate School and University Ctr., 25 W. 43rd St., Rm. 620, New York, NY 10036. Call (212) 354-8525; FAX: (212) 642-1956.

National Mental Health Consumers Self-Help Clearinghouse, 1211 Chestnut St., Philadelphia, PA 19107-4103. Call 800-553-4-KEY, FAX: (215) 735-0275.

National Empowerment Center, 20 Ballard Rd., Lawrence, MA 01843. Call (508) 685-1518 or 800-POWER-2-U; FAX: (508) 681-6426; TTY: 800-889-7693.

Self-Help Clearinghouses in Other Countries

ARGENTINA

Fundación Precavida Espinosa 1885, 2nd Floor "B" Capital Federal, Buenos Aires, Argentina. Phone: (011) 54-1-582-8680; FAX: (011) 54-1-951-5925.

AUSTRALIA

Western Institute of Self-Help, 80 Railway Street, Cottesloe, Western Australia 6011. Phone: (09) 383-3188; FAX: (09) 385-1476.

The Collective of Self-Help Groups, P.O. Box 251, Brunswick, East Victoria 3057, Australia. Phone: (03) 388-1777.

AUSTRIA

Servicestelle Für Selbsthilfegruppen, Schottenring 24 A-1160, Vienna, Austria. Phone: 0222/53-114/81223; FAX: 0222/53-114/9981221.

BELGIUM

Trefpunt Zelf Hulp, E. Van Evenstraat 2 C 3000, Leuven, Belgium. Phone: 0032-16-23-65-07; FAX: 0032-16-32-33-65.

CANADA

Self-Help Resource Center, 40 Orchard View Blvd., Suite 219 Toronto, Ontario Canada M4R 1B9. Phone: (416) 487-4355; FAX: (416) 487-0624 (Information for all of Canada).

The Self-Help Connection Mental Health Association, 63 King Street, Dartmouth, Nova Scotia, Canada B2Y 2R7. Phone: (902) 466-2011; FAX: (902) 466-3300.

Self-Help Resource Association of B.C. Winnipeg Self-Help Resource Clearinghouse NorWest Coop & Health Center 103-61, Tyndall Avenue, Winnipeg, Manitoba Canada R2X 2T4. Phone: (204) 589-5500 or (204) 633-5955.

Prince Edward Island Self-Help Clearinghouse Box 785 Charlottetown, PEI Canada C1A 7L9. Phone: (902) 566-3034; FAX: (902) 566-4643.

CROATIA

College of Nursing, University of Zagreb, Mlinarska 38 Y-41000, Zagreb, Croatia. Phone: (050) 28-666.

DENMARK

Lailos - National Tordenjkjoldsvei 20 3000, Helsinor, Denmark.

Center for Frivilligt Socialt Arbejde Pantheonsgade 5,3 5000 Odense C., Denmark. Phone: 66-14-60-61; FAX: 66-14-20-17.

Sr - Bistand Social Radgivning og Bistand Sortedam Dosseringen 3, st. th. 2200 Kobenhavn N, Denmark. Phone: 31-31-71-97.

Selvhjaelps-Grupper Centre in Kolding Vesterskovog 19 6091 Bjest, Denmark.

ENGLAND

The Self-Help Team, 20 Pelham Road, UK-Nottingham NG5 1AP, England, United Kingdon. Phone: 44-0115-969-1212; FAX: 44-1159-602049.

GERMANY

Nationale Kontakt-Und Informationsstelle Zur Anregung Und Unterstützung Von Selbsthilfegruppen (NAKOS), Albrecht-Achilles-Strasse 65 D-10709, Berlin, Germany. Phone: 30-891-4019; FAX: 30-893-4014.

Deutsche Arsseitsgemeinschaft Selbsthilfegruppen e.v. (DAG SHG), c/o Friedrichstrasse 28 D-6300, Giessen, Germany. Phone: 641-702-2478.

HUNGARY

Self-Help Groups Team National Committee of Mental Health, P.O. Box 39, H-1525, Budapest, Hungary.

ISRAEL

National Self-Help Clearinghouse, 37 King George Street, P.O. Box 23223, Tel-Aviv 61231, Israel. Phone: 03-299389.

JAPAN

The Osaka Self-Help Support Center, 6-998-3-3-225 Nakamozu-cho, Osaka 591, Japan. Phone: 722-57-3667; FAX: 722-54-6075.

Self-Help Clearinghouse for Children with Serious Diseases, Japan Welfare of Children & Families Association, Bancho Palace, Bldg. 2, Gobancho, Chiyoda-ku Tokyo, 102 Japan. Phone: 3-3261-3696; FAX: 3-3261-9249 Contact: Tomofumi Oka.

POLAND

Working Group of the Self-Help Movements, Dluga 38/40 00-238, Warszawa, Poland. Phone: 22-314551; FAX: 22-314712.

SPAIN

Institut Municipal de la Salut Pa. Lesseps, 1 08023, Barcelona, Spain.

SWEDEN

Distriktlakare (Lapland only), Villavagan 14 S-9390, Arjeplog, Sweden. Phone: 961-11230.

SWITZERLAND

Selbsthilfezentrum Hinderhuus Feldbergstrasse 55 CH-4057, Basel, Switzerland. Phone: 061-692-8100; FAX: 061-692-8177.

Team Selbsthillfe Zürich Wilfiedstrasse 7 CH-8032, Zürich, Switzerland. Phone: 01-252-3036.

Condensed and reprinted with permission from the American Self-Help Clearinghouse.

REFERENCES

Ablon, J. (1974). Al-Anon family groups: Impetus for change through the presentation of alternatives. *American Journal of Psychotherapy, 28,* 30-45.

Abramowitz, I. A., & Coursey, R. D. (1989). Impact of an educational support group on family participants who take care of their schizophrenic relatives. *Journal of Consulting and Clinical Psychology, 57*(2), 232-236.

Adam, D., & Hoehne, D. (1989). Mutual aid in remote areas: Addressing the obstacles. *Canada's Mental Health 37,* 18-21.

ADRDA. (1990). *Standing by you: Family support groups.* Chicago: Author.

ADRDA. (1993). *Alzheimer's Association: Factsheet.* (Available from the Alzheimer's Association, 919 N. Michigan Ave., Suite 1000, Chicago, IL 60611.)

ADRDA. (1995). *The Alzheimer's Association.* Chicago: Author.

Al-Anon Family Groups. (1966). *Al-Anon family groups.* New York: Author.

Al-Anon Family Groups. (1986). *First Steps: Al-Anon . . .36 years of beginnings.* New York: Author.

Al-Anon Family Groups. (1993). *Who are the members of Al-Anon and Alateen? 1993 Survey.* New York: Author.

Al-Anon Family Groups. (1995). *'95 Summary: Al-Anon Family Groups world service conference.* New York: Author.

Alcoholics Anonymous. (1952). *Twelve steps and twelve traditions.* New York: Alcoholics Anonymous World Services.

Alcoholics Anonymous. (1989). *Analysis of the 1986 survey of the membership of AA.* New York: General Service Office.

Alcoholics Anonymous World Services. (1996, June-July). Estimates of groups and members as of January 1, 1996. *Box 459: News and Notes from the General Service Office of AA, 42*(3), 3.

Alcoholics Anonymous World Services (n.d.). *CPC workbook: Cooperation with the professional community.* New York: General Service Office.

Alcoholics Anonymous World Services (n.d.). *Treatment facilities workbook.* New York: General Service Office.

Alcoholics Anonymous World Services. (1957). *Alcoholics Anonymous comes of age.* New York: Author.

Alcoholics Anonymous World Services. (1976). *Alcoholics Anonymous: The story of how many thousands of men and women have recovered from alcoholism.* New York: Author.

Alcoholics Anonymous World Services. (1984). *Pass it on: The story of Bill Wilson and how the AA message reached the world.* New York: Author.

Alcoholics Anonymous World Services. (1986). *The twelve concepts for world service illustrated.* New York: Author.

Alcoholics Anonymous World Services. (1990). *The AA group: Where it all begins* (Rev. ed.). New York: Author.

Alcoholics Anonymous World Services. (1992). Alcoholics Anonymous 1992 membership survey. New York: Author.

Alcoholics Anonymous World Services. (1995, June-July). Estimates of groups and members as of January 1, 1995. *Box 459: News and Notes from the General Service Office of AA, 41*(3), 3.

Alford, G. S., Koehler, R. A., & Leonard, J. (1991). Alcoholics Anonymous-Narcotics Anonymous model inpatient treatment of chemically dependent adolescents: A 2-year outcome study. *Journal of Studies on Alcohol, 52*(2), 118-126.

Anderson, D. B., & Shaw, S. L. (1994). Starting a support group for families and partners of people with HIV/AIDS in rural settings. *Social Work, 39*(1), 135-138

Antze, P. A. (1979). The role of ideologies in peer psychotherapy groups. In M. A. Lieberman & L. Borman (Eds.), *Self-help groups for coping with crisis* (pp. 272-304). San Francisco: Jossey-Bass.

Arkin, R. M., & Burger, J. M. (1980). Effects of unit relation tendencies on interpersonal attraction. *Social Psychology Quarterly, 43*, 380-391.

Auslander, B. A., & Auslander, G. K. (1988). Self-help groups and the family service agency. *Social Casework, 69*, 74-80.

Bailey, M. (1965). Al-Anon family groups as an aid to wives of alcoholics. *Social Work, 10*, 68-74.

Barouh, G. (1992). *Support groups: The human face of the HIV/AIDs epidemic.* Huntington Station, NY: Long Island Association for AIDS Care, Inc.

Bateson, G. (1972). *Steps to an ecology of the mind.* San Francisco: Chandler Publishing.

Bauman, L. J., Gervey, R., & Siegel, K. (1992). Factors associated with cancer patients' participation in support groups. *Journal of Psychosocial Oncology, 10*(3), 1-20.

Beckman, L. (1993). Alcoholics Anonymous and gender issues. In B. S. McCrady & W. R. Miller (Eds.), *Research on Alcoholics Anonymous: Opportunities and alternatives* (pp. 233-248). New Brunswick, NJ: Rutgers Center for Alcohol Studies.

Bernstein, A. (n.d.). *How to build shared leadership.* Denville, NJ: New Jersey Self-help Clearinghouse.

Bertcher, H. (1994). *Tell-A-Group: How to set up and operate group work by telephone.* (Available from Harvey Bertcher, The University of Michigan School of Social Work, Ann Arbor, MI 48109.)

Bittle, W. E. (1982). Alcoholics Anonymous and the gay alcoholic. *Journal of Homosexuality, 7*(4), 81-88.

Bond, G., McDonel, E. C., Miller, L. D., & Pensec, M. (1991). Assertive community treatment and reference groups: An evaluation of their effectiveness for young adults with serious mental illness and substance abuse problems. *Psychosocial Rehabilitation Journal, 15*, 31-43.

Borkman, T. (1990). Experiential, professional, and lay frames of reference. In T. J. Powell (Ed.), *Working with self-help* (pp. 3-30). Silver Spring, MD: NASW Press.

Borkman, T. (1991). Introduction to the special issue. *American Journal of Community Psychology, 19*(5), 643-650.

Borkman, T. (1995, June 15-17). *Viewing mutual help groups as experientially-based commons in the voluntary sector: Beyond the human service paradigm.* Paper presented at the Community Psychology Biennial conference, Chicago, IL.

Borkman, T. (1996). *Experiential learning in self-help groups.* Manuscript submitted for publication.

Borkman, T., & Schubert, M. (1995). Participatory action research as a strategy for studying self-help groups internationally. In F. Lavoie, T. Borkman, & B. Gidron (Eds.), *Self-help and mutual aid groups: International and multicultural perspectives* (pp.45-68). New York: Haworth.

Borman, L. D. (1980). The professional as facilitator: Helping self-help groups help themselves. *D. D. Polestar,* newletter of Developmental Disabilities Training Systems and Technical Resource Center-Region II, 1 (9), 7.

Bouricius, J. K., Kersten, E., Nagy, M., McCartney, P. L., & Stein, R. (1994). Family support groups—AMI of Western Mass. Style. *Innovations and Research, 3*(3), 33-40.

Brennan, P. F., Moore, S. M., & Smyth, K. A. (1991). ComputerLink: Electronic support for the home caregiver. *Advances in Nursing Science, 13*(4), 14-27.

Brennan, P. F., Ripich, S., & Moore, S. M. (1991). The use of home-based computers to support persons living with AIDS/ARC. *Journal of Community Health Nursing, 8*(1), 3114.

Browne, B. R. (1991). The selective adaptation of the Alcoholics Anonymous program by Gamblers Anonymous. *Journal of Gambling Studies, 7*(3), 187-206.

Browne, B. R. (1994). Really not God: Secularization and pragmatism in Gamblers Anonymous. *Journal of Gambling Studies, 10*(3), 247-260.

Budman, S. H. (1975). A strategy for preventive mental health intervention. *Professional Psychology, 6*, 394-398.

CCCF. (n.d.a). *Twenty-five years of candlelighters milestones.* (Available from CCCF, 7910 Woodmont Ave, Suite 460, Bethesda, MD, 20814.)

CCCF. (n.d.b). *Candlelighters Childhood Cancer Foundation: Ombudsman Program.* (Available from CCCF, 7910 Woodmont Ave, Suite 460, Bethesda, MD, 20814.)

CCCF. (1995a). Statement of purpose. *Candlelighters Quarterly Newsletter, 20*(2), 2.

CCCF. (1995b). *Ombudsman program overview.* (Available from CCCF, 7910 Woodmont Ave, Suite 460, Bethesda, MD, 20814.)

Carey, D., Griffin, K., & Hastings, J. (1992). Alzheimer's patients: strength in numbers. *Health, 8*, 22-23.

Chamberlin, J., Rogers, E. S., & Ellison, M. L. (1996). Self-help programs: A description of their characteristics and their members. *Psychiatric Rehabilitation Journal, 19*(3), 33-42.

Cherniss, C., & Cherniss, D. S. (1987). Professional involvement in self-help groups for parents of high-risk newborns. *American Journal of Community Psychology, 15*, 435-444.

Chesler, M. A. (1990). The "dangers" of self-help groups: Understanding and challenging professionals' views. In T. J. Powell, *Working with self-help* (pp. 301-324). Silver Spring, MD: NASW Press.

Chesler, M. A. (1991). Participatory action research with self-help groups: An alternative paradigm for inquiry and action. *American Journal of Community Psychology, 19*(5), 757-768.

Chesler, M. A., & Chesney, B. K. (1995). *Cancer and self-help: Bridging the troubled waters of childhood illness.* Madison, WI: University of Wisconsin Press.

Chesney, B. K., & Chesler, M. A. (1993). Activism through self-help group members: Reported life changes of parents of children with cancer. *Small Group Research, 24*(2), 258-273.

Chesney, B. K., Rounds, K. A., & Chesler, M. A. (1989). Support for parents of children with cancer: The value of self-help groups. *Social Work with Groups, 12*(4), 119-139.

Christo, G., & Franey, C. (1995). Drug users' spiritual beliefs, locus of control and disease concept in relation to Narcotics Anonymous attendance and six-month outcomes. *Drug and Alcohol Dependence, 38,* 51-56.

Christo, G., & Sutton, S. (1994). Anxiety and self-esteem as a function of abstinence time among recovering addicts attending Narcotics Anonymous. *British Journal of Clinical Psychology, 33*(2), 198-200.

Clore, G. L., and Byrne, D. (1974). A reinforcement-affect model of attraction. In T. Huston (Ed.), *Foundations of interpersonal attraction.* New York: Academic Press.

Cohn, A. H. (1979). Effective treatment of child abuse and neglect. *Social Work, 24*(6), 419-513.

Collier, G. (1991, May). The essential role of language in the Recovery method. Paper presented at the Conference on Mental Illness, Stigma, and Self-Help, Chicago, IL.

Coremblum, B., & Fischer, D. G. (1975). Some correlates of Al-Anon group membership. *Journal of Studies on Alcohol, 36*(5), 675-677.

Cutter, C. G. (1985). How do people change in Al-Anon? Reports of adult children of alcoholics. (Doctoral dissertation, Brandeis University, 1985) *University Microfilms International,* 85-18894.

Cutter, C. G., & Cutter, H. S. G. (1987). Experience and change in Al-Anon Family Groups: Adult children of alcoholics. *Journal of Studies on Alcohol, 48*(1), 29-32.

Davidson, H. (1979). Development of a bereaved parents groups. In M. A. Lieberman & L. D. Borman, *Self-help groups for coping with crisis: Origins, members, processes, and impact* (pp. 80-94). San Francisco: Jossey-Bass.

Ditman, K. S., Crawford, G. G., Forgy, E. W., Moskowitz, H., & MacAndrew, D. (1967). A controlled experiment on the use of court probation for drunk arrests. *American Journal of Psychiatry, 124,* 160-163.

Emerick, R. (1990). Self-help groups for former patients: Relations with mental health professionals. *Hospital and Community Psychiatry, 42* (4), 401-407.

Emotions Anonymous. (1978). *Emotions Anonymous.* St. Paul, MN: Emotions Anonymous International.

Emrick, C., Tonigan, J. S., Montgomery, H., & Little, L. (1993). Alcoholics Anonymous: What is currently known. In B. S. McCrady & W. R. Miller, *Research on Alcoholics Anonymous: Opportunities and alternatives* (pp. 41-76). New Brunswick, NJ: Rutgers Center for Alcohol Studies.

Fairchild, M. W. (1995). Women with postpartum psychiatric illness: A professionally facilitated support group. In M. J. Galinsky & J. H. Schopler (Eds.), *Support groups: Current perspectives on theory and practice* (pp. 41-54). New York: Haworth.

Ferguson, T. (1996). *Health online: How to go online to find health information, support forums, and self-help communities in cyberspace.* New York: Addison-Wesley.

Festinger, L. A. (1954). A theory of social comparison processes. *Human Relations, 7,* 117-140.

Finn, J. (1995). Computer-based self-help groups: A new resource to supplement support groups. *Social Work With Groups, 18*(1) 109-117.

Finn, J., & Lavitt, M. (1994). Computer-based self-help groups for sexual abuse survivors. *Social Work with Groups, 17*(1/2), 21-46.

Flynn, K. A. (1994). Performing sobriety: Story and celebration in Alcoholics Anonymous. *Dissertation Abstracts International,* 56-03, 0758. (University Microfilms No. 95-21702.)

Fox, P. (1989). From senility to Alzheimer's Disease: The rise of the Alzheimer's Disease movement. *The Milbank Quarterly, 67*(1), 58-102.

Fritz, M. E. (1989). Full circle or forward. *Child Abuse and Neglect, 13,* 313-318.

Furlong, M. S. (1989). An electronic community for older adults: The seniornet network. *Journal of Communication, 39*(3), 145-153.

Galanter, M. (1988). Zealous self-help groups as adjuncts to psychiatric treatment: A study of Recovery, Inc. *American Journal of Psychiatry, 145*(10), 1248-1253.

Galinsky, M. J., & Schopler, J. H. (1985). Patterns of entry and exit in open-ended groups. *Social Work with Groups, 8*(2), 67-80.

Galinsky, M. J., & Schopler, J. H. (1994). Negative experiences in support groups. *Social Work in Health Care, 20,*(1), 77-95.

Gamblers Anonymous. (1984). *Sharing recovery through Gamblers Anonymous.* Los Angeles: Author.

Gidron, B., & Chesler, M. (1995). Universal and particular attributes of self-help: A framework for international and intranational analysis. In F. Lavoie, T. Borkman, & B. Gidron, *Self-help and mutual aid groups: International and multicultural perspectives* (pp. 1-44). New York: Haworth.

Gifford, P. D. (1991). AA and NA for adolescents. *Journal of Adolescent Chemical Dependency, 1*(3), 101-120.

Gilbert, S. (1996, April 10). On-line tips about health offer mountains of gems and junk. *New York Times,* online edition.

Gitterman, A., & Shulman, L. (Eds.). (1994). *Mutual aid groups, vulnerable populations and the life cycle.* New York: Columbia University Press.

Glajchen, M., & Magen, R. (1995). Evaluating process, outcome, and satisfaction in community-based cancer support groups. In M. J. Galinsky & J. H. Schopler (Eds.), *Support groups: Current perspectives on theory and practice* (pp. 27-40). New York: Haworth.

Goffman, E. (1963). *Stigma: Notes on the management of spoiled identity.* Englewood Cliffs, NJ: Prentice-Hall.

Gonyea, J. G. (1989). Alzheimer's disease support group: An analysis of their structure, format and perceived benefits. *Social Work in Health Care, 14*(1), 61-72.

Gonyea, J. G., & Silverstein, N. M. (1991). The role of Alzheimer's Disease support groups in families' utilization of community services. *Journal of Gerontological Social Work, 16*(3/4), 43-55.

Goodman, G., & Jacobs, M. K. (1994). The self-help, mutual-support group. In A. Fuhriman & G. Bulingame, *Handbook of comprehensive psychotherapy,* (pp. 489-526). New York: John Wiley.

Gorman, J. M., & Rooney, J. F. (1979). The influence of Al-Anon on the coping behaviors of alcoholics. *Journal of Studies on Alcohol 40,* 1030-1038.

Gottlieb, B. H. (1982). Mutual-Help groups: Members views of their benefits and of roles for professionals. *Prevention in Human Services, 1*(3), 55-68.

Gottlieb, B. H., & Peters, L. (1991). A national demographic portrait of mutual aid group participants in Canada. *American Journal of Community Psychology, 19*(5), 651-666.

Grosz, H. (1972). *Recovery, Inc. survey: A preliminary report.* Chicago: Recovery, Inc.

Gussow, Z., & Tracy, G. S. (1976). The role of self-help clubs in adaptation to chronic illness and disability. *Social Science and Medicine, 10,* 407-414.

Gustafson, D., Wise, M., McTavish, F., Taylor, J. O., Wolberg, W., Stewart, J., Smalley, R. V., & Bosworth, K. (1993). Development and pilot evaluation of a computer-based support system for women with breast cancer. *Journal of Psychosocial Oncology, 11*(4), 69-93.

Hall, J. M. (1994, September). *Lesbians' experiences in Alcoholics Anonymous.* Paper presented at the International Conference on Addiction and Mutual Help Movements in a Comparative Perspective, Toronto, Ontario.

Hatfield, A. B. (1981). Self-help groups for families of the mentally ill. *Social Work, 26*(5), 408-413.

Hatfield, A. B., Coursey, R. O., & Slaughter, J. (1994). Family responses to behavior manifestations of mental illness. *Innovations and Research, 3*(4), 41-49.

Heil, R. A. (1992). A comparative analysis of therapeutic factors in self-help groups (Alcoholics Anonymous, Overeaters Anonymous). *Dissertation Abstracts International, 53/8-B*, 4373.

Henderson, J. N., Gutierrez-Mayka, Garcia, J., & Boyd, S. (1993). A model for Alzheimer's Disease support group development in African-American and Hispanic populations. *The Gerontologist, 33*(3), 409-414.

Hermann, J. F., Cella, D. F., & Robinovitch, A. (1995). Guidelines for support group programs. *Cancer Practice, 3*(2), 111-113.

Hogan, R., Curphy, G. J., & Hogan, J. (1994). What we know about leadership: Effectiveness and personality. *American Psychologist, 49* (6), 493-504.

Hollander, J. P. (1989). Restructuring lesbian social networks: Evaluation of an intervention. *Journal of Gay and Lesbian Psychotherapy, 1*(2), 63-71.

Howe, C. (1995). A history of NAMI CAN. *NAMI CAN News, 2*(5), 1-3.

Howe, C. W., & Howe, J. W. (1987). The National Alliance for the Mentally Ill: History and ideology. In A. Hatfield (Ed.), *Families of the mentally ill: Meeting the challenges* (pp. 23-34). San Francisco: Jossey-Bass.

Humphreys, K., & Kaskutas, L. A. (1994, September). *World views of Alcoholics Anonymous, Women for Sobriety, and Adult Children of Alcoholics/Al-Anon mutual help groups.* Paper presented at a meeting of the Kettil Bruun Society International Conference on Addiction and Mutual Help Movements in a Comparative Perspective, Toronto, Ontario.

Humphreys, K., & Kaskutas, L. A. (1995). World views of Alcoholics Anonymous, Women for Sobriety, and Adult Children of Alcoholics/Al-Anon Mutual Help Groups. *Addiction Research, 3*(3), 231-243.

Humphreys, K., Mavis, B., & Stöfflemayr, B. (1995). Are Twelve Step programs appropriate for disenfranchised groups? Evidence from a study of posttreatment mutual help involvement. In F. Lavoie, T. Borkman, & B. Gidron (Eds.), *Self-help and mutual aid groups: International and multicultural perspectives* (pp. 165-179). New York: Haworth.

Humphreys, K., & Rappaport, J. (1994). Researching self-help/mutual aid groups and organizations: Many roads, one journey. *Applied & Preventive Psychology, 3*, 217-231.

Humphreys, K., & Woods, M. D. (1993). Researching mutual help group participation in a segregated society. *Journal of Applied Behavioral Science, 29*(2), 181-201.

Humphreys, K. N. (1993). *World view transformations in adult children of alcoholics mutual help groups.* Unpublished doctoral dissertation, University of Illinois at Urbana-Champaign.

Hunka, C. D., O'Toole, A. W., & O'Toole, R. (1985). Self-help therapy in Parents Anonymous. *Journal of Psychosocial Nursing, 23*(7), 25-32.

Jacobs, M. K., & Goodman, G. (1989). Psychology and self-help groups: Predictions on a partnership. *American Psychologist, 44,* 536-544.

James, W. (1958). *Varieties of religious experience.* New York: Mentor Books. (Original work published 1902)

Jenson, A. (n.d.). [Data from "every member survey" research project]. (Available from NAMI, 200 N. Glebe Road, Arlington, VA).

Johnsen, E., & Herringer, L. G. (1993). A note on the utilization of common support activities and relapse following substance abuse treatment. *Journal of Psychology, 127*(1), 73-78.

Jurik, N. C. (1987). Persuasion in a self-help group: Processes and consequences. *Small Group Behavior, 18,* 368-397.

Kadushin, A. (1977). *Consultation in social work.* New York: Columbia University Press.

Kaminer, W. (1992). *I'm dysfunctional, you're dysfunctional: The recovery movement and other self-help fashions.* Reading, MA: Addison-Wesley.

Karp, D. A. (1992). Illness ambiguity and the search for meaning: A case study of a self-help group for affective disorders. *Journal of Contemporary Ethnography, 21*(2), 139-170.

Kaskutas, L. A. (1994). What do women get out of self-help? Their reasons for attending Women for Sobriety and Alcoholics Anonymous. *Journal of Substance Abuse Treatment, 11*(3), 185-195.

Katz, A. H. (1965). Applications of self-help concepts in current social welfare. *Social Work, 10*(3), 68-74.

Katz, A. H. (1993). *Self-help in America: A social movement perspective.* New York: Twayne.

Katz, A. H., & Bender, E. I. (1976). *The strength in us: Self-help groups in the modern world.* New York: New Viewpoints.

Katz, A. H., & Maida, C. A. (1990). Health and disability self-help organizations. In T. J. Powell (Ed.), *Working with self-help* (pp. 141-155). Silver Spring, MD: NASW.

Kaufman, C. L., Schulberg, H. C., & Schooler, N. R. (1995). Self-help group participation among people with severe mental illness. In F. Lavoie, T. Borkman, & B. Gidron, *Self-help and mutual aid groups: International and multicultural perspectives* (pp. 315-331). New York: Haworth.

Kennedy, M., & Humphreys, K. (1995). Understanding worldview transformation in members of mutual help groups. In F. Lavoie, T. Borkman, & B. Gidron, *Self-help and mutual aid groups: International and multicultural perspectives* (pp. 181-198). New York: Haworth.

Kessler, R. C., Zhao, S., Katz, S. J., Kouzis, A. C., Frank, R. G., Edlund, M., & Leaf, P. (1996). *Use of outpaitent services for psychiatric problems 1990-1992 in the National Comorbidity Survey.* Manuscript submitted for publication.

Kieffer, C. H. (1984). Citizen empowerment: A developmental perspective. In J. Rappaport, C. Swift, and R. Hess (Eds.), *Studies in empowerment* (pp. 9-35). New York: Haworth Press.

King, S. A. (1994, July). Analysis of electronic support groups for recovering addicts. *Interpersonal Computing and Technology, 2* (3), 47-57.

King, S. A. (1996). Researching internet communities: Proposed ethical guidelines for the reporting of reality. *The Information Society, 12*(2), [online serial].

Kirschenbaum, H., & Glaser, B. (1978). *Developing support groups: A manual for facilitators and participants.* La Jolla, CA: University Associates.

Klass, D. (1984-1985). Bereaved parents and the Compassionate Friends: Affiliation and healing. *Omega: Journal of Death and Dying, 15,* 353-373.

Klass, D. (1993). Solace and immortality: Bereaved parents' continuing bond with their children. *Death Studies, 17,* 343-368.

Kostyk, D., Fuchs, D., Tabisz, E., & Jacyk, W. R. (1993). Combining professional and self-help group intervention: Collaboration in co-leadership. *Social Work with Groups, 16*(3), 111-124.

Krezman, J. (1985). Averageness. *The Recovery Reporter, 48*(5), 1-2.

Kropotkin, P. (1955). *Mutual aid: A factor in evolution.* Boston: Porter Sargent Publishers. (Original work published 1914).

Kurtz, E. (1979). *Not-God: A history of Alcoholics Anonymous.* Center City, MN: Hazelden.

Kurtz, E. (1982). Why AA works: The intellectual significance of Alcoholics Anonymous. *Journal of Studies on Alcohol, 42,* 38-80.

Kurtz, E. (1992). Commentary. In J. W. Langenbucher, B. S. McCrady, W. Frankenstein, & P. E. Nathan (Eds.), *Annual Review of Addictions Research and Treatment: Volume 2,* (pp. 397-400). New York: Pergamon.

Kurtz, E. (1996). Twelve-Step programs. In E. Cousins (Series Ed.) & P. H. VanNess (Vol. Ed.), *World spirituality: An encyclopedic history of the religious quest, Vol. 22. Spirituality and the secular quest,* (pp. 277-302). New York: Crossroad/Continuum.

Kurtz, E., & Ketcham, K. (1992). *The spirituality of imperfection: Modern wisdom from classic stories.* New York: Bantam.

Kurtz, L. F. (1985). Cooperation and rivalry between helping professionals and members of AA. *Health and Social Work, 10,* 104-112.

Kurtz, L. F. (1988). Mutual aid for affective disorders: The Manic Depressive and Depressive Association. *American Journal of Orthopsychiatry, 58,* 152-155.

Kurtz, L. F. (1990a). The self-help movement: Review of the past decade of research. *Social Work With Groups, 13*(3), 101-115.

Kurtz, L. F. (1990b). Twelve step programs. In T. J. Powell (Ed.), *Working with self help* (pp. 93-119). Silver Spring, MD.: NASW.

Kurtz, L. F. (1992). Group environments in self-help groups for families. *Small Group Research, 23,* 199-215.

Kurtz, L. F. (1994). Self-help groups for families with mental illness or alcoholism. In T. J. Powell, *Understanding the self-help organization: Frameworks and findings* (pp. 293-313). Thousand Oaks, CA: Sage.

Kurtz, L. F., Garvin, C. D., Hill, E. M., Pollio, D., McPherson, S., & Powell, T. J. (1995). Involvement in Alcoholics Anonymous by persons with dual disorders. *Alcoholism Treatment Quarterly, 12*(4), 1-18.

Kurtz, L. F., Mann, K. B., & Chambon, A. (1987). Linking between social workers and mental health mutual aid groups. *Social Work in Health Care, 13*(1), 69-78.

Kurtz, L. F., & Powell, T. J. (1987). Three approaches to understanding self-help groups. *Social Work with Groups, 10,* 69-80.

Kus, R. J. (1988). Working the program: the Alcoholics Anonymous experience and gay American men. *Holistic Nursing Practice, 2*(4), 62-74.

Kus, R. J. (1992). Spirituality in everyday life: Experiences of gay men in Alcoholics Anonymous. *Journal of Chemical Dependency Treatment, 5*(1), 49-66.

Kus, R. J., & Latcovich, M. A. (1995). Special interest groups in Alcoholics Anonymous: A focus on gay men's groups. In R. J. Kus (Ed.), *Addiction and recovery in gay and lesbian persons.* Binghamton, NY: Harrington Park Press.

Lavoie, F. (1984). Action research: A new model of interaction between the professional and self-help groups. In A. Gartner & F. Riessman, *The self-help revolution.* New York: Human Sciences Press.

Lavoie, F., Borkman, T., & Gidron, B. (Eds.). (1995). *Self-help and mutual aid groups: International and multicultural perspectives.* New York: Haworth.

Lee, D. T. (1991, May). *Abraham A. Low: Pioneer in cognitive behavioral therapy.* Paper presented at the Conference on Mental Illness, Stigma, and Self-Help, Chicago, IL.

Lee, D. T. (1995). Professional underutilization of Recovery, Inc. *Psychiatric Rehabilitation Journal, 19*(1), 63-70.

Leslie, J. (1994, March). Mail bonding. *Wired,* 2.03. Available at http://www/hotwired.com/Lib/Wired/2.03.

Leventhal, G. S., Maton, K. I., & Madara, E. J. (1988). Systemic organizational support for self-help groups. *American Journal of Orthopsychiatry, 58*(4), 592-603.

Levy, L. H. (1979). Processes and activities in groups. In M. A. Lieberman & L. D. Borman, *Self-help groups for coping with crisis: Origins, members, processes and impact* (pp. 234-271). San Francisco: Jossey-Bass.

Levy, L. H. (1984). Issues in research and evaluation. In A. Gartner & F. Riessman (Eds.), *The self-help revolution* (pp. 155-172). New York: Human Sciences Press.

Levy, L. H., & Derby, J. F. (1992). Bereavement support groups: Who participates; who does not; and why. *American Journal of Community Psychology, 20*(5), 649-662.

Lieber, L. L. (1983). The self-help approach: Parents Anonymous. *Journal of Clinical Child Psychology, 12* (1), 288-291.

Lieberman, M. A. (1990). A group therapist perspective on self-help groups. *International Journal of Group Psychotherapy, 40*(3), 251-278.

Lieberman, M. A. (1979). Analyzing change mechanisms in groups. In M. A. Lieberman & L. Borman (Eds.), *Self-help groups for coping with crisis: Origins, members, processes, and impact* (pp. 194-233). San Francisco: Jossey-Bass.

Lieberman, M. A., & Borman, L. D. (1979). *Self-help groups for coping with crisis: Origins, members, processes, and impact.* San Francisco: Jossey-Bass.

Lieberman, M. A., & Snowden, L. R. (1993). Problems in assessing prevalence and membership characteristics of self-help group participants. *Journal of Applied Behavioral Science, 29,* 166-180.

Litwak, E., & Meyer, H. J. (1966). A balance theory of coordination between bureaucratic organizations and community primary groups. *Administrative Science Quarterly, 11,* 31-58.

Llewelyn, S. P., & Haslett, A. V. J. (1986). Factors perceived as helpful by the members of self-help groups: An exploratory study. *British Journal of Guidance and Counseling, 14*(3), 252-262.

Lotery, J. L., & Jacobs, M. K. (1995). The involvement of self-help groups with mental health and medical professionals: The self-helpers' perspective. In F. Lavoie, T. Borkman, & B. Gidron, *Self-help and mutual aid groups: International and multicultural perspectives* (pp. 279-302). New York: Haworth.

Low, A. A. (1943a). *The techniques of self-help in psychiatric after-care.* (Available from Recovery, Inc., Chicago, IL.)

Low, A. A. (1943b). *Lectures to relatives of former mental patients.* Boston: Christopher.

Low, A. A. (1950). *Mental health through will training.* Chicago: Willett Publishing.

Low, A. A. (1967). *Peace versus power in the family: Domestic discord and emotional distress.* Glencoe, IL: Willett.

Luke, D. A. (1989, June). Assessing individual change in a mutual help organization. Paper presented at the Biennial Conference on Community Research and Action, East Lansing, MI.

Luke, D. A., Roberts, L., & Rappaport, J. (1993). Individual, group context, and individual-group fit predictors of self-help group attendance. *The Journal of Applied Behavioral Science, 29,* 216-238.

Madara, E. J. (1993, July). *Tapping mutual aid self-help opportunities on-line.* Paper presented at the First National Consumer Health Informatics Conference, Stevens Point, WI.

Madara, E. J. (1995, May). *On-line self-help: National and world-wide networks.* Paper given at Harvard University Conference, The Computer as a Patient's Assistant, Cambridge, MA.

Mäkelä, K. (1993a). Implications for research of the cultural variability of Alcoholics Anonymous. In B. S. McCrady & W. R. Miller (Eds.), *Research on Alcoholics Anonymous: Opportunities and Alternatives* (pp. 189-208). New Brunswick, NJ: Rutgers Center of Alcohol Studies.

Mäkelä, K. (1993b). International comparisons of Alcoholics Anonymous. *Alcohol Health & Research World, 17,* (228-234).

Mäkelä, K. (Ed.). (1996). *Alcoholics Anonymous as a mutual-help movement: A study in eight societies.* Madison, WI: University of Wisconsin Press.

Malenbaum, R., Herzog, D., Eisenthal, S., & Wyshak, G. (1988). Overeaters Anonymous: Impact on bulimia. *International Journal of Eating Disorders, 7*(1), 139-143.

Martin, J. E. (1992). The evolution of Al-Anon: A content analysis of stories in two editions of its "Big Book." *Contemporary Drug Problems, 19,* 563-585.

Maton, K. I. (1988). Social support, organizational characteristics, psychological well being, and group appraisal in three self-help group populations. *American Journal of Community Psychology, 16*(1), 53-77.

Maton, K. I. (1989). Community settings as buffers of life stress? Highly supportive churches, mutual help groups, and senior centers. *American Journal of Community Psychology, 17,* 203-232.

Maton, K. I. (1993). Moving beyond the individual level of analysis in mutual help group research: An ecological paradigm. *Journal of Applied Behavioral Science, 29*(2), 272-286.

McCarthy, K. (1984). Early alcoholism treatment: The Emmanuel Movement and Richard Peabody. *Journal of Studies on Alcohol, 45,* 59-74.

McCrady, B. S., & Delaney, S. I. (1995). Self-help groups. In R. K. Hester & W. R. Miller (Eds.), *Handbook of alcoholism treatment approaches: Effective alternatives* (2nd ed., pp. 160-175). Boston: Allyn and Bacon.

McKay, M., & Paleg, K. (Eds.). (1992). *Focal group psychotherapy.* Oakland, CA: New Harbinger.

McNally, E. B. (1989). Lesbian recovering alcoholics in Alcoholics Anonymous: A qualitative study of identity transformation. *Dissertation Abstracts International,* 50/09-B, 4227.

Medvene, L. J. (1990). Family support organizations: The functions of similarity. In T. J. Powell (Ed.), *Working with self-help* (pp. 120-140). Silver Spring, MD: NASW.

Medvene, L. J., & Krauss, D. (1985). *An exploratory case study of a self-help group for families of the mentally ill.* Unpublished manuscript, Yale University, New Haven, CT.

Medvene, L. J., & Krauss, D. (1989). Causal attributions about psychiatric disability in a self-help group for families of the mentally ill. *Journal of Applied Social Psychology, 19,* 1413-1430.

Medvene, L. J., Lin, K., Wu, A., Mendoza, R., Harris, N., & Miller, M.(1995). Mexican American and Anglo American parents of the mentally ill: Attitudes and participation in family support groups. In F. Lavoie, T. Borkman, & B. Gidron (Eds.), *Self-help and mutual aid groups: International and multicultural perspectives* (pp.141-164). New York: Haworth.

Meier, A., Galinsky, M. J., & Rounds, K. A. (1995). Telephone support groups for caregivers of persons with AIDS. In M. J. Galinsky & J. H. Schopler (Eds.), *Support groups: Current perspectives on theory and practice* (pp. 99-108). New York: Haworth.

Meissen, G. J., Gleason, D. F., & Embree, M. G. (1991). An assessment of the needs of mutual-help groups. *American Journal of Community Psychology, 19*(3), 427-442.

Meissen, G. J., Mason, W. C., & Gleason, D. F. (1991). Understanding the attitudes and intentions of future professionals toward self-help. *American Journal of Community Psychology, 19*(5), 699-714.

Meissen, G. J., & Volk, F. (1995). Predictors of burnout among self-help group leaders. In F. Lavoie, T. Borkman, & B. Gidron (Eds.), *Self-help and mutual aid groups: International and multicultural perspectives* (pp. 241-262). New York: Haworth.

Michels, R. (1978). *Political parties: A sociological study of the oligarchical tendencies of modern democracy.* (E. & C. Paul, Trans.). Gloucester, MA: Peter Smith. (Original work published 1915)

Miller, W. R., & Kurtz, E. (1994). Models of alcoholism used in treatment: Contrasting AA and other perspectives with which it is often confused. *Journal of Studies on Alcohol, 55,* 159-166.

Molinari, V., Nelson, N., Shekelle, S., & Crothers, M. K. (1994). Family support groups: An analysis of attendees and nonattendees. *Journal of Applied Gerontology, 13*(1), 86-98.

Monaco, G. P. (1993). Family issues. *Cancer, 71*(Suppl., May 15) 3370-3376.

Montgomery, H. A., Miller, W. R., & Tonigan, J. S. (1993). Differences among AA groups: Implications for research. *Journal of Studies on Alcohol, 54,* 502-504.

Moore, J. B. (1983). The experience of sponsoring a Parents Anonymous group. *Social Casework, 64,* 585-592.

Moos, R. H. (1974). *Evaluating treatment environments: A social ecological approach.* New York: John Wiley.

Moos, R. H. (1986). *Group environment scale manual* (2nd. ed.). Palo Alto, CA: Consulting Psychologists Press.

Moos, R. H., Finney, J., & Maude-Griffon, P. (1993). The social climate of self-help and mutual support groups: Assessing group implementation, process, and outcome. In B. S. McCrady & W. R. Miller, *Research on Alcoholics Anonymous: Opportunities and alternatives* (pp. 251-270). New Brunswick, NJ: Rutgers Center for Alcohol Studies.

NAMI. (1993). Families of the world unite. *NAMI Advocate, 14*(2), 1.

NAMI. (1995a). Home Page (//www.cais.com/vikings/nami/index.html).

NAMI. (1995b). Results of 1995 NAMI member survey. *NAMI Advocate, 17*(3), 23.

Narcotics Anonymous. (1987). *Narcotics Anonymous* (4th ed.). Van Nuys, CA: Narcotics Anonymous World Service Office.

Norman, W. H. (1983-1984). Self-blame in self-help: Differences in two weight-loss groups. *The Journal of Applied Social Sciences, 8*(1), 137-153.

Norton, S., Wandersman, A., & Goldman, C. R. (1993). Perceived costs and benefits of membership in a self-help group: Comparisons of members and nonmembers of the Alliance for the Mentally Ill. *Community Mental Health Journal, 29*(2), 143-160.

Oka, T. (1995). Self-help groups in Japan: Trends and traditions. In F. Lavoie, T. Borkman, & B. Gidron, *Self-help and mutual aid groups: International and multicultural perspectives* (pp. 69-95). New York: Haworth.

Overeaters Anonymous. (1980). *Overeaters Anonymous.* Torrance, CA: Author.

Overeaters Anonymous. (1992). *Membership survey summary*. Torrance, CA: Author.

Parents Anonymous. (n.d.). Parent leadership strengthens families. *The parent networker, 1*(1), 1-2.

Parents Anonymous. (1975). *Chairperson—Sponsor Manual*. Claremont, CA: Author.

Parents Anonymous. (1982). *Chairperson—Sponsor Manual* (2nd ed.). Claremont, CA: Author.

Parents Anonymous. (1993). *Hope for our future*. Claremont, CA: Author.

Parents Anonymous. (1995a). *Perspectives on the Parents Anonymous national network. 1994 Database analysis*. Claremont, CA: Author.

Parents Anonymous. (1995b). A parent's story. *The Parent Networker, 1*(1), 3.

Parker, S., Hutchinson, D., & Berry, S. (1995). A support group of families of armed services personnel in the Persian Gulf War. In M. J. Galinsky & J. H. Schopler (Eds.), *Support groups: Current perspectives on theory and practice* (pp. 89-98). New York: Haworth.

Peabody, R. R. (1931). *The common sense of drinking*. Boston: Little, Brown.

Perkins, D. V., Lafuze, J. E., & Van Dusen, C. (1995). Social climate correlates of effectiveness in Alliance for the Mentally Ill groups. In F. Lavoie, T. Borkman, & B. Gidron (Eds.), *Self-help and mutual aid groups: International and multicultural perspectives* (pp. 263-277). New York: Haworth.

Peterson, M. G. E., & Rippey, R. M. (1992). A computerized cancer information system. *Patient Education and Counseling, 19*, 81-87.

Peyrot, M. (1985). Narcotics Anonymous: Its history, structure, and approach. *International Journal of Addictions, 20*(10), 1509-1522.

Pittman, B. (1988). *AA: The way it began*. Seattle: Glen Abbey Books.

Pollen, D. A. (1993). *Hannah's heirs: The quest for the genetic origins of Alzheimer's Disease*. New York: Oxford University Press.

Post-Kammer, P. (1988). Effectiveness of Parents Anonymous in reducing child abuse. *The School Counselor, 35*(5), 337-342.

Powell, T. J. (1979). Comparisons between self-help groups and professional services. *Social Casework, 60*, 561-565.

Powell, T. J. (1987). *Self-help organizations and professional practice*. Silver Spring, MD: NASW.

Powell, T. J. (1990). *Working with self help*. Silver Spring, MD: NASW.

Powell, T. J. (1990). Differences between national self-help organizations and local self-help groups: Implications for members and professionals. In T. J. Powell, *Working with self-help* (pp. 50-70). Silver Spring, MD: NASW.

Powell, T. J., Hill, E. M., Gutfreund, M. J., Warner, L., Yeaton, W., Pollio, D., & Silk, K. R. (1995). *An intervention to encourage people with mood disorders to attend a self-help group following hospitalization*. Manuscript submitted for publication.

Prochaska, J. O. (1994). Strong and weak principles for progressing from precontemplation to action on the basis of twelve problem behaviors. *Health Psychology, 13*(1), 47-51.

Prochaska, J. O., DiClemente, C. C., & Norcross, J. C. (1992). In search of how people change: Applications to addictive behaviors. *American Psychologist, 47*(9), 1102-1114.

Prochaska, J. O., Norcross, J. C., & DiClemente, C. C. (1994). *Changing for good*. New York: Morrow.

Raiff, N. R. (1978). Recovery, Inc.: A study of a self-help organization in mental health. *Dissertation Abstracts International, 40* (2-A), 1085. (University Microfilms No. 79-17472)

Raiff, N. R. (1984). Some health-related outcomes of self-help participation: Recovery, Inc. As a case example of a self-help organization in mental health. In A. Gartner and F. Riessman (Eds.), *The self-help revolution* (pp. 183-193). New York: Human Sciences Press.

Rappaport, J. (1993). Narrative studies, personal stories, and identity transformation in the mutual help context. *Journal of Applied Behavioral Science, 29,* 239-256.

Rappaport, J., Seidman, E., Toro, P. A., McFadden, L. S., Reischl, T. M., Roberts, L. J., Salem, D. A., Stein, C. H., & Zimmerman, M. A. (1985). Finishing the unfinished business: Collaborative research with a mutual-help organization. *Social Policy, 15,* 12-24.

Rau, N., & Rau, M. (1971). *My dear ones.* Englewood Cliffs, NJ: Prentice Hall.

Recovery, Inc. (n.d.). *RX: Recovery, Inc.* Chicago: Author.

Recovery, Inc. (1993). Recovery, Inc. Historical and projected growth charts (1961-2000). (Available from Recovery, Inc., Chicago, IL)

Recovery, Inc. (1995). *1995 directory of group meeting information.* Chicago: Author.

Revenson, T. A., & Cassel, J. B. (1991). An exploration of leadership in a medical mutual help organization. *American Journal of Community Psychology, 19*(5), 683-698.

Rheingold, H. (1993). *The Virtual Community.* New York: Harper Perennial. (Also available at http://www.well.com/user/hlr.)

Riessman, F. (1965). The 'helper therapy' principle. *Social Work, 10,* 27-32.

Riessman, F., & Carroll, D. (1995). *Redefining self-help: Policy and practice.* New Resources for Human Services.

Rittner, B., & Hammons, K. (1992). Telephone group work with people with end stage AIDS. *Social Work With Groups, 15*(4), 59-72.

Roberts, L. J. (1985, August). *Measures of self-help group quality: Observer and participant views.* Paper presented at the 93rd Annual Convention of the American Psychological Association at Los Angeles, CA.

Roberts, L. J. (1987, May). *The appeal of mutual help: Paper presented at the Community Research and Action Conference, Columbia, SC.*

Roberts, L. J., & Rappaport, J. (1989, June). *Empowerment in the mutual help context: An empirical analysis of the value of helping others.* Paper presented at the Second Biennial Conference on Community Research and Action, East Lansing, MI.

Romness, S., Bruce, V., & Smith-Wilson, C. (1992). Multiple sclerosis telephone self-help support groups. In A. H. Katz, H. L. Hedrick, D. H. Isenberg, L. M. Thompson, T. Goodrich, & A. H. Kutscher (Eds.), *Self-help concepts and applications* (pp. 220-223). Philadelphia: The Charles Press.

Room, R. (1993). Alcoholics Anonymous as a social movement. In B. S. McCrady & W. R. Miller (Eds.). *Research on Alcoholics Anonymous: Opportunities and alternatives.* New Brunswick, NJ: Rutgers Center of Alcohol Studies.

Rorty, M., Yager, J., & Rossotto, E. (1993). Why and how do women recover from bulimia nervosa? The subjective appraisals of forty women recovered for a year or more. *International Journal of Eating Disorders, 14*(3), 249-260.

Rounds, K. A., Galinsky, M. J., & Stevens, L. S. (1991). Linking people with AIDS in rural communities: The telephone group. *Social Work, 36*(1), 13-21.

Rudy, D. R. (1986). *Becoming alcoholic: Alcoholics Anonymous and the reality of alcoholism.* Carbondale, IL: Southern Illinois University Press.

Salem, D. (1987, May). *The culture of mutual help: Characteristics of the GROW membership.* Paper presented at the Community Research and Action conference, Columbia, SC.

Salem, D. A., Bogat, G. A., & Reid, C. (1996). *Mutual-help goes on-line.* Manuscript submitted for publication.

Salem, D., Gant, L., & Campbell, R. (1996). *The initiation of self help groups within residential treatment settings.* Manuscript submitted for publication.

Salem, D. A., Seidman, E., & Rappaport, J. (1988). Community treatment of the mentally ill: The promise of mutual-help organizations. *Social Work, 33,* 403-410.

Salzer, M. S., McFadden, L., & Rappaport, J. (1994). Professional views of self-help groups. *Administration and Policy in Mental Health, 22*(2), 85-95.

Schene, A. H., & van Wijngaarden, B. (1995). A survey of an organization for families of patients with serious mental illness in the Netherlands. *Psychiatric Services, 46*(8), 807-813.

Schopler, J. H., & Galinsky, M. J. (1993). Support groups as open systems: A model for practice and research. *Health and Social Work, 18,* 195-207.

Schopler, J. H., & Galinsky, M. J. (1995). Expanding our view of support groups as open systems. *Social Work With Groups, 18*(1), 3-10.

Schubert, M. A., & Borkman, T. J. (1991). An organizational typology for self-help groups. *American Journal of Community Psychology, 19*(5), 769-787.

Sherman, B. (1979). The emergence of an ideology in a bereaved parents group. In M. A. Lieberman & L. D. Borman (Eds.), *Self-help groups for coping with crisis: Origins, members, processes and impact* (pp. 305-322). San Francisco: Jossey-Bass.

Silverman, P. R. (1978). *Mutual help groups: A guide for mental health workers.* Rockville, MD: NIMH.

Silverman-Dresner, T. (1989-1990). Self-help groups for women who have had breast cancer. *Imagination, Cognition and Personality, 9*(3), 237-243.

Skinner, E. A., Steinwachs, D. M., & Kasper, J. A. (1992). Family perspectives on the service needs of people with serious and persistent mental illness: Part I: Characteristics of families and consumers. *Innovations and Research, 1*(3), 23-30.

Smith, A. R. (1991). *Alcoholics Anonymous: A social world perspective.* Unpublished Doctoral Dissertation, University of California, San Diego.

Smith, A. R. (1993). The social construction of group dependency in Alcoholics Anonymous. *The Journal of Drug Issues, 23,* 689-704.

Snow, D. A., & Machalek, R. (1983). The convert as a social type. In R. Collins (Ed.), *Sociological Theory* (pp. 259-289). San Francisco: Jossey-Bass.

Snowden, L. R., & Lieberman, M. A. (1994). African-American participation in self-help groups. In T. J. Powell, *Understanding self-help organizations: Frameworks and findings* (pp. 50-61). Thousand Oaks, CA: Sage.

Stein, L., Rothman, B., & Nakanishi, M. (1993). The telephone group: Accessing group service to the homebound. *Social Work With Groups, 16*(1/2), 203-213.

Steinwachs, D. M., Kasper, J., & Skinner, E. A. (1992). *Final report. Family perspectives on meeting the needs for care of severely mentally ill relatives: A national survey.* Unpublished manuscript.

Stephens, S. (1972). *Death comes home.* New York: Morehouse-Barlow.

Stewart, M., Banks, S., Crossman, D., & Poel, D. (1995). Partnerships between health professionals and self-help groups: Meanings and mechanisms. In F. Lavoie, T. Borkman, & B. Gidron, *Self-help and mutual aid groups: International and multicultural perspectives* (pp. 199-240). New York: Haworth.

Stewart, M. J. (1990).Expanding theoretical conceptualizations of self-help groups. *Social Science and Medicine, 31*(9), 1057-1066.

Taylor, M. C. (1977). Alcoholics Anonymous: How it works recovery processes in a self-help group. *Dissertation Abstracts International*, 39, 7532A. (University Microfilms No. 79-13241).

TCF. (1991). *The principles of the Compassionate Friends*. Oak Brook, IL: Author.

TCF. (1993). *When a child dies.* . . Oak Brook, IL: Author.

Thibaut, J. W., and Kelley, H. H. (1959). *The social psychology of groups*. New York: John Wiley.

Tonigan, J. S., & Ashcroft, F. (1995). *Group dynamics and content in alcohol self-help groups: Comparison of Alcoholics Anonymous and rational self-help programs*. Manuscript submitted for publication.

Toro, P. A., Rappaport, J., & Seidman, E. (1987). A social climate comparison of mutual help and psychotherapy groups. *Journal of Consulting and Clinical Psychology, 55*, 430-431.

Toro, P. A., Reischl, T. M., Zimmerman, M. A., & Rappaport, J. (1988). Professionals in mutual help groups: Impact on social climate and members' behavior. *Journal of Consulting and Clinical Psychology, 56*, 631-632.

Torrey, E. F. (1995). *Surviving schizophrenia: A family manual* (3rd. ed.). New York: Harper & Row.

Toseland, R. W., & Rivas, R. F. (1995). *An introduction to group work practice*. 2nd ed. Boston: Allyn & Bacon.

Toseland, R. W., Rossiter, C. M., Peak, T., & Smith, G. C. (1990). Comparative effectiveness of individual and group interventions to support family caregivers. *Social Work, 35*(3), 209-216.

Trang, T., & Urbano, J. (1993). A telephone group support program for the visually-impaired elderly. *Clinical Gerontologist, 13*(2), 61-71.

Traunstein, D. M. (1984). From mutual-aid self-help to professional service. *Social Casework, 65*, 622-627.

Trice, H. M. (1957). A study of the process of affiliation with Alcoholics Anonymous. *Quarterly Journal of Studies on Alcohol, 18*, 39-54.

Trice, H. M., & Roman, P. M. (1970). Sociopsychological predictors of affiliation with Alcoholics Anonymous: A longitudinal study of "treatment success." *Social Psychiatry, 5*, 51-59.

Trojan, A. (1989). Benefits of self-help groups: A survey of 232 members from 65 disease-related groups. *Social Science and Medicine, 29*(2), 225-232.

Tuchman, K. (1995). *Long-term recovery: Characteristics, processes and challenges*. Unpublished paper.

Unruh, D. H. (1983). *Invisable lives: Social worlds of the aged*. Newbury Park, CA: Sage.

Uttaro, T., & Mechanic, D. (1994). The NAMI consumer survey analysis of unmet needs. *Hospital and Community Psychiatry, 45*(4), 372-374.

Videka-Sherman, L. (1982). Effects of participation in a self-help group for bereaved parents: Compassionate Friends. *Prevention in Human Services, 1 (3)*, 69-78.

Videka-Sherman, L. (1990). Bereavement self-help organizations. In T. J. Powell (Ed.), *Working With Self-Help* (pp. 156-174). Silver Spring, MD: NASW.

Videka-Sherman, L., & Lieberman, M. A. (1985). The impact of self-help and professional help on parental bereavement: The limits of recovery. *American Journal of Orthopsychiatry, 55*, 70-87.

Vincke, J., & Bolton, R. (1994). Social support, depression, and self acceptance among gay men. *Human Relations, 47*(9), 1049-162.

Von Appen, U. (1995). The development of self-help in Germany's new provinces (former East Germany): The case of Schwerin. In F. Lavoie, T. Borkman, & B. Gidron,

Self-help and mutual aid groups: International and multicultural perspectives (pp. 97-116). New York: Haworth.

Wasserman, H., & Danforth, H. E. (1988). *The human bond: Support groups and mutual aid.* New York: Springer.

Wasow, M. (1986). Support groups for family caregivers of patients with Alzheimer's Disease. *Social Work, 31*(2), 93-97.

Wechsler, H. (1960). The self-help organization in the mental health field: Recovery, Inc., A case study. *Journal of Nervous and Mental Disease, 130, 297-314*).

Weinberg, N., Schmale, J. D., Uken, J., & Wessel, K. (1995). Computer-mediated support groups. *Social Work With Groups, 17*(4), 43-54.

Weinberg, N., Uken, J. S., Schmale, J., & Adamek, M. (1995). Therapeutic factors: Their presence in a computer-mediated support group. *Social Work With Groups, 18*(4), 57-69.

Westefeld, J. S., & Winkelpleck, J. M. (1983). University counseling service groups for gay students. *Small Group Behavior, 14*(1), 121-128.

Wheelan, S. A. (1994). *Group processes: A developmental perspective.* Boston: Allyn and Bacon.

Wheeler, I. P. (1990). *The role of meaning and purpose in life in parental bereavement.* Dissertation, University of Georgia, Athens, GA.

White, B. J., & Madara, E. J. (Eds.). (1995). *The self-help sourcebook: Finding and forming mutual aid self-help groups* (5th ed.). Denville, NJ: American Self-Help Clearinghouse.

Wiener, L. S., Spencer, E. D., Davidson, R., & Fair, C. (1993). National telephone support groups: A new avenue toward psychosocial support for HIV-infected children and their families. *Social Work with Groups, 16*(3), 55-72.

Wollert, R. W., Knight, B., & Levy, L. H. (1980). Make today count: A collaboarative model for professionals and self-help groups. *Professional Psychology, 1, 130-138.*

Wright, S. D., Lund, D. A., Pett, M. A., & Caserta, M. S. (1987). The assessment of support group experiences by caregivers of dementia patients. *Clinical Gerontologist, 6*(4), 35-59.

Wright, K. D., & Scott, T. B. (1978). The relationship of wives' treatment to the drinking status of alcoholics. *Journal of Studies on Alcohol, 39*(9), 1577-1581.

Yager, J., Landsverk, J., & Edelstein, C. K. (1989). Help seeking and satisfaction with care in 641 women with eating disorders: Patterns of utilizaton, attributed change, and perceived efficacy of treatment. *Journal of Nervous and Mental Disease, 177*(10), 632-637.

Yalom, I. D. (1995). *The theory and practice of group psychotherapy* (4th ed.). New York: Basic Books.

Yeary, J. (1987). The use of Overeaters Anonymous in the treatment of eating disorders. *Journal of Psychoactive Drugs, 19*(3), 303-309.

Yoak, M., & Chesler, M. (1985). Alternative professional roles in health care delivery: Leadership patterns in self-help groups. *Journal of Applied Behavioral Science, 21*(4), 427-444.

INDEX

ABOUT THE AUTHOR

Linda Farris Kurtz is a professor in the Department of Social Work at Eastern Michigan University, where she teaches courses on self-help and support groups, chemical dependency and mental illness, and human behavior theory. She has presented Professional Development Institutes on self-help and support groups at the University of Chicago's School of Social Service Administration and has published numerous articles related to her research on this topic. Dr. Kurtz received her D.P.A. from the University of Georgia in 1983 and her M.S.W. from the University of Pittsburgh in 1965. She has taught in schools of social work at the University of Georgia, the University of Chicago, and Indiana University. Prior to her teaching career, she practiced social work in Chicago, Illinois, and Atlanta, Georgia. She and her husband, Ernest Kurtz, live in Ann Arbor, Michigan.